B000719

The Social Roots of Basque Nationalism

The Basque Series

ALFONSO PÉREZ-AGOTE

The Social Roots of Basque Nationalism

TRANSLATED BY CAMERON WATSON
AND WILLIAM A. DOUGLASS

FOREWORD BY WILLIAM A. DOUGLASS

University of Nevada Press   Reno   Las Vegas

The Basque Series

Series Editor: William A. Douglass

University of Nevada Press

Reno, Nevada 89557 USA

The paper used in this book meets the

requirements of American

National Standard for Information

Sciences—Permanence of Paper

for Printed Library Materials, ANSI z.48-

1984. Binding materials were selected for

strength and durability.

First Printing

15 14 13 12 11 10 09 08 07 06

5 4 3 2 1

Library of Congress Cataloging-in-

Publication Data

Pérez-Agote, Alfonso.

The social roots of Basque nationalism /

Alfonso Pérez-Agote Poveda ; translated by

Cameron Watson and William A. Douglass ;

foreword by William A. Douglass.

p. cm. — (The Basque series)

Includes bibliographical references and

index.

ISBN 0-87417-605-0 (hardcover : alk. paper)

1. País Vasco (Spain)—Politics and

government—20th century. 2.

Nationalism—Spain—País Vasco—

History—20th century. 3. Political

persecution—Spain—País Vasco—

History—20th century. 4. Spain—Politics

and government—1939–1975. 5. Spain—

Politics and government—1975– 6.

Basques—Ethnic identity. 7. Basques—

Social life and customs—History—20th

century. I. Title. II. Series.

DP302.B53P48 2006   2005020357

320.54′09466—dc22

To Purífica

Contents

Chapter Six

Tables

Foreword

The literature on Basque nationalism is enormous and growing exponentially. Nevertheless, the contribution of Alfonso Pérez-Agote stands out as remarkably unique and evocative—distinguished by four characteristics. First, it was pioneering in that Pérez-Agote was the first (1978) investigator after the death of Spanish dictator Francisco Franco in 1975 to initiate research on the theretofore forbidden topic of Basque nationalism.

Second, it is sustained in that Pérez-Agote has monitored Basque (and Spanish) political developments throughout the entire post-Franco period, while initiating ambitious new research projects regarding the reproduction of Basque nationalism in 1984 and again in 1998.

Third, Professor Pérez-Agote is a sociologist by training, one of the few to embrace a topic dominated by historians and political scientists. Therefore, his analysis of core structures and focal events germane to Basque nationalism differs from that of most other investigators. His point of departure is to accept the existence of Basque nationalism as a given during the terminal years of the Franco regime (his temporal baseline) in order to understand how, despite dictatorial countermeasures, Basque nationalist sentiment not only survived but prospered—both broadening its base and assuming additional guises, including that of a Basque radical left movement disposed to support ETA's violence. Rather than a conventional focus on the historiography of Basque politics (electoral results, shifting alliances, proliferating parties, changing leadership), the present work introduces the reader to the social pillars of Basque nationalism itself: the private realms of the household, the informal *cuadrillas* (generational peer groups) engaged in *poteo* (frequent rounds of barhopping), folk dance groups and hiking clubs whose stated purposes often masked a hidden nationalist agenda, and the critical role of Catholic youth associations shielded from the scrutiny of civil authorities by sympathetic parish priests.

Fourth, unlike most of the literature on Basque nationalism, which tends to be myopically self-referential, Pérez-Agote situates his text within the wider frameworks of sociological theory regarding identity and group dynamics, as well as political theory on the nature of nationalism. By framing its analysis in broadly sociological rather than narrowly Basque historiographic terms, the present work becomes highly accessible (and useful) to scholars of other contemporary ethnonationalist movements throughout the world.

The present text is a translation, but one of an unusual sort. About ten years ago, I broached with Professor Pérez-Agote the possibility of translating one of his works for publication in the Basque series that I edited for the University of Nevada Press. The problem was that his existing monographs were somewhat dated, and he was contemplating revisiting the topic in the near future by launching another formal research project. We therefore decided to await its results in order to include them in a general overview of the entire corpus of his research on Basque nationalism. The present text is a translation of that synthesis—a work that has yet to appear as such in the original Spanish that is Professor Pérez-Agote's customary language of publication.

William A. Douglass

Introduction

It is the purpose of this book to identify and analyze some of the features and social processes that have nurtured, maintained, and even intensified Basque nationalist political consciousness in Spain, particularly during the Franco post-Franco historical period. Nationalism is a social phenomenon because, in the strictest sense, it belongs to the realm of the consciousness of social actors. Furthermore, as Walker Connor maintains, sociologists are interested in the nation not merely as the product of an elitist process, which in fact it normally is during its formative stages, but as a mass phenomenon (Connor 1994, 352).

Currently the paradigm of rational choice theory is fashionable within sociology, and renowned specialists have tried to apply it to the field of nationalism. Rogowski, for example, attempts to construct a "strictly rationalist theory" of nationalism (1985, 87), while Hechter tries to apply the theory of group solidarity to its analysis, an approach that "shows that it is indeed possible to explain variations in intergroup solidarity on the basis of the rational action of individuals. The theory proposes that groups will form when individuals desire to attain jointly produced private goods that cannot be obtained by following individual strategies" (Hechter 1989, 24). However, the present work argues that instrumentality (although very important) is only one of the many elements that inform human behavior (Weber 1978, 24–26) and that it should not be understood as referring only to the acquisition of material and private benefits.[1] An approach based solely on Hechter's (1989) restricted instrumental rationality is perhaps more relevant when predicting the future of nationalist movements that act in consolidated democratic states structured by political parties that play the parliamentary game. Under authoritarian regimes, however, the nationalist ideology is relegated and reduced to private and clandestine circles and means, as was the case in Spain during the Franco years. In such cases, both nationalist movements and individuals within them operate reactively (that is to say, without previously establishing defined objectives) on most occasions. Consequently, the overly restrictive instrumentalist approach becomes too narrow—even more so when, as a part of the response to repression, there is recourse to violence, as is characteristic of the Basque case. Indeed, the virulence and aggressiveness of such behavior corresponds to the traumatically felt renting of the emotional shield that normally protects values, concepts, and symbols transmitted through the family. In this respect, Douglass cautions that a strictly instrumentalist interpretation of ethnic nationalism "fails totally when it seeks an explanation of the inclination to violence of certain factions within ethno-nationalist movements" (1989, 101).

On the other hand, ascertaining instrumental behavior requires meeting a series of logical prerequisites. First, the social actors must establish objectives or goals. Second, and for the present study this is more interesting, one must address the subject's response to the social acceptance of his or her identity. When an identity is not accepted, that is, is either ignored or negatively valued, some individuals develop behavior that, while affirming their identity, in general is reactive. Social behavior based on the affirmation of a rejected social identity is grounded not in irrationality (as some observers tend to regard nationalist behavior) but in prerationality, because, viewed from without, it might be seen as intended to establish the prerequisites for subsequent instrumental behavior. I employ the term "from without" because often the actor does not even think about potential instrumental rational behavior, but simply responds to a given situation.

Clearly, in the early stages of nationalism many thinkers, social scientists as well as the implicated social and political elites, participate in the initial definition and configuration of a nation. When the outcomes reach the masses, or, as Connor would say, are transformed into social definitions, social scientists can operate in one of two ways. Either they can emulate and echo social actors by formulating supposedly objective definitions of the nation, or, as is the object of this work, they can ask themselves why and how social actors come to categorize their social reality thus, that is, in terms of nation, and the consequences of this.

Naturally, the actor's definitions of reality are subject to evaluation; they can be judged either true or false. However, even allowing for this, we must recognize that not all human activity is reducible to truth and error. Language clearly demonstrates this. For example, the statement "Tom's car is green" does not have the same logical set as "I advise you not to go." The former states something about something and is therefore subject to potential verification, whereas the latter refers to doing something, giving advice, and is therefore a "performative" expression (Austin 1982) that can be subjected to certain judgments (moral, for example) but not to verification of its truthfulness or objective nature. Even in human activity that can be examined in scientific terms (demonstrable truth or falsifiable error) by being predicative linguistic activity or, more generally, definitions of reality, meaning's existence and efficiency do not depend on veracity. Accordingly, a false definition can shape behavior just as much as a true one. Moreover, some definitions are impossible to verify. In any case, it is not the responsibility of the social scientist to submit the actors' definitions to scientific judgment. Sociologists of religion would not consider beginning their research asking themselves if a particular religious belief is true or false; rather, they would ask how beliefs were produced and reproduced, and how they shaped the actors' behavior. For the social effectiveness of an idea,[2] that is, its capacity to influence behavior, does not depend on its scientific veracity, but rather on the degree of certainty it achieves, on its capacity to assert itself as true, which in turn depends on the mechanisms of social gestation and reproduction of the idea—as will be demonstrated in the present work.

Social reality is very conventional, and when social actors define a collective or group reality, their behavior is predicative in that they configure something—that is, they say something about something. But it is also performative in the sense that they do something, since they generate the same reality that they define. For a statistical category to become a social aggregate—the number of redheads in a given population, for example (Nisbet 1970)—the members need to have a sense of belonging. This occurs when an objective, or supposedly objective, feature is transformed into a social symbol. The existence or not of a social aggregate does not depend on the existence of the objective feature per se, but on the perception of it as a differentiating symbol. The defining of individuals of an aggregate as social is performative in the sense that it is specifically generated or defined by them. Its persistence is then dependent on the social success of the definition, as well as on the extent to which others accept it, thus producing and reproducing a general feeling of belonging among the collectivity's adherents. A social meaning (in the sense that it is produced through a social process) is experienced by the actor as something that emanates directly from an original feature projected into the consciousness (or onto the screen of consciousness) of the individual. However, a feature can have social or political meaning in one situation and not in another. The Basque language, for example, has one significance in the Spanish Basque Country and another in the French Basque Country.

For a group definition to succeed, it requires social, rather than logical or scientific, plausibility. In other words, it needs a social milieu in which the definition makes sense for the actors; it depends more on their perceptions than on the objective reality of the defining feature itself.[3] In many cases, when movements emerge to defend a supposedly true cultural identity, we find that they are at a critical juncture where their supposedly objective differentiating features have all but disappeared and the process of disappearance may have been traumatic. This makes for an excellent cultural medium or structure of social plausibility in which movements can define themselves in terms of an identity based on supposedly objective features. Social definitions of identity are essentialist; they refer to the seemingly objective features that constitute a collectivity's essence, and the very consciousness of its members' identity is then presented as a product of these objective features.

A group definition becomes objective through various means: mutual recognition by actors who define themselves as a group, recognition of the group by others, and the politico-administrative stance toward the group, which might involve force or coercion. The relations among these forms in a particular aggregate might or might not be coterminal. They are analyzed in this work specifically in terms of the Spanish Basque Country vis-à-vis the Spanish state.

Flowing from the foregoing theoretical baseline, what separates a statistical aggregate (a number of individuals sharing a common feature) from a social aggregate (a collectivity of individuals that feel a sense of belonging to a whole, generally based on claimed possession of a common feature) is logically or theoretically arbitrary. There is no logical or theoretical reason why a social aggregate or group (understood as a consciousness of belonging) forms, and therefore one cannot predict group formation. Groups form through the arbitrary definition of inclusion-exclusion. The actors or group members, however, cannot think in terms of logical arbitrariness. Rather, they formulate a rationalizing discourse about the collective existence and insulate the group, and its survival, from arbitrariness by consecrating or naturalizing discourse about it.[4]

However, the formation of social groups is ultimately not arbitrary, since groups, or social definitions of them (evident to the members or politically objectified), are the product of a historico-social process. The theory of social aggregation contradicts the methodological premises outlined by Marx in developing his ideas of objective interest, class in itself, and class for itself. Objective interest is when a class in itself, a statistical aggregate, is transformed into a class for itself, a social aggregate, once it is objectified by science. For me what transforms a statistical aggregate into a social aggregate is an arbitrary logic (and social determination), however, in Marx what separates a class for itself (social aggregate) from a class in itself (statistical aggregate) is the group's grasp of scientific knowledge of reality. The distinction makes salient the restrictive assumptions—illusions—that are underlined in Marx with respect to the role of reason and objective knowledge in history.

Given my belief in the importance of the logical arbitrariness and social determination of social phenomena in general, and of social aggregates in particular,[5] in the present work I examine the twin phenomena of nation and nationalism in terms of two inescapable and fundamental methodological moments: the phenomenological and the generative. If an idea's social effectiveness, in the previous sense of its capacity for behavioral determination, does not particularly depend on greater or lesser truth but on its capacity to impose itself as true through social mechanisms, then (1) the phenomenological moment guarantees that a scientific judgment of social imagery or beliefs is ineffective, and that its determination will be as value judgmental as any based on morality, justice, or political convention; and (2) the generative moment guarantees, on the contrary, a distancing from an idealist stance by considering images, beliefs, and the like to be dependent variables, thereby drawing us toward an idea's objective resolutions and the social mechanisms that generate its production and reproduction. Both moments must be considered, because, at one extreme, to ignore the fetishes and dreams of a historical period is to discount the driving forces of humanity and, at the other, to recognize them as the sole reality would be acknowledging that there is no better sociology than common sense expressed in statistics.

Today, there seems to be a growing consensus that the nation is something phenomenological, something that belongs, fundamentally, to the consciousness of social actors. The nation is an imagined community (Anderson 1983); or a reality born through mutual recognition (Gellner 1983); or belongs to the field of social phenomena (Pérez-Agote 1984b); or possesses a phenomenological charter (Tiryakian and Nevitte 1985); or, as with any identity, is perception (Greenfeld 1992); or is an intangible reality, a psychological bond.

The nation is therefore a social categorization (made by social actors) of a collective reality, and as such is not a scientific categorization (made by social scientists) of a social reality. When sociologists become interested in the concept of nationhood, they do so for the why and how—the causes and social mechanisms by which actors come to categorize reality in terms of the nation.

To whom we refer when thinking of the nation as a categorization of reality undertaken by actors can vary considerably. Thus, while for Walker Connor nationalism is a mass phenomenon (1994), the objective of Liah Greenfeld's book *Nationalism: Five Roads to Modernity* "is to explain the evolution of a particular set of ideas and to show how they permeate the attitudes of relevant actors" (1992, 24). The former regards acting out the nation, the latter conceiving it. The dilemma, I would argue, is not resolved simply by pointing to the effect of different periods of research. Nor is it simply about pointing out that for something to become a mass phenomenon it must previously have been an elite idea.

There is something more. While the majority of theorists, including Connor, think of nationalism as a phenomenon that began in Europe in the eighteenth century, Liah Greenfeld tries to demonstrate that the concept of the national community emerged in England during the first third of the sixteenth.

Furthermore, it should be remembered that nationalism involves not only the cognitive dimension (ideas) but others, among which satisfaction based on an emotionally protective sense of belonging stands out. Related to this, the wide scope both of an idea and of a broad feeling raises the question of how effective the transmission mechanisms are, in particular the educational system (Gellner 1983) and certain mechanisms of ritual identity maintenance, along with the historical myths on which the identity was founded (A. Smith 1971; Douglass 1989, 103 ff.).

A sociological model confronting the concept of the nation must include both internal elements, belonging to the social world of the actors, and external elements. For this reason, the rudimentary model outlined here contains elements from the social actors' world of representation and elements imposed by the sociologist from the outside by asking questions that the actors do not generate themselves. This dual level of observation, from both within and without, may introduce aspects of the object termed the nation that are apparently contradictory. However, in reality they are characteristics that belong to different levels of observation (Pérez-Agote 1996b).

From within, the nation is a specific social reading by a particular collectivity. The idea of nation functions socially in a kind of essentialist way, as actors affirm that a collective reality is (or is not) a nation, as if it were a changeless essence, a biological entity or a natural given.

However, from an external point of view, the challenge is to explain the process whereby a social convention is generated, rather than to presuppose or prejudge its scientific veracity or nature. All research that derives from the positing of an objective a priori concept of the nation falters over its own premise. From such a viewpoint, rejected here, national history is constructed ad probandum, as a supposedly discernible process that produces a nation's objective features.

In this sense, the history of Western nation-state building—at least of those that were constructed according to the model that Smith has termed the political or civic nation (an ethnic group defining itself and other ethnic groups inhabiting a constituted given state as a single supraethnic nation) (A. Smith 1994)—is, in a way, the history of progressive negation of the social and political significance or meaning of specific and varied territories that make up the state. This is a potential source of political instability owing to a possible crisis of legitimacy. The state may be successful in forging a collective national consciousness whereby the citizens as a whole are convinced that they belong to the same community, considering any differences as simply local particularities. However, it may not be entirely successful. Success, to whatever degree, does not depend so much on the scientific objectivity of the supposed national community but rather on the social mechanisms that contribute to the formation and acceptance of social evidence.[6]

This is the case with the relation between the national state and the social aggregation within it. Simple mutual recognition is the weakest form of objectification of the aggregate. Recognition of their relationship by others is another form. And its objectification in politico-administrative arrangements is the strongest. Of greatest interest are the configurations of the extreme forms of objectification and the relations between them, since the definition of the state and the nation, the state and we the people, may or may not coincide.

The case examined in this book is the conflict over the "we" that emerges within a state (Spain) already territorially defined five centuries earlier, but in which the symbolic order has been unable to develop a national Spanish collective consciousness embraced by the entire population residing within those old borders.

Within the officially demarcated territory of the Spanish state are specific territories in which (to a certain extent and varying according to political factions and historical moments) representations of an alternative or incompatible political community coexist with a countervailing consistent affirmation of a Spanish nation. In a latent or explicit way, alternating or continuous, a particular sense of "we" among specific populations of defined territories within Spain has favored the constitution of a more or less different political order. Historically, this social phenomenon occurs, at the very least, in Catalonia, the Basque Country, and, to a lesser extent, Galicia.

Therefore, in the Basque case, the present conflict is about the definition of "we"—between a "we" that is objectified and promulgated by the state and a "we" that emerges from the Basque Country itself. When a politically objectified "we" is called into question, but without the superimposed political order disappearing, there is a crisis of political legitimacy.

In such "we" conflicts the intensity and depth of the struggle can vary from a regionalist claim to greater administrative autonomy to the quest for political secession. In every case the "we" conflict necessarily retains a form of political expression because politics is a necessary referent for social synthesis (Balandier 1967, 58).[7]

An individual living in society belongs to numerous groups. This group continuum (which sociology considers a complex matrix of objective and intersubjective relations) is circumscribed by time and space. Discontinuity bounds meaning for individuals, since beyond its limits there is an abrupt decline in the individual's symbolic and emotional involvement and commitment. In the modern Western states the boundary of discontinuity is objectified in both political and territorial terms.

The problem of discontinuity is precisely that of the society. Mauss, in his "plan of descriptive sociology," privileges social cohesion among the "general phenomena of intrasocial life." A society defines itself in two ways: politically through its self-recognition and assertion (establishment of its name, borders, rights of citizenship, and so on), and psychologically as a collective representation of a single totality of individuals sharing such attributes in a certain place and time (1967, 100–101).

The objective and subjective aspects of social cohesion are anchored within spatial and temporal coordinates: on the one hand, there are individuals in given places and moments and, on the other, there is a collective representation of this distribution, marked by a sense of "social territory" and by the myth of "common descent" (Mauss 1967, 100–101). Time and space (history and territory) define the "we"—a tautological and arbitrary "we" (since its existence cannot be deduced from a prior or universally valid concept), yet historically and socially determined.

The question arises: what is the relationship between social cohesion and its political equivalent? Statist political power always imposes a certain social cohesion, but other forces can exist as well. One or more of these can prove incompatible with cohesive state authority. This is not a logical problem but a power relationship and, defined thus, it is very complex.

The Basque case appears as a tension and conflict between two social cohesions, between two historically determined arbitrary logics. Conflict emerges over power—a "we" conflict. It is about space and time and their social representation, about their "objectification" in territory and history, on the border and in common descent, in a mother earth concept and as myth.

Like history, territory has twin dimensions: the objective and the symbolic. The modern state differs from previous forms of political association in being primarily territorial in an objective sense, since the "monopoly of physical coercion" is devoted to defending boundaries. For this reason Weber speaks of territory as "an essential element in the definition" of the state (Weber 2002). However, territory has a symbolic dimension beyond mere geographic or political expressions, which may or may not coincide with Weber's definition. In the contemporary Spanish Basque Country there is a territorial political objectification, the so-called Basque Autonomous Community of Euskadi (a name originally coined in the nineteenth century to refer to the whole Basque Country), which is included in the present Spanish State of the Autonomies. However, the symbolic territory of Basque nationalists comprises not only this objectified territory, but also that which corresponds to another autonomous community, Navarre, and the nonadministratively objectified (within France) territory of the French Basque Country.

Although territory and history might be two fundamental symbolic elements, their objective dimensions may operate in different realms. Territory is a determinant objective element of the modern state, whereas history, in its most objective dimension, pertains to the symbolic realm.

"Objective history" refers not to the historian's claim to objectivity, but to a certain hypostasis that the institutions of intergenerational symbolic transmission (the educational system) objectify as national history (or what might be termed "sacred" history), as opposed to the less objectified versions that operate within lived history (that of the actors themselves) and in narrated history (that experienced not by the actors but by the generation preceding them).

Mills (1959) contends that it is the responsibility of the social scientist to explain the contemporary features of a society in terms of their current functions. This piece of advice might be translated as the priority of the present over the past: if a phenomenon has a past or historical reason, this must be translated into contemporary meaning. Among the different aspects that history presents to the social scientist, priority is given in the present text to contemporary collective representations of history (shared memory, narrated history, lived history). Some reasons for this priority are theoretical, since individuals try to justify the community to which they belong in social terms by constructing an ad hoc history. Other reasons are more specific: for example, a fundamental element of the Basque problem during the Franco years was the overdramatization of the Spanish regime by various generations of Basques, a phenomenon still evident within certain factions of Basque nationalism.

In the Basque case there was also a change, or historical evolution, in the perception of history. One might speak of, as an initial change, a transformation from a consciousness defined by the ethnocentric defense of traditional forms of existence, sustained by classes tied to the Old Regime (Carlism), in the face of the repeated assaults of political centralization and modernization, to a political consciousness of national affirmation, sustained by new urban classes against political centralization and new forms of urban and industrial life (Basque nationalism). It was a move from an attitude of withdrawal and isolation toward a specific political project with an ideology and a political party. However, Basque nationalism did not dissolve (or resolve) ethnocentrism. A traditional way of life survived in some form, and nationalist ideology invoked the existence of a historical ethnic group with mythical repercussions. In its ideological development Basque nationalism would evolve from a natural to a cultural objectivism. In recent times less objectivist or primordialist formulations have emerged that, although far from accepted orthodoxy, show that ideological projects favoring a civic (ethnically heterogeneous) political nation are socially acceptable and sustainable inside the Basque nationalist world.[8] Furthermore, levels of nationalist radicalism (political independence as an end and military violence as a means) and political radicalism (a left-wing project) have also varied over time.

Recent history, from the Spanish Civil War (1936–39) onward, produced a curious effect in historical representation within the core of Basque nationalism. The Franco period and social life under its authoritarian political regime were overdramatized, so that recent, and therefore "lived," history was framed as fundamental, even foundational. Franco's state imposed a repressive system proscribing all forms of Basque nationalism and leftist politics, a policy that legitimated, to the regime's regret, Basque nationalist sentiment and social concern. Basque nationalist consciousness during this period did not need to refer to some mythical age, given that repressed social life itself was experienced as foundational, as a founding myth. As social life was experienced as foundational, so the nation was framed as a symbolic project, both national and social, for future generations. For them the rational political institutionalization of this symbolic synthesis was difficult to bring about, but the quest for it, along with the formation and dissolution of political organizations, is one of the keys to understanding the transformation of Basque nationalist consciousness during the Franco years. This process cannot be understood if one does not take into account the attempt to synthesize the "national question" and the "social question of class" that occurred within Basque nationalism's political organizations, and particularly within the armed Basque nationalist movement during the Franco regime.

The first consideration of the present work (part II) is Basque nationalism during the Franco years (1939–75). This is not to ignore the earlier historical genesis of Basque nationalism, but rather to distinguish two different theoretical problems: the generative matrix of Basque nationalism and its operation from the beginning of the Franco period onward. Removing (rather than ignoring) historical origins is a methodological device that facilitates treating Basque nationalism in 1939 as a *primitive accumulation of symbolic nationalist capital*, capital that had a fixed geographic and social base.

Thus, a distinction is made here between *primitive accumulation* (Marx 1977,

xxii   *The Social Roots of Basque Nationalism*

chap. 26), governed by precise sociohistorical laws, and the operation and social reproduction of this initial *symbolic capital* (Bourdieu 1988, 137–41) from the Spanish Civil War onward, governed by other laws and sustained through other social
mechanisms. The latter, less explored by sociologists than the first is by historians, is
my principal focus. In addition, I examine the essential means through which
Basque nationalism was transformed after Franco's death and once the democratiz-
ing of Spain had begun (part III and epilogue).

After the Spanish Civil War, this initial symbolic capital found itself in a new
sociopolitical context that projected nationalist consciousness into new arenas and
social sectors of the Basque Country. This consciousness also intensified into more
reactive and virulent forms. At the same time, and as a direct consequence of such
developments, the social meaning of this capital was transformed, since it was symbolic. This transformation was effected further by the introduction of both democracy and a degree of political decentralization through creation of the current autonomous communities in Spain.

This book is composed of three parts and an epilogue. Part I is theoretical and
outlines a theory of the social roots of nationalism, understood as a specific historical form of politicizing collective identity. It consists of two chapters: chapter 1 tack-
les the theoretical problem of collective identity, while chapter 2 addresses how a
specific form of politicizing collective identity takes place and the consequences. Peripheral nationalisms in Western nation-states are viewed as a consequence of the
unsuccessful construction of a supraethnic political identity in a multiethnic state.
The basic conclusion of an analysis of Basque nationalism within the Spanish state,
which is the goal of the subsequent parts of the book, is that the social success of a
nationalist (centralist or peripheral) definition of collective identity relies above all
on its mechanisms of social diffusion.

Part II, consisting of chapters 3 and 4, looks at the mechanisms that Basque nationalism employed to sustain its reproduction during the Franco years. Chapter 3 is
principally devoted to explaining Basque nationalism's historical development and
demonstrating how the installation of Franco's authoritarian regime unintentionally caused, by its persecution of Basque ideology, culture, and language (which remained virulent until the late 1960s), the extension and radicalization of nationalist
consciousness. Chapter 4 argues that, given the regime's authoritarian control (especially from the end of the Spanish Civil War through the 1960s, since later this
control would be significantly less effective) of the public sphere of social reproduction (educational system, mass media, political association), nationalism took refuge
in those areas of life that the state found more difficult to penetrate: the family, inter
pares groups, private associations, friendship groups, and the Catholic Church. Because of this withdrawal and the political pressure exercised by the state, there was a
generational radicalization within Basque nationalism, eventually resulting in the
formation of an armed wing that, on eliciting the increased emotional support of

important sectors of the population, itself became a mechanism for reproducing nationalist consciousness.

Part III analyzes both the changes that occurred in the reproduction of Basque nationalism during the establishment of the democratic regime and the subsequent institutionalization of autonomous political power. Chapters 5 and 6 focus on the transformations in the two kinds of reproduction mechanisms that emerged during the Franco years. Chapter 5 analyzes changes in the different types of violence, the physical and symbolic forms of the state and the physical acts of a sector of Basque nationalism, and especially social perceptions of the types of violence. Chapter 6 addresses changes in the associative and intersubjective network that had been inaccessible to Franco's state; and, above all, it examines the loss of political momentum and vision within this network.

Finally, the epilogue outlines a series of elements that describe the current political situation in the Basque Country, with the aim of presenting this work as a step toward elaborating a new, more complex, model of Basque nationalist reproduction, a model that takes into account the current twin dimensions of this process: that deriving from the institutionalization of autonomous power connected to the central state and that originating in the former reproduction mechanisms within a significant sector of the population—as well as the interrelation between the two dimensions.

This book incorporates a series of theoretical works (the oldest being Pérez-Agote 1980 and the most recent being Pérez-Agote 1996 and Pérez-Agote et al. 1999a,b) and summarizes the observations of other analysts. The essential empirical data stem from two books (Pérez-Agote 1984 and 1987), while the epilogue is original and part of work in progress (Pérez-Agote et al. 1999a,b). Qualitative empirical data from three different fieldwork projects have been included in this text. The first was initiated as soon as possible after the death of Franco (November 1975), or once sociological investigation of political questions was again feasible. The object of the research was an analysis of the reproduction process and the radicalization of Basque nationalist consciousness during the Franco years, the results of which correspond to part II of this book.

The second field research project, corresponding to part III, took place in 1984 and was commissioned by the Centro de Investigaciones Sociológicas (CIS; Center for Sociological Research) in Madrid with the objective of understanding how the mechanisms of political radicalization generated during the Franco period evolved during the political transition to democracy. Finally, the third piece of fieldwork, commissioned by the Gabinete de Prospecciones Sociológicas del Gobierno Vasco (Cabinet of Sociological Research of the Basque Government), was undertaken in 1998, or at a time when, it could be said, Spanish democracy was totally consolidated; whereas in the Basque Country the politico-symbolic conflict was far from being resolved, despite the political solutions designed into the so-called State of the

Autonomies in the prevailing Spanish constitution. This fieldwork has been used to write the epilogue, which attempts to outline, in a provisional way, the loci of Basque nationalization processes of reproduction and transformation. For analyzing the politico-symbolic universe, that is, the political culture of Basque nationalism, I've selected a qualitative approach for both methodological and theoretical reasons, as well as for more practical reasons stemming from the political circumstances of the subjects' social reality.

Regarding the latter, it must be said that during the whole period of study, given the delicate nature of the subject matter, it was not easy to find good informants or a comfortable context in which they could fully and freely express themselves. Gaining access to the most profound dimensions of people's identity, as well as their attitudes toward both state and ETA violence, has required earning the utmost trust of the informants, which in turn has meant guaranteeing safeguards and devoting much time to breaking down the barriers of suspicion. In many cases, informants were naturally reluctant to speak about criminal, or at least indictable, behavior—their own or that of someone close to them. However, at other times their reticence was due simply to what they felt they could or could not say. In general, it became progressively more difficult to obtain information from people in those social sectors that sympathized with armed nationalist violence.

Under these conditions a quantitative methodology based on opinion and attitude polls would not have been very appropriate. Furthermore, there were both methodological and theoretical reasons, deriving from the object of study itself, to use a qualitative methodology. On the one hand, an attempt was made to understand the most profound dimensions of Basque political culture and identity, adapting the idea of culture as advocated by Geertz (1973) to the political realm in order to interpret a political reality through thick description and in terms of its deepest human meaning. I seek to understand the mechanisms whereby this meaning is extended to new social sectors. Wuthnow and Witten demonstrate the existence of four types of qualitative cultural studies in sociology. The first, in which culture is understood as an implicit feature of social life, and the fourth, which concerns the institutional contexts in which culture is produced and diffused, are very close to the direction of this research (Wuthnow and Witten 1988; Potter 1996).

The cognitive dimension of nationalism consists of the socially constructed definition of a collective (group) reality, a definition the nationalist social actor accepts, thereby making that definition true (performativity). The initial point of interest for this research was the definition and its transformation, in transmission-adhesion mechanisms. These twin points of interest might be compared to the *emic-etic* distinction (A. Smith 1971; Potter 1996, 84–86). An *emic* perspective was adopted because the definition was retained without directing attention to defined reality; the comparison between definition and defined reality would be an *etic* position, which in this case would make no sense given that the definition, after obtaining support, generates defined reality (performativity). In this perspective, termed *contingent accuracy* by Potter, it is more a matter of intersubjectivity than of objectivity per se. Methodologically, the perspective is strictly phenomenological, although not regarding epistemology, for through representation-definition no attempt is made to reach a represented-defined reality. Instead, a mixed methodological approach was adopted, termed *subjective valuing* by Potter: the actors' view is accepted but elements not provided by the actors are introduced to describe a process of reproduction and transformation.

In general, qualitative methodology is useful when one cannot understand something by any other means; therefore it tends to be valuable when one wants to understand subjective human experience (Valle 1997, 104–5). More specifically, qualitative methodology is more useful the more this human experience is sensitive and hidden and the greater the social or political (including police) control there is over subjective expression. For both reasons, the qualitative approach was unavoidable in this study.

Searching for a base of *statistical representativeness* was unattainable through qualitative means, and so not a problem. Rather, the challenge was achieving *social representativeness*, something more difficult to define and control in this fieldwork. One wants a guarantee of credibility that what is stated by informants in a limited number of responses is applicable to the majority of the social sector. The guarantee is never strong enough to convert credibility into certainty, and therefore the information obtained has its limits. The best way to clarify those limits is to explicate my research design.

First Stage of the Research

No doubt one of the potential benefits of qualitative methodology is its capacity to expose sociological inquiry to a social phenomenon where the basic elements in play are unknown. In applying qualitative techniques, the researcher very openly (and less forcefully) accesses the deepest experience of some social actors in order to gain an idea of the kinds of social elements, mechanisms, and institutions (along with experiences, important events, and processes) that constitute the phenomenon under investigation. This was certainly true of this study.

From initial observations, it was clear that, despite the political persecution of nationalist ideology and the prohibitions on the learning and use of the language, Basque nationalist consciousness during the Franco years not only held its ground but penetrated new social and geographic realms. It also became more radicalized, both in its sociopolitical dimension, incorporating ideological elements from the Left, and in its purely nationalist one, adopting more openly pro-independence postures. Moreover, all this took place over two decades, the 1950s and 1960s, during which important contingents of people from different Spanish provinces flocked to the Basque Country, provoking a greater penetration and radicalization of nationalist sentiment among the nonimmigrant population.[9] The initial presumption, in fact, was that Franco's political regime and its persecutory politics produced the spread and radicalization of Basque nationalist consciousness. However, the question remained: how and through which mechanisms? There was no available research on the topic. Historians had studied the origins of Basque nationalism at the end of the nineteenth century and its initial development in the beginnings of the twentieth. However, sociologists and political scientists had done nothing to determine the social roots of nationalist consciousness and their transformation during the Franco years; and there was no data on political opinions about these changes. Nor were there any electoral data to examine as a true social barometer. This situation meant that the research, starting with an heuristic analysis, veered toward more systematic collection of information, which then implied a continual revision of the theoretical-analytical model.

In 1979, the first round of interviews was conducted with five university students about twenty-one years old (individuals 1 to 5).[10] The main aim was to ascertain the principal socialization mechanisms and the means and forms of confronting (during adolescence) social, political, and nationalist problems in general. Special emphasis was placed on examining intergenerational family relations and the universe of the respondents' associations. The students were offered the possibility of taking part in a political sociology seminar on the Basque nationalist phenomenon as experienced personally and in one's family. The selected students possessed a range of relevant factors. As was reasonable to expect at the time, the participants had, at the very least, a certain sympathy for Basque nationalism. Each one of the five was given a guide to what was called *social biography,* which emphasized personal and family geographic origin (rural or urban residence); social, cultural, religious, ideological, and linguistic background; political, cultural, and religious environment in the family's home life; education and inter pares groups; personal evolution in the attitudes of friends and family in relation to politics; periods, moments, or events judged to be key in socialization; personal experience of politics and political repression; and personal view of the national question.

In each seminar session a student responded extensively to the questions posed in the guide, having forty-five minutes to an hour to do so. Afterward, the organizers led a group discussion of the case. Notes could be taken, but the students decided that the sessions should not be tape-recorded. So after each session it was necessary to think about and jot down the most relevant aspects for interpretation.

Once a detailed analysis of the interviews and their resulting discussions had been made, an interview plan could be designed to target those sectors of social life that appeared critical. Associations (in particular those in which adult leaders devoted time to organizing activities for young people) and the *cuadrilla* (group of friends) appeared to be especially relevant in political socialization.

From the process there emerged different nationalist prototypes discriminated by age cohort. Among individuals over sixty, who had experienced the Spanish Civil War when they were young, were those from the moderate Basque Nationalist Party (PNV) milieu. Among the first nationalist generation of the postwar era, politically socialized during the triumphant years of the Franco regime and who were then around forty or forty-five years of age, were the early members of ETA. Those who were socialized during the declining years of the dictatorship (from 1960 onward) were about thirty years old. They had been born around 1950, and became aware of the political arena toward the end of that decade. Among them were those of the nationalist Left who rejected its own political inability to control military nationalist violence, or even dismissed the violence itself as illegitimate in a political context (that of 1980) considered different from that of the Franco years. The youngest individuals would be approached through interviews concerning the cuadrilla and their other associations. The corresponding series of interviews specified below sought to take account of all of the foregoing considerations.

In 1980, two rounds of interviews were conducted: the first of these (individuals 9 to 17) with young members of a politically radicalized but nonactivist cuadrilla of friends. The world of the cuadrilla was touched on in practically all the responses, the questions being specifically designed to elicit this, and an attempt was made to discover the keys in their operation and the possibility of maintaining, through intersubjective relationships, a *world* (Schutz 1974; Berger and Luckmann 1966) or specific conceptual universe. The symbolic role of violence in this world was of particular interest. Using a snowball sampling approach, an attempt was made, through those previously interviewed, to establish contact with a cuadrilla of young people between twenty and twenty-five years old and drawn from the widest social and cultural spectrum possible (which was easier to accomplish in an urban neighborhood than in a smaller town or village). Arrangements were made to interview young people from the same cuadrilla so as to be able to understand what membership meant from within as intersubjective space, although this required reducing the potential diversity of those questioned. These young people did not allow tape-recording either, so notes and subsequent postinterview reconstruction were utilized.

The second round of interviews from this year (individuals 18 to 23) was devoted to former members of the armed organization ETA, who were approximately forty years old. The specific focus of interest was on the mechanisms by which they were attracted to the nationalist cause—particularly their social ties, family relationships, and the transformation of certain symbolic structures within such arrangements. Four of the respondents (I-18 to I-21) came from nationalist families; the remaining two (I-22 and I-23) did not. Obviously, it was not easy to make contact with this type of interviewee. Snowball sampling was also utilized here, using the contacts made with the individuals interviewed in the cuadrilla. The interviews were tape-recorded and subsequently transcribed.

The 1981 round of interviews (individuals 24A to 24B) focused on two leaders of youth organizations well established during the Franco years. Through them we attempted to understand the climate of opinion and forms of socialization present among young people prominent in these groups during the Franco period, especially regarding social and political problems. The selection of such groups was an easy task since they were large and diffuse, as well as well known in nationalist circles. The interviews were tape-recorded and subsequently transcribed.

Finally, in 1982, two more rounds of interviews were undertaken. The first of these (individuals 6 to 8) was devoted to members (around thirty years old) of the so-called *izquierda abertzale* (nationalist Left) that had explicitly rejected the use of armed violence for political purposes. Through these interviews we attempted to understand the degree to which emotional support of Basque nationalism—expressed nonpolitically—persisted despite democratization of Spain. Furthermore, we attempted specifically to understand *lived history* during the Franco period: the degree to which that period had served as a foundational moment. Again snowball sampling was used in selecting the individuals. These interviews could not be tape-recorded, so we reconstructed the interviews through notes.

The second of the 1982 rounds (individuals 25 to 30) was devoted to former nationalist combatants from the Spanish Civil War, of which four were members and the rest supporters of the PNV (Basque Nationalist Party). They ranged in age from sixty-five to seventy-five. The interviews attempted to understand what life was like for nationalist families in the aftermath of the war, especially from a symbolic point of view—that is, how they strategically approached the socialization of their children, raising them to live in an environment that was hostile to their specific symbolic universe and that rendered them publicly voiceless, but without renouncing their political beliefs for that reason. In sum, it was revealing to know how they perceived this hostile environment and how, in spite of it, they transmitted the symbolic nationalist universe. Again, respondents were identified by means of snowball sampling. They did not consent to being tape-recorded, and notes were taken for subsequent reconstruction.

This stage of the research was necessarily very heuristic, and a certain redundancy was evident. Because of greater freedom in all public spheres at that time, society was changing rapidly. Consequently, we decided to embark on another stage of research that was more systematic in its collection of information and, in every facet of the new fieldwork focused on the two historical moments that were most interesting for the study: the repression by the Franco regime of Basque nationalism and the current political changes being experienced. This, moreover, strengthened the analysis of the first stage of the research.

Second Stage of the Research

The Spanish transition to democracy brought about fundamental changes in the political and other spheres of social life, substantially altering the model of reproduction and radicalization of Basque nationalism. Passed by referendum in Spain, the new 1978 Spanish constitution failed to obtain conclusive approval in the Basque Country (as can be seen in table 6.1), and gave rise to the Statute of Gernika, which allowed for the formation of a Basque government and parliament. From the death of Franco onward, freedom of political association was gradually permitted, so that a new framework of old (until that time clandestine) and new parties emerged in the Basque Country (Llera 1993 and 1994). The establishment of political parties had very important consequences: a decrease in political pressure on the population and the shattering of a certain anti-Franco unanimity, along with a similar breaking up of pro-Basque nationalist unanimity. On the other hand, the creation of autonomous power meant, in part, the formation of a new local center of power, as well as tolerance of Basque cultural and linguistic symbols.

This second stage of the research had two fundamental objectives. The first was to examine the place of violence in both a general Basque worldview and, more especially, in political culture. It involved exploring more deeply the role played by violence and the attitudes starting to emerge toward it—particularly in the social images of the armed conflict—as a result of the political change associated with the Spanish transition to democracy. Rather than speak of just one type of violence, one should refer to the constellation of interwoven physical and symbolic violence during the Franco years. We identified three facets or factors of violence: Factor A refers to the symbolic violence practiced by the state through its general control of expression in the public sphere and its particular measures against the Basque language and culture, as well as against a nationalist ideology. Factor B refers to the physical violence practiced by the state. Factor C refers to the physical violence practiced by ETA.

The second objective was to understand what was happening with the intersubjective associative framework that had established the structure of social plausibility for the reproduction and radicalization of Basque nationalist consciousness at the beginning of a climate of progressive political modernization and rationalization. To what degree did this framework and its political projection remain intact? Had there occurred (or not) a certain depoliticization of social life? Or, to put it more succinctly, who still advocated Basque radical nationalism and who did not?

Once established, these objectives were broken down into what might be called central variables:

Factor A: state violence toward language and culture, and later liberalization
Factor B: physical state violence and change in the legitimacy of the state and its violence

Factor c: physical violence of ETA and changes in the perception of it and its
legitimacy
Intersubjective world: (a) cuadrillas and *poteo* (going round the bars): changes
in their form and political function; and (b) associative world: changes in its
form and political function
Relative autonomy of political life: perception of political change

To get at these dimensions of social and political life, a dual approach was proposed. The first would employ interviews with strategic informants to determine
the critical dimensions of study. The exercise required considerable sensitivity to
subtleties, since the very posing of the issues was likely to be received and processed
differently by each of the social sectors. It became necessary to conduct long,
semidirected interviews with key social actors and qualified politicians. An attempt
was made to interview leaders who had a general overview of the problem, which
normally meant those holding the highest position possible in different organizations. This was the selection criterion in the interviews with 1-31 to 1-58 (according
to the outline below).

The second approach consisted of trying to observe the same dimensions operating on the ground and to discern the interactions among different points of view.
The two sites where fieldwork was eventually carried out were selected according to
the following considerations: Of the four Spanish Basque provinces (Araba, Gipuzkoa, and Bizkaia, which make up the current Autonomous Community of Euskadi,
and Navarre, presently constituted in the Community of Navarra) affected by the
phenomenon of Basque nationalism, two were selected for the fieldwork—Bizkaia
and Gipuzkoa. There, Basque nationalism retained a strong base of support. In 1977,
during the first general elections of the democratic era, the Basque nationalist vote
reached 46 percent in Gipuzkoa and 39 percent in Bizkaia; in Araba it scarcely attained 20 percent (Gurrutxaga, Pérez-Agote, and Unceta 1991, 24, 198, 388) and in
Navarre still less.[11]

Basque nationalism was born in Bizkaia in the 1890s as a response to the several
waves of immigration during the industrialization of the second half of the nineteenth century; and from the fact that the new arrivals tended to concentrate in the
dense urban areas of greater metropolitan Bilbao. Gipuzkoa's industrialization process began somewhat later and to a certain extent derived from that of Bilbao. That
said, industrial and population growth were more geographically widespread in
Gipuzkoa than in Bizkaia; so, immigration undoubtedly was experienced less traumatically. Lacking Bilbao's urban concentration of non-Basques, newcomers were
less evident throughout Gipuzkoa. In 1975, the population of Gipuzkoa's capital city
represented but 25 percent of the provincial total, while that of Bilbao was close to 40
percent, rising to 80 percent if greater metropolitan Bilbao is taken into account

(Gurrutxaga, Pérez-Agote, and Unceta 1991, 24, 198, 388). However, once Basque cultural and linguistic characteristics had been highlighted through the felt trauma of their imperilment by such concentrated immigration, nationalism tended to develop more extensively.

After the two provinces were selected, we discussed whether to undertake fieldwork throughout each territory or simply select a representative population nucleus. The second option was chosen because one of the principal goals of the analysis was to examine everyday life as expressed and experienced in a compact network of intersubjective relationships maintained through the ritualized movements of cuadrillas during poteo and the intense socializing within an extensive associative network. The premise was that an authoritarian regime, at least that of Franco, controlled public spaces (political representation, education, media, civic order), which forced the reproduction of nationalist consciousness to withdraw into the private spaces of family and friendship, to the discrete arena of religious institutions, and to the concealed world of certain groups with ostensibly politically insignificant or benign purposes (gastronomy, dance, hiking, culture, athletics). So an understanding of community life, within a specific place, was particularly relevant to the overall objectives of the study.

Therefore a compact urban place was selected in each province. In Gipuzkoa, Tolosa was chosen because it best represented the Basque reality of the province. Tolosa had a stable population from 1970 onward of about eighteen thousand inhabitants, belonging to that region of Gipuzkoa with a low percentage of immigrants (around 11 percent in 1981). Among municipalities of approximately twenty thousand inhabitants, it had the greatest number of Basque speakers, and its level of industrial development was similar to that of Gipuzkoa as a whole (in 1981 55 percent of the active population was employed in industry or construction in both Tolosa and Gipuzkoa). Above all, the community had a very high degree of social and political mobilization in the era when these became important factors (from 1970 onward) (Gurrutxaga, Pérez-Agote, and Unceta 1991, vol. 1).[12]

In Bizkaia, the greater metropolitan area of Bilbao was an obvious choice, for, as previously mentioned, it accounted for 80 percent of the province's population in 1975. Its largest component was Bilbao proper, with 431,000 inhabitants, or half the total population of the metropolis and 40 percent of the province. Therefore, Bilbao itself was selected, but, because its size would not allow us to become familiar with community life, we chose one of the neighborhoods. Not having in hand at that time data about the social structure of the city below the municipal level, we consulted experts (sociologists and town planners) in order to identify a Bilbao neighborhood that would comply with a series of criteria. Santutxu seemed the most appropriate, since in that district native and immigrant populations coexisted, along with a relatively broad range of social strata (from the middle lower class to the middle class).

Above all, in this neighborhood there was a very high level of social and political mobilization. The percentage of Basque speakers was very low, practically nil in the public sphere, which corresponded to the general reality of Bizkaian urban areas. It was thus agreed that Tolosa and Santutxu were good examples of the multipolarity and predominance of the Basque language found in Gipuzkoa and the concentration and cultural clash of Bizkaia, respectively.

In the field research, the decision was made to undertake individual interviews, but to also work with groups and elicit a wealth of hybrid discourse by encouraging informants to meet and discuss the issues.[13] Both in Santutxu and Tolosa, the first task was to identify two strategic informants (I-59 and I-60 for Tolosa, I-69 and I-70 for Santutxu). An attempt was made to choose people who had a good general perspective of the context in question and who were not active in a political party. As expected, priests were selected—individuals who were very involved in the social life of the community. These men, in addition to offering a general perspective on social and political life in Tolosa and Santutxu, helped to identify informants conversant with the life of political parties as well as the young people and cuadrillas. It is worth noting that in each of the nuclei two owners of popular bars on the ritual poteo circuit were interviewed. Indeed, they were extraordinarily perceptive about changes in this complex interaction ritual among friends, cuadrillas, and the generations. The leaders of each political party were asked to choose six actively affiliated members of specified age. These individuals had to have lived through the hard postwar years, in order to have a greater perspective of the changes since then. In the case of the PNV, it was a requirement that informants' personal experiences include the immediate postwar years.

All the individual interviews and meetings with groups were tape-recorded and later transcribed. A considerable effort was made to be credible at the initial interviews, but it should be noted that there was a preexisting climate of trust.

This phase of the fieldwork took place in 1984 and was undertaken according to the following guidelines:

Individual Interviews

FACTOR A

Language
I-31: general informant on the circumstances of the language
I-32: typical member of a very radical linguistic organization (Euskalherrian Euskaraz, or The Basque Country in Basque)
I-33: highly placed official in the highest Basque government institution for the teaching of the Basque language (HABE)
I-34: privileged observer of a pragmatic assessment of the language (School of Education, highly placed official in the teaching of the language)

Culture

1-35: general information about the situation of Basque culture (diverse fields: principally knowledgeable about audiovisual aids)

1-36: general information about the situation of culture (diverse fields: principally music, plastic arts, and publication)

FACTORS B AND C

Physical Violence

1-37: former *etarra (mili)* (ETA member of the military, or "m," faction)

1-38: former *etarra (poli-mili)* (ETA member of the politico-military, or "pm," faction)

1-39, 1-40: two active members of the EE party (Euskadiko Ezkerra, or Euskadi Left)

1-41, 1-42: two members of the PNV, from traditionally nationalist families that at the time had relatives in political exile or prison

1-43, 1-44: two active members of the HB party (Herri Batasuna, or Popular Unity), with a minimally critical stance toward ETA violence

Political Parties

1-45: general qualified informant on the functioning, organization, and internal life of the PNV

1-46: general qualified informant on the functioning, organization, and internal life of EE

1-47: general qualified informant on the functioning, organization, and internal life of HB

INTERNAL CRITICISM IN POLITICAL PARTIES

1-48: member of a critical faction of the PNV

1-49: member of a critical faction of EE

1-50: member of a critical faction of HB

The Associative World

1-51: generally privileged informant from the pro-amnesty committees

1-52: generally privileged informant from neighborhood groups

1-53: generally privileged informant on church groups

1-54: generally privileged informant on Christian associations

1-55: generally privileged informant on folkloric groups

1-56: generally privileged informant on youth groups

1-57: generally privileged informant on hiking groups

1-58: informant on youth groups already analyzed in part II (interviews 1-24 to 1-24B)

I-59, I-69: general informants on life in Tolosa-Santutxu

I-60, I-70: general informants on life in Tolosa-Santutxu

I-61, I-71: qualified (high-ranking) informant on life in the PNV in Tolosa-Santutxu

I-62, I-72: qualified (high-ranking) informants on life in EE in Tolosa-Santutxu

I-63, I-73: qualified (high-ranking) informant on life in HB in Tolosa-Santutxu

I-64, I-74: leading member of cuadrilla in Tolosa-Santutxu

I-65, I-75: youth leader in Tolosa-Santutxu

I-66, I-76: youth leader in Tolosa-Santutxu

I-67, I-77: owners of bars typically frequented during the rounds of poteo in Tolosa-Santutxu

I-68, I-78: owners of bars typically frequented during the rounds of poteo in Tolosa-Santutxu

I-79: general informant on youth questions, especially in Santutxu[14]

Group Interviews (Approximately Five or Six People)

G-I: adults older than 40, active members of the PNV, with responsibility in Tolosa

G-II: adults between 30 and 40, active members of EE, with responsibility in Tolosa

G-III: adults between 30 and 40, active members of HB, with responsibility in Tolosa

G-IV: young people between 18 and 25, belonging to different cuadrillas in Tolosa

G-V: adults older than 40, active members of the PNV, with responsibility in Santutxu

G-VI: adults between 30 and 40, active members of EE, with responsibility in Santutxu

G-VII: adults between 30 and 40, active members of HB, with responsibility in Santutxu

G-VIII: young people between 18 and 25, belonging to different cuadrillas in Santutxu

Epilogue

As previously stated, the epilogue does not provide closure to the research, but, on the contrary, looks toward the future. Since 1984, the year when the second stage of fieldwork just described was undertaken, important changes have occurred. Furthermore, the pace of change and the extent of its oscillations have grown extraordinarily. For these reasons, and remembering that the aim is not to reach a conclusion, we decided to provide a schematic view of the central elements defining the so-called Basque problem. Such an overview is based on previous experience and on the systematic day-to-day monitoring of the problem. It is also informed by certain ancillary results of empirical research undertaken concerning other aspects of Basque social reality.

Specifically, for the writing of the epilogue, three interviews were conducted in 1998 with three strategic general informants conversant with the social and community life in Tolosa and Santutxu (I-80 and I-82 referred to Santutxu, I-81 to Tolosa). Three group meetings were also held with members around age sixty from the PNV (G-IX), with members around age fifty from HB (G-X),[15] and with members around age sixty from EA (G-XI). The empirical material is quite fragmentary, which forces a careful and humble interpretation of the results. For this reason, the material presented here is at best only illustrative of the overview of the current situation set out in the epilogue.

Without Professor William A. Douglass's interest this book would not have been possible. It took a long time to reach the final manuscript. During this journey our friendship increased, and this is a second reason to thank him.

PART ONE

Theoretical Questions

Chapter One

Collective Identities

and Their Political Dimension

The General Problem of Collective Identity

Employing the concept of identity to unravel any social problem comes with serious risks. The broadest risk might be of raising more problems than one resolves. For the term *identity* is central to the history of Western thought in general and to any specialized area. In the human sciences one of the principal divisions of the past few centuries derives from the resort to essentialist thinking: that is, from the substitution of essence, or the identity question, for concerns with social functioning, dynamics, or change.

While within sociology the idea of personal identity consciousness, or the permanence of a dynamic "I" over time, is generally accepted, many social scientists see the notion of *collective* identity as open to the charge of essentialism. To the extent that such social scientists accept the notion of collective identity at all, they analyze it from the perspective of personal identity. Consequently, they either regard collective identity as but one of the dimensions of personal identity or treat the formation processes of personal identity as social. The critics who most adamantly equate collective identity with essentialism routinely attack (a misinterpreted) Durkheim when he speaks of collective consciousness.

If, despite such considerations, I broach the subject of collective identity, it is with two beliefs: first, that social definitions of reality (that is, those by the social actors themselves) constitute an important part of reality, independently of the scientific validity of the definitions; and second, that the dangers of invoking essentialist ideas in sociology, or of making them a by-product of psychology, can be avoided by specifying the problem (rather than the premise) of collective identity as an object of analysis.

That social definitions constitute an important part of reality is evident in many social phenomena. In modern society social problems are increasingly seen by the actors themselves as ones of social and cultural identity. African political leaders, for instance, speak of the need for a new African identity, defined by a unified African ideal—that of negritude. Social minorities demand political recognition of their national, cultural, and ethnic identity. Homosexuals demand the collective recognition

3

and acceptance of their sexual predilection as central to their personal lives. Urban social movements seek to control a given social space by identifying residents as synonymous with that space. And so on.

Faced with these social phenomena, scientists normally adopt two different positions or strategies. The first consists of privileging one's own interpretation over that of social leaders and their followers to ascertain whether social definitions are true or false—false in the sense that they are purely ideological or of questionable "scientific" validity. If the definition is of questionable validity, one tries to redirect the problem toward a more scientific approach. However, what normally happens in such cases is that social scientists lose a part (and by no means the least important part) of the reality they originally sought to analyze. In addition, they forsake the possibility of including social definitions and discourse in the very reality that is the object of their study. Furthermore, one should not overlook the capacity of scientific discourse itself to shape dominant social definitions. The social importance of this discourse depends on the type of cosmology specific to each society and, therefore, on the social importance and power of the scientific community within it. Those who embrace this strategy should recall Kierkegaard's admonition that "they do not even use in science the precaution they use on a daily basis: listen attentively to the problem before trying to solve it" (1963, 14).

Prudence dictates, then, that we "listen attentively to the problem before trying to solve it." We need to accept social definitions as an object of study. In reality, when social actors define problems of collective identity in more or less explicit terms, sociologists are presented with social definitions of collective realities.

Such is the posture of the present work. This position is phenomenological but not entirely so, because the research does not end with treatment of the phenomenological moment. Rather, it transforms representation or belief into an object, but requires the origin of representation be further questioned. The sociologist needs to move both within and outside the social world. Examining the genesis of representation or the definition of reality is even more necessary when the defined reality is a collective one. For in this case one might face a process that can be termed *performative*, in that socially produced definitions may, according to how successful they are and precisely because of such success, gradually generate the defined reality.

However, one also needs a truly social phenomenology. This must be made explicit, because even those, such as Berger and Luckmann, who adopt a phenomenological position in their social analyses often have problems utilizing the idea of collective identity, although they do not hesitate to draw in the idea of personal identity. Berger and Luckmann's denunciation of the idea of collective identity is, in this author's opinion, especially vague and even inconsistent with their own approach. For example, in referring to identity as a key element of subjective reality and, as such, found in a dialectic relationship with society, they state that "if one is mindful of this dialectic one can avoid the misleading notion of 'collective identities' without having to resort to the uniqueness, *sub specie aeternitatis*, of individual existence" (Berger and Luck-mann 1966, 159). Their assertion is less bold in the footnote corresponding to the above-cited passage: "it is inadvisable to speak of 'collective identity' because of the danger of false (or reifying) hypostatization. The *exemplum horribile* of such hypostatization is the German 'Hegelian' sociology of the 1920s and 1930s (such as the work of Othmar Spann). This danger is present in greater or lesser degree in various works of the Durkheim school and the 'culture and personality' school in American cultural anthropology" (Berger and Luckmann 1966, 191).

The ill-defined nature of this criticism is evident from a comparison of the two quotes; Berger and Luckmann refer to collective identity as a misleading concept (in the first) and as an idea to be avoided (in the second). The theoretical grounding of the criticism is also not entirely clear: that is, does using collective identity as a scientific or theoretical concept necessarily impede thinking of collective identity as a phenomenon, that is, as the representation of reality by social actors themselves? The following several observations will help to clarify the position of the present work.

Berger and Luckmann do not explain why using the concept of subjective identity does not entail the same risks of reifying hypostatization as using the concept of collective identity, nor why, in the event these risks become evident, the concept of subjective identity must still be employed. The criticism seems so uneven as to become psychologizing. These authors use the concept of subjective identity based on its existence as a phenomenon, which seems perfectly reasonable—just as it is reasonable to consider this "identity" "a phenomenon that emerges from the dialectic between individual and society." Indeed, their underscoring of this last point continues to be, in this author's opinion, correct: "Identity types . . . are social products *tout court*, relatively stable elements of objective social reality. . . . As such, they are the topic of some form of theorizing in any society. . . . Theories about identity are always embedded in a more general interpretation of reality; they are 'built-into' the symbolic universe and its theoretical legitimations." Thereafter, and conscientiously following their reasoning, they add: "It should be stressed again that we are here referring to theories about identity as a social phenomenon; that is, without prejudice as to their acceptability to modern science. Indeed, we will refer to such theories as 'psychologies' and will include any theory about identity that claims to explain the empirical phenomenon in a comprehensive fashion, whether or not such an explanation is 'valid' for the contemporary scientific discipline of that name. . . . Psychology always presupposes cosmology" (Berger and Luckmann 1966, 160–61). However, just as a specific cosmology or objectified reality includes a psychology that explains the phenomenon of individual identity in a social group, this cosmology must also explain the phenomenon of a relationship, or relationships, of inclusion-exclusion produced within each group. In other words, the cosmology should explain the "I" and the "we," and this same cosmology, as a phenomenon, is an objectified reality.

This does not mean that a group feels or possesses consciousness in the same way as an individual, but various relationships of inclusion-exclusion are produced in a group, and the self is one of these. Similarly, this does not mean that the explanation contained in a cosmology is necessarily scientifically valid. This explanation can, therefore, be essentialist, and it undoubtedly usually is since cosmological explanations explain anything that is socially necessary except themselves. One cannot explain the "from whence" one looks, interprets, and understands: for example, only after secularization could religion be converted into a scientific object and subjected to explanation, because until then everything was explained by religion itself. In this sense, from a theoretical point of view, all cosmology definitely has some essentialist content. It is akin to a point of view or, more precisely, the point from whence it is seen.

For the same reason, Berger and Luckmann could have just as mistakenly categorized the theoretical concept of personal identity as erroneous. However, as will be seen, this would imply casting doubt on the very representational bases of science that require a subject-object relationship and, specifically, the concrete relationship between each particular researcher and the object of study. For although researchers might conclude of their object that it has no subjects (as in structuralism, for example), they must also recognize that, in order to make this forecast, they are themselves subjects. This ultimately requires accepting nonreflexive premises, however much Berger and Luckmann might have postulated that the fundamental dimension of learning rooted in socialization is more a relationship among subjects than between subject and object.

In the same year that Berger and Luckmann's *The Social Construction of Reality* appeared, the former also published an article entitled "Identity as a Problem in the Sociology of Knowledge." The result of his attempt to construct an all-embracing theory of the relationship between the individual and society is a vision in which the individual is converted into the fundamental focus of the relationship. In other words, Berger offers a somewhat psychologized vision of sociology. He concludes, "The purpose of these brief considerations has been to indicate what theoretical gains might be expected from an integration of the approaches of social psychology in the Meadian tradition and the sociology of knowledge" (1966, 114).

"Every society," says Berger, "contains a repertoire of identities that is part of the 'objective knowledge' of its members. It is 'known' as a matter 'of course' that there are men and women, that they have such-and-such psychological traits and that they will have such-and-such psychological reactions in typical circumstances. As the individual is socialized, these identities are 'internalized.' These are then not only taken for granted as constituents of an objective reality 'out there' but as inevitable structures of the individual's own consciousness. . . . Socialization brings about symmetry between objective reality and subjective reality, objective and subjective identity" (1966, 107).

This raises the central scientific problem of the existence of reality outside consciousness and of the social construction of its image, a problem whose resolution is beyond the scope of this work. However, it is very important to recognize with Berger that socially constructed reality—that is, the representation or arrangement of specific historical reality—is, for social actors, objective. The challenge of socialization is to internalize a vision of reality. Further, this vision exists objectively independent of its scientific validity and is socially constructed. Yet this internalization is not experienced by the individual as the assumption of one version of reality, but as learning about reality itself: for the individual it is *the* reality.

Understanding why an individual exits the socially constructed order is a central problem. Berger speaks of the fear of anomie, which occurs when individuals find themselves submerged in a world of disorder and are faced with an absence of meaning that is anomic, a nightmare par excellence (Berger 1967, 42). D. L. Carveth later led a furious assault on Berger's thought, premised in part on his interpretation (somewhat restrictive in this author's opinion) of Berger's notion of anomic fear. According to Carveth, "The question concerns the reality status of what is experienced in anomy: Is it Nothing (Berger's 'irreality,' chaotic emptiness) or is it Something (the return, say, of repressed impulses)?" (Carveth 1977, 85). I would argue that Carveth's approach is mistaken in that, for Berger, "irreality" is not inexistent at all. Rather, he views it as a lack of feeling something. In other words, it is the confrontation with something that escapes the subject's notice and, consequently, cannot be allocated a reality status by the subject in question. That said, when the issue (raised by Berger) is focused on the fear of homosexuality, Carveth is right in affirming that such urges are not "irrealities." Instead, what emerges within the homosexual is "the growing consciousness of the *existence* of real, morally proscribed sexual appetites" (Carveth 1977, 85). In effect, the individual is confronted by these urges independent of their provenance, and, in this sense, they are real. However, Berger's concept of anomic fear refers more to a void of meaning and sense that this confrontation produces.

Furthermore, if conversation (a relationship with others) is perhaps the primary verification mechanism in our world and of our reality (already by speaking with another we take a certain "reality" for granted), homosexuals must confront a visibly and verbally approved objectified social order with an established sexual agenda. Their urges will not meet with approval in the social order in which they live, consequently reinforcing their fears. The social consequences, either merely anticipated or truly experienced, of fulfilling these impulses will reinforce their fears, because they will be persecuted and marginalized. Homosexuals will therefore try to find a compatible setting in which to be able not only to satisfy their urges, but also to construct and reside in an environment in which homosexuality has positive meaning and can be taken for granted and verified on a daily basis. They look for a structure of social plausibility wherein their condition might be considered normal.

Within Berger's range of identities are some, termed *collective identities,* that specify for individuals their group membership. For example, in a given city where Catholics and Protestants coexist, a male Catholic is both a man and Catholic, but, further, he "belongs" to a church of which he is a known member. In most social environments there is a range of groups, objectified by being clearly recognized by members and nonmembers alike. Obviously, however, there is another kind of objectification, namely a politico-administrative one. For example, the state objectifies the nation as the political order's basic community; consequently, current national conflicts within nation-states raise the interesting problem of two legitimating orders and two kinds of objectification competing for control of a fixed territory. This implies, at the very least, some confusion and loss of social obviousness. Furthermore, each of these two orders will have its own structure of social plausibility. There will be those, who, in relation to this single territory, affirm their exclusive membership in one of the two communities. This crisis of legitimacy and lack of obviousness reveal the struggle for absolute objectification within each social identity. That is, one social identity will struggle to establish the social obviousness of its politically objectified identity, while the other will seek to infuse a community rejected by the state with political objectification. Once the latter, in its own view, has sufficient political recognition, it might struggle to establish the social obviousness of the territory in its own terms. What is at stake, therefore, is the objectification of society's symbolic center (Shils 1975; Eliade 1992; Eisenstadt 1969).

However, the struggle for objectification does not occur only in the realm of social identities. Many social groups, such as feminists and gays, struggle to change society's objectified sexual agenda. Socially objectified reality is maintained through social life, through social relations among individuals that have internalized it. Within Berger's (1967, 15 ff.) triple dialectical moment (objectification, internalization, and externalization), externalization explains both the maintenance and the transformation of symbolic universes. Within each society there exist groups, structures, and organizations (both formal and informal) that are especially relevant because of their specific weight in the processes of producing meaning in everyday life—that is, in the maintenance and transformation of objectified social reality. This means that sociology cannot give priority to the "human being" as the main "locus" of society. If a feeling of group belonging is the psychological projection of an objective feature, the outward expression of it—what here is termed collective identity— will be a psychological rather than a sociological concept. However, because the processes of socially producing and diffusing a feature's meaning are social (socially constructed meaning), and because all actors are not equally situated when this meaning is produced, reproduced, and changed,[1] it is clear that the problem of collective identity cannot be removed from sociological analysis.

The most important consequence of Berger and Luckmann's proscribing of the notion of collective identity is that it forces a debate on both the concept and its use in the field of sociology. This debate should, moreover, take into account that the meaning of collective identity is contested by both essentialist and psychological explanations. Logically, then, sociology is once more confronted, in establishing its objects of study, by essentialist thought and psychology, realms in which the term *identity* enjoys a scarcely debated natural status.

Thus the issue of collective identity once again highlights questions that in the human sciences have their own historical and philosophical precedents, above all in a metaphysical sense. The greatest difficulties the social sciences have faced when addressing the problem of the nation ensued from (and to a great extent continue to ensue from) considering it as a collective identity. In such contexts, identity is understood as, and equated to, essence. Identity thus evokes itself: it is a fundamental something that makes a particular thing and no other. It evokes substance and essence as opposed to form and accident. Furthermore, identity unequivocally reveals the impossibility of its own incoherence or discontinuity (there is permanence of the fundamental, change only in the accidental). This is the case with research that, either covertly or explicitly, starts from an a priori or objective concept of nation. It is also true of those who attempt, through the more or less recurrent features found in the national phenomena they investigate, to find the minimum common denominator in the idea of nation, that is, the real content constituting it.[2]

As noted earlier, a fundamental aspect of the historical division in the human sciences regarding essentialist interpretations of analogous phenomena has been the substitution of the essence, or identity, question for concerns with social functioning, dynamics, and change. This division has never been total, however, and one still finds more or less camouflaged "essentialist" echoes within scientific discourse. Here the issue arises of essentialist influence on the identity question, within both sociology and psychology. In particular, essentialist thought is disguised in sociological and psychological discourse rather than presented openly.

An example of essentialism's infiltration of social science can be found in some sociological and social anthropological treatments of so-called primitive and traditional societies. Many of these approaches base their arguments on dichotomies, such as historical societies versus societies without history, societies with cumulative history versus societies with repetitive history, and so forth.[3] According to such views, some societies have been founded in identity, being therefore always identical to themselves. For that reason, in general, uses of the idea of social identity within sociological models that attempt to uncover the differences between so-called traditional and modern societies invite confusion: mechanical and organic solidarity, a frozen society and one of institutionalized change, the evolution from ascribed to acquired status, from reproduction to production, and so on.

An essentialist view is introduced into the analysis when identity is considered in light of a permanent social reality through time: "A society appears to have a much stronger identity when its change is less rapid and when it reproduces its codes of conduct more precisely" (Touraine 1980, 20). Here the term *identity* is used in the stated sense. However, if a complementary phenomenological point of view is adopted, the proposition can be reversed. When change is slow, identity will not be questioned or thematicized, but becomes rather something given as fact or as an inactive behavioral principle. Breaking this harmony will produce the thematicization of identity and its transformation into an active principle. For example, a consciousness traumatized by the danger of an esteemed cultural feature disappearing can imbue the topic with fundamental identity meanings.

A human science's rupture with previous essentialist thought, as is the case with Freud and his "I" dynamic, entails establishing a concern for change, a dynamic approach as opposed to a static essentialist one. The problem of collective identity is not so much a society's identity per se but social identity consciousness. Consciousness refers here to the threat an identity faces at times of traumatically experienced crisis and/or change.

Simmel clearly sensed the need to speak of consciousness or representation when posing the question of a society's identity. "What the problem of social groups' own permanence most commonly poses is the fact that they remain identical to themselves while their members change or disappear. We say that it is the same state, the same army, the same association, that exists today and that existed already tens and even hundreds of years ago; however, among members of the group there is no one who remains the same as before. . . . The temporal separation of generations does not impede its succession from forming, for our representation, an uninterrupted whole" (1896–97, 75–76). It is one thing for both group members and outside observers (and between them the sociologist, who needs to identify or delimit reality as an object of study) to represent an uninterrupted unity and quite another to postulate the existence of an essence that is maintained through time. However, it should be immediately added that, from the perspective defended here, psychology is faced with the same problem. For psychology the individual is not an unchangeable essence, however much the person represents himself or herself as such. Consequently, in psychological terms, the individual is also a constructed reality and therefore as sui generis as social reality is.

Introducing the mediation of consciousness into the identity question should not be considered essentialist, even though the definition of consciousness itself might possess some essentialist content. Social actors tend to essentialize their social identity in their own discourse—with a twofold consequence. On the one hand, Schutz's distinction between the sociologist and the actor is evoked. Each of them considers the same group life cultural pattern in different ways, since the actor organizes knowledge of his or her social world "not in terms of a scientific system, but from the significativity for his or her actions" (Schutz 1974, 96–97). On the other hand, introducing this mediation leads to a distinction between two already cited methodological moments. The first considers consciousness exactly as it is, as a social phenomenon, as a means of observing its consequences for behavior without criticizing it in terms of scientific truth or falsity. The second moment is generative in that it attempts to understand the social mechanisms whereby consciousness is produced, reproduced, and changed.

The preceding discussion emphasizes the need in the human sciences to again raise the problem of identity in the field of consciousness, separating it from the issue of essence. Individual consciousness is understood as both existing and substantive, although its content cannot be scientifically verified. The challenge is to move from concern with the individual to analysis of the social—in other words, from the realm of the psychological to that of the sociological. However, the question remains whether a collective or social identity can exist as something distinct from an individual or personal one.

"Most authors establish a distinction between personal and social identity." However, as Luckmann emphasizes "all identity is personal in the sense that it is located in one person and social in the sense that its formation processes are social" (noted in Kasterztein 1981, 99). Luckmann's formulation is so vague that it is difficult not to agree with it. However, it still seems a little unfocused since it proposes personal identity as a "place" and, therefore, as a point of view. This might tempt one to reduce the problem to that of subjective consciousness and feeling of identity. On the contrary, I would argue that Luckmann's assertion does little to resolve the problem of whether one can constitute collective identity as an object of study, as a "sui generis reality." I do refer to such a reality in the present work, but not in the sense of identifying a *social body* (to use an analogy from the physical sciences) that maintains consciousness or a feeling of identity, but potentially the very opposite, in that kind of reality where a feeling or consciousness, the social link, might form the basis of the group. Indeed, this might be a different kind of reality from that of the individual and different still from the individuals who form it.

Pierre Bourdieu criticizes "the personification of collectives" (in phrases like "the bourgeoisie thinks that" or "the working class refuse to accept that"), which leads, assuredly as Durkheim's professions of faith, to postulating the existence of a group or class "collective consciousness": "by crediting groups or institutions with dispositions which can be constituted only in individual consciousness, even when they are the product of collective conditions, such as the awakening of awareness (*prise de conscience*) of class interests, one gets out of having to analyze conditions, in particular those determining the degree of objective and subjective homogeneity of the group in question and the degree of consciousness of its members" (1977, 203 n. 49).

Clearly, personifying collective identity is not the same as trying to frame it as an object of study, or indeed as something greater than, different from, and at the same time intimately related to personal identity. Behind this issue lurks the traditional debate about the nature of sociology and what we sociologists make of the relations between the individual and society. It is well and useful to caution against personifying collective identities, but Bourdieu's take on Durkheim is too facile. A good while ago, Nisbet warned against such readings:

> To be sure, there are and have been distinguished sociologists, including Emile Durkheim, who occasionally seem to be suggesting that there *is* a kind of metaphysical reality to society that separates it from the behavior of individuals. We may generally charge such statements, however, to excess zeal or ill-advised terminology in their worthy effort to highlight irreducibility of the social bond to forces which are purely psychological or physiological. As the following passage makes clear, not even Durkheim believed, really believed, that society was something which could be detached from concrete human beings in interaction. (1970, 48)

Nisbet goes on to cite the passage from Durkheim:

> On the one hand, the individual gets from society the best part of himself, all that gives him a distinct character and a special place among other beings, his intellectual and moral culture. If we should withdraw from men their language, sciences, arts and moral beliefs, they would drop to the level of animals. So the characteristic attributes of human nature come from society. But, on the other hand, society exists and lives only in and through individuals. If the idea of society were extinguished in individual minds and the beliefs, traditions, and aspirations of the group were no longer felt and shared by the individuals, society would die. We might say of it . . . : It is real only insofar as it has a place in human consciousness, and this place is whatever one we may give. . . . Society cannot do without individuals anymore than these can do without society. (48–49)

In many cases, when sociologists reduce objective reality to the individual level, they are revealing their own inferiority complex. For they tend to believe that psychologists, in so far as they target the individual as the object of their study, are closer to the "certainty" (the objectivity of their field of study) of the natural sciences. However, I would argue (remaining true to Nisbet's understanding of the term *social*) that either psychologists should not accept such scientific certainty so uncritically or that sociologists should believe more in what they do. In other words, sociologists should accept more that they really do study reality.

In the first volume of *L'Année Sociologique* (1896–97), Simmel published the already cited interesting and illustrative article "How Social Forms Are Maintained." In it he argues:

> I understand society as not only the complex whole of groups and individuals united in one political community. I see society everywhere in that man finds

himself in a state of reciprocal action and building a permanent or transitory unit. . . . It is fair to present society as a sui generis unit, different from its individual elements. . . . All these phenomena (languages and customs, church and law, political and social organization) appear as products and functions of an impersonal being in which undoubtedly individuals participate, as in the public good, but not so much that one particular individual stands out as the productive cause or key reason for the rest.

Simmel clearly establishes, in Durkheimian fashion, the sui generis character of social reality as an autonomous reality different from the individuals that constitute it. Nor should the other aspect of the antinomy—that is, that society cannot exist without individuals—be overlooked. However, the way he addresses this second concern is very telling:

On the other hand, it is true that only individuals exist, that outside the human world human products have no reality beyond that of the material nature from which they stem, and that the creations referred to here, in that they are spiritual, live only in individual minds. How, then, if individual beings alone exist, can the supra-individual character of collective phenomena, the objectivity and autonomy of social forms, exist? There is only one way to resolve this antinomy. For a perfect understanding, one must accept that only individuals exist. In order to examine things more closely, all phenomena made up of some unit above that of the individual level should be understood through the exchange of reciprocal actions by their constituent individuals. Unfortunately we are prevented from attaining perfect knowledge. Human relations are so complex that it is impossible to reduce them to their basic elements. Rather, they should be treated as realities that are self-sufficient in themselves. It is therefore only for methodological purposes that one speaks of the state, law, fashion, and so on. . . . Thus, the conflict posed between an individual and what one might term a monist understanding of society is resolved; one concerns reality, while the other refers to a state achieved through our analytical faculties; one is the ideal aspired to by knowledge, the other expresses the current situation. (73–74)

Simmel correctly understands that sociological reality is conceptual. Nevertheless, he grants to individuals a different reality status, because they belong, in the Simmelian way of thinking, to reality in itself. All this demonstrates the inferiority complex (in terms of certainty or proximity to reality) of sociologists compared to psychologists. This is paradoxical (if one considers the efforts of sociologists at this time, and especially in the journal in which Simmel published,[4] to establish sociology as a positivist science among the others) because either that knowledge termed perfect is psychological and thus sociology is a lesser evil because it recognizes the impossibility of achieving perfection, or relations among individuals constitute an objective reality and as such perfect knowledge can never be attained through exclusive observation of individuals. Therefore, this knowledge is not psychology but a potential science of the future whose objective would be to comprehend the "complex" relations among individuals: in other words, this is sociology.

Simply put,[5] the *reality* of every science is conceptual. "Sociological data," observes Nisbet, "scarcely differs from the data of other social sciences and even from that of some biological sciences. Concepts are the means we use to perceive some *aspects* of common data and, currently, the differences between the social sciences are basically those of the aspects that are illuminated through the use of concepts" (Nisbet 1975, ix). For this reason it is highly likely that psychology's individual will differ from that of sociology, since the two disciplines employ different concepts to analyze what can often be the same piece of information: "As sociologists, we do not deal with man alone. We deal with *man-in-society*. . . . But if we say that our subject is man-in-society, it is equally important, and not at all inconsistent, to say that in sociology we deal with *society-in-man*" (Nisbet 1970, ix–x). Nisbet goes on to say that, "Given the nature of the human mind, it is not merely possible, it is *necessary* to say that when human beings interact with one another, social elements, forces, and mechanisms are established which are no more capable of being reduced only to supposedly underlying psychological forces within human beings than to physiological or chemical forces. Assuredly, the levels overlap and interact. But each has its own *conceptual* reality" (1970, 47).

That a determined notion of the individual in and of society is the reality (conceptual) of sociologists is a vision of our science that permits us to avoid certain blind alleys—fundamentally the epistemological one that the concept never possesses its object (as Spinoza would say, that the concept of the dog cannot bark),[6] as well as the blind alley of regarding the individual or society as determinative of the other. Such a vision allows us to employ our own conceptual reality and adapt it to our only possible form of reflection, which is lineal. That is to say, we should not preach a single approach to understanding reality. Rather, our understanding can and should be the result of diverse and successive methodologies.

Nisbet himself falls into the trap he wants to avoid, for in his determination not to detach society from the individuals that constitute it he reaches the conclusion that "society is not something abstract and external that is *out there*" (Nisbet 1975, xv). However, in a way society is *out there* because there is a methodological moment in which sociologists must consider that society is indeed *over there:*

> If culture is credited with the status of objectivity, there is a double meaning to this appellation. Culture is objective in that it confronts man as an assemblage of objects in the real world existing outside his own consciousness. Culture is *there*. But culture is also objective in that it may be experienced and appre-

hended, as it were, in company. Culture is *there for everybody*. This means that the objects of culture (again, both the material and non-material ones) may be shared with others. This distinguishes them sharply from any constructions of the subjective consciousness of the solitary individual. (Berger 1967, 10)

To recap, then, here is a series of ideas in synthetic form. This set of ideas allows us to think about collective identity as a sociologically constructed reality, as an object of sociological analysis:

1. In order to sociologically approach the concept of collective identity, it is necessary to include some discussion of, on the one hand, the semantic limits of the idea and, on the other, the framing of collective identity as an object of study or, in other words, as a conceptual reality.

2. One must distance oneself from the essentialist semantic perspective. For the sociologist, collective identity refers primarily to the world of representations and images of (a socially objectified) reality and, in its individual projection, to the world of consciousness. Here representation and consciousness, when observed by the sociologist, must be taken literally insofar as they remain phenomena. This means that the sociologist must not judge their scientific validity and, therefore, that representation and consciousness can be (and usually are) essentialist. Instead, the sociologist must analyze how and why they are produced and reproduced, and how they determine social behavior.

3. Regarding sociology's semantic perspective, sociologists must watch for any essentialist incursion into their work. Such an incursion typically involves thinking of societies and groups as possessing an essence or something immutable through time. Such temporal permanence of a collective subject belongs more to the realm of representing reality.

4. Regarding psychology's semantic perspective, sociologists cannot analogically assume that society or social groups possess consciousness in the same way that an individual does. Collective identity does not imply transferring the consciousness of personal identity to the consciousness of a collective identity. Rather, collective identities are socially produced objective realities that, through socialization processes, transform into elements of personal identity.

5. Regarding the need to contemplate social representations of collective realities that reside in the consciousness of individuals, along with the social processes of constructing and diffusing these representations, two moments must be understood when analyzing collective identity. During the phenomenological moment, representation and consciousness are objectively established, thereby avoiding any judgment about their true or scientific nature. During the generative moment, the emphasis shifts to the production of rep-

resentation, the mechanisms of social diffusion and the performative process by which social definitions of collective realities are, to some extent at least, successful. This occurs when they generate the same reality that they define.

6. The social representation and individual consciousness of collective identity do not emerge out of a material reality but rather are socially constructed symbolic realities in a social world composed of unequal subjects (unequal in terms of their capacity to produce and diffuse collective representations). This leads collective identity to become an object of sociological analysis.

7. All societies contain multiple forms of identity that belong to a socially objectified reality.

8. In every society tensions and alterations can occur when there is explicit disagreement about certain definitions of identity.

9. Within these multiple forms of identity there exists one type that can be termed collective or social, which also possesses a subjective projection through the consciousness or feeling of belonging.

10. Here the term *objectification of collective or group identity* refers to the level of independence that identity achieves for its individual members. Given the performative potential of actors to produce a collective identity, the weakest level of objectification is that which is simply foundational, that is, mutual recognition among members of a group. This therefore coincides with the very existence of the group, which in turn achieves a minimum degree of independence. The second level would be recognition by others, with group conflict emerging as one possible form of recognition. The existence of both levels can be symbolically very effective in that it usually constitutes social evidence of the group's existence. The third level is that of politico-administrative objectification, which implies political recognition of the group's existence. The existence of the three levels of objectification in one group indicates the existence of the group. If only the first level (mutual recognition) is present, then there is either no social recognition or a lack of understanding, as is the case with clandestine groups, secret societies, and so forth. There might be cases where the second level exists but not that of the first. A renegade or someone who abandons the group might still be considered a member of it even against his or her own will. Saint Peter, for example, refused to acknowledge he was from Jesus Christ's circle, but the people *recognized* him as such by his accent. Similarly, the first and third levels might not coincide.

11. Within a society, subsystems (with a corresponding structure of social plausibility) can emerge. This implies objectification in the form of *mutual recognition* as opposed to the existent *political objectification*. These cases are particularly interesting when composed of an exclusive collective identity in which it is incompatible to belong to two or more identities from the same order. Especially apparent after that historic moment when political legiti-

macy came to be based in a specific and exclusive collective identity, namely the nation, the tension between different kinds of objectification can often result in a crisis of legitimacy for the state itself, as will be demonstrated in this work.

Collective Identities of the Social Actor

As Turner argues, there are at least three important levels in defining the "I." The first is that of a given "I" as human being who consists of determined characteristics shared with all other humans, as opposed to different forms of life. The second is intermediate, composed of "categorizations in terms of in-group/out-group, based on social similarities and differences among human beings that define someone as a member of certain groups and not of others (for example, 'American,' 'woman,' 'black,' 'student,' 'working class')." The third is a subordinate level of personal "I" characteristics based on the differences that an individual possesses in relation to other members of the in-group (J. C. Turner n.d., 77).

It is my purpose to concentrate on the second, or intermediate, categorization level, although social interaction occurs both here and on the third level. As Tajfel and Turner observe, in the relationship that one individual establishes with another, the one person locates the other on a *continuum* that starts with the purely group perception and ends in a purely individual (or personal) reflection. In a friendly relationship, with the gradual development of more intimacy, the individual tends to progressively approach the friend on the third (personal) level, although, in the process of building friendship, one may experience vicissitudes.[7] The reverse is also possible, as when a *racial* conflict is increasingly exacerbated and radicalized. In such a context personal relationships between members of different *racial* communities will be more and more difficult to establish or maintain. In the first process one eventually arrives at an individualized and personal definition of the friend, while in the second there is the tendency to generalize the other's image according to a social stereotype. Over the span of a lifetime the form in which one thinks about others is typically found somewhere between the two poles of this ideal continuum (Tajfel and Turner 1986, 227).

On the second level, every individual possesses a series of attributes that imply belonging to several collectivities. The unique quality of each individual (third level) stems from characteristics that might be considered personal (the arrangement and combination of personal and second-level attributes into one's unique self). It is conditioned as well by the consideration of how others perceive one's individuality.

On this second level, therefore, the individual comes to see himself or herself as formed by a series of attributes. These attributes are socially constructed and conceived by the individual through his or her interactions with others.

All attributes are social in the sense that their meaning is socially constructed. Even those that are biological, such as skin color, are in reality social in as much as social meaning attributed to a biological characteristic is hardly neutral. Rather, for all individuals the important element of the attribute is the social meaning that accompanies the purely biological fact. To be black is of little importance in itself. Its meaning depends on the social context in which an individual lives. To be black might be insignificant in a sub-Saharan African community and very significant in a city inhabited by black and white people. Furthermore, in this same city what it means to be black may vary over time.

Attributes, then, may be of a biological nature (gender, skin color, age, and so on), while others are more obviously social, such as religious or political affiliation, social class, and the like. These two classes of attributes differ in terms of their social significance, especially according to the arbitrariness of a feature's meaning and the identity deriving from it. Collective identity always implies a degree of arbitrariness. Even when a feature that symbolically anchors an identity in one context exists in another (for example, skin color), it doesn't inevitably have the same meaning. This original arbitrariness of all social qualities tends to be conservative. Such designation seeks security in presumed objectivity that symbolically establishes identity beyond all doubt. For this reason, individuals tend to naturalize (in a biological sense) collectivities and objectify them culturally as well. Social actors need to ground their identities in something objective that is more obvious than specific social processes that create meaning or a particular individual wanting to identify his/her self. From a cultural perspective, biological explanations tend to carry more objective weight than social observations. However, within the social order itself objectivity can be achieved through other means. This is Durkheim's principal argument in *The Elementary Forms of Religious Life* (1915), which posits that consecrating a group's foundational quality is equivalent to freeing it from physical or mental manipulation, since it is placed off limits, out of our reach, through a whole series of interdictions (Pérez-Agote 1984b).

As previously mentioned, one form of meaning a biological or social attribute can have is conferring membership in a collectivity. Membership is an extensive and diffuse area that can range from belonging to a social category (as described by Merton)[8] to membership in a collectivity (with members in general sharing a common sense of belonging) or group (where members maintain a sense of both belonging and frequent face-to-face interaction). In switching the emphasis from the individual perspective to the realm of social life in which these different senses of belonging are relevant, one can observe a dynamic process of relationships among diverse levels of belonging. If the realm is gender, for example, the attribute of being female gives rise to groups and collectivities whose goal is the transformation of the prevailing meaning of gender-based identities. The general interest in the identity paradigm for the study of contemporary social movements stems from the capacity of such movements to transform the cultural meaning of at least some features that people use to define their identity (age, gender, work, citizenship, territory, and so on). Such movements, in addition to those relatively few mobilized individuals, may have the capacity to transform basic cultural meanings in the social consciousness. This takes place not only through a state-centered political process, but also by spectacular dramatization and dissemination of such activities through the mass communication media (Gusfield 1994).

Features or attributes may be biological or social, but their meaning is always social or socially constructed. Moreover, features can be individual, personal (the third level of "I" categorization), or even social in the sense of implying membership in a (second level) collectivity. A theoretical relationship between the second and third levels can be established through two axes. The first axis is social interaction among individuals through time, with a general trend toward the personalization or depersonalization of the other within the previously discussed continuum. The second axis is social mobilization based on a particular feature. In some cases new social movements erase the border between the public and private. In those movements whose objective is to change the cultural meaning (gender or the social meaning of homosexuality, for example) of an individual's personal attribute (sex or homosexuality), members may journey from the private to the public and possibly return again to the private realm. A personal feature's negative meaning is ameliorated through group membership. In cases where a movement's goal is directly public (an environmental movement, for example), its members' journey may be from the public to the private if belonging to the movement becomes the central feature of the members' identity (Pérez-Agote 1996a).[9]

While still focusing on the individual, and before embarking on a macrosocial analysis, I offer (schematically) a list of characteristics relating to collective identities (the second categorization level) of the social actor:

THE MULTIPLICITY OF IDENTITIES

Within each individual different senses of belonging function simultaneously. At any given time, individuals have feelings of belonging to different yet compatible groups, among which particular relationships may or may not exist. Here, the image of the individual surrounded by ever-expanding concentric circles emanating from his or her being is relatively valid and helps to underscore the fact that the bigger the circle the more that individuals within it need shared symbols, because the possibility of their maintaining direct interaction with the other members is progressively undermined, as is the likelihood of their mutual personal recognition. However, the fact that one circle might be bigger than another does not imply that an identity is less emotionally protected. Affectivity has a lot to do with proximity to one's inner being, but intense emotional commitment to a big circle can be inculcated within a reduced group setting, such as that of the family.

THE TEMPORAL NATURE, LATENCY, AND RITUALIZATION
OF COLLECTIVE IDENTITY

Some feelings of belonging can last a lifetime, but all are subject to expiration and latency if they are not ritually rejuvenated in some way.

In some groups, and especially the more informal ones, the decline in regular interaction among members over time can lead to progressive loss of their sense of belonging. Sometimes, however, members of such groups try to halt this reversal by consciously intensifying and formalizing their mutual encounters. Ultimately, the dispersal of group members in space and time can be partly compensated for by the overritualization of encounters and interaction.

For the individual, circumstances (such as economic emigration or political exile) that introduce a sudden break in the interaction with notable reference groups produce complex emotions, and these have often been examined by social science. Elsewhere, for example, the author has analyzed the meaning of political exile (for Basques exiles of the Spanish Civil War in Argentina) in terms of an unresolved mourning (Freud 1972, 2881 ff.). For years a struggle persisted between the reality principle, derived from everyday life, and the libido, which refused to recognize the loss of the cherished object (territory—an emotionally denoted and familiar space). Here, the lost territory's meaning is maintained through plausibility structures linked to a certain collective and affective nostalgia. Specifically, the Basque center of Buenos Aires, Laurak Bat, was examined as the context where exiles relived and symbolically reconstructed their lost territory (Pérez-Agote, Azcona, and Gurrutxaga 1997, chap. 8).

COLLECTIVE IDENTITY ORIENTS SOCIAL BEHAVIOR

As has been mentioned, following Tajfel (1981), interaction involves situating the other—as one is always situated in turn by the other—at some point in the ideal continuum that runs from a purely collective to a purely individual characterization. Therefore, at any given time, one also acts either more individually or more collectively, thereby bringing into play a collective identity—one among the various identities that one possesses.

In situations where a collective identity is problematic, in that it is not obvious or commonly accepted, lack of recognition by the other often impedes instrumental and rational interaction. In these situations, mutual recognition of collective identity—that is, of the collective identity of every actor who is party to the interaction—emerges as a logical prerequisite of instrumental rationality. For example, in social realities where central and peripheral nationalisms coexist, to the degree the collective identity of a peripheral nationalist is not recognized by the centralist, the former's behavior is not accepted as being rational or instrumental. Because the relationship is not symmetrical, because one collective identity is objectified by the state and the other is not, the central nationalist lays claim to a more instrumental and rational behavior since his or her identity "goes without saying." However, the peripheral nationalist's behavior is both prerational (not irrational) in relation to the other and also rational, in a different degree, in the sense that it is designed to achieve recognition. As there is no recognition of the other's collective identity, the scope of behavioral meaning within the interaction becomes more complex and multiple.[10]

Initially, one observes that the collective identity an actor embraces guides his or her behavior. It gives him or her a sense of purpose, in the ample sense in which Schutz (1974, 96) opposes meaning and scientific knowledge. This does not prevent a collective identity from having a cognitive dimension (discussed below), but in the present work the practical aspect of collective identity as a means of directing behavior and constructing meaning for an actor is emphasized. Consequently, when two actors meet and there is no immediate consensus about each other's collective identity, common sense comes into play as they negotiate the meaning of behavior itself.

NONREFLEXIVE OR AUTOMATIC PERFORMANCE OF COLLECTIVE IDENTITY

For actors, operationalizing a collective identity, from the many that they might possess, can be nonreflexive or automatic. Although they may do so, actors do not need to think about establishing a collective identity. In their day-to-day social interactions, actors employ different group identities depending on the situation and the identity of the other(s).

THE STRATEGIC USE OF IDENTITY

However, the actor may think about and strategically employ his or her group identity. This issue has been examined in regard to interethnic relations by Lyman and Douglass (1973). As always, however, in the social world some social features are more difficult to manage than others. In particular, visible biological features are especially difficult to strategically control.

In social contexts where identity problems exist, either because collective identity is problematic in itself or because there are inequalities, competition, or conflict among different groups, it is logical that strategic behaviors are adopted more frequently.

THE SITUATIONAL NATURE OF COLLECTIVE IDENTITY

Given that each actor has multiple collective identities, the activation of one of these by him or her depends on the social situation. As has been stated, this activation may be either automatic or thought out.

THE FINITE QUALITY OF COLLECTIVE IDENTITY

There is a limit to how many collective identities an individual can have. A kind of boundary exists beyond which the proliferation of collective identities no longer makes sense in the aggregate. In other words, there is a point of diminishing return.

Furthermore, belonging to two social aggregates of the same order (in terms of both size and general substance) might cause incompatibility, whether emotional or even juridical. Dual or multiple membership does exist, but such belonging can cause problems.

Nowadays it appears that the nation may constitute maximal membership for the individual in terms of both substance and compatibility. In other latitudes and at other times, other forms of collective identity bounded this general and all-inclusive world that framed the limits of symbolic meaning and so also set restrictions and boundaries on dual or multiple belonging—serfdom on the manor of a particular lord and not another, for example.

Nationalism, among other things, connotes a species of identity and, in the psychological sense of the term, denotes self-definition. In this sense, any identity is a set of ideas, a symbolic construct. It is a particularly powerful construct, for it defines a person's position in his or her social world. It carries within itself expectations of the person and of people from different classes within that individual's social settings, and thus orients his or her actions. The least specialized identity, the one with the widest scope, which is believed to define a person's very essence and guide his or her actions in many spheres of social life is, of course, the most powerful. The image of social order is reflected therein most fully; indeed, this essence of identity is a microcosm of the social order. In the course of history people's essence has been defined by different identities. In numerous societies, religious identity performed this function. In many orders an estate or a castle did the same. The nation is the generalized identity in the modern world (Greenfeld 1992, 20).

In modern times, complex combinations of political and religious identity boundaries can also occur. This is clearly the case in the current political conflicts of eastern European countries that have experienced the re-ethnicization of political identity. We will return to this problem when we consider the politicization of collective identity.

In these times of globalization, there are problems in delimiting the meaning of identity. For modernity implies, as Thomas warned as long ago as 1923, a profound weakening of the local community as the defining agent of a *situation:* "The community is now so weak and vague," he wrote, "that it gives us no idea of the former power of the local group in regulating behavior. Originally the community was practically the whole world of its members. It was composed of families related by blood and marriage and not so large that all members could not come together; it was a face-to-face group. I asked a Polish peasant what was the extent of an *'okolica'* or neighborhood—how far it reached. 'It reaches,' he said, 'as far as the report of a man reaches—as far as a man is talked about'" (Thomas 1923, 44).

What challenges globalization, in large measure, is also found in the nation-state: the harmony between what the individual knows and what affects him or her. In respect to economic globalization, individuals know relatively little of what affects them, given that many of the decisions affecting their lives are made in remote places. And because of cultural globalization, they strive to know realms that do not touch their daily lives. As such, the balance between knowledge and emotions is, at least for the moment, upset.[11]

LACK OF A NEED FOR COHERENCE AMONG COLLECTIVE IDENTITIES

Given the situational character of collective identity, the individual normally has more than one. This may appear contradictory, since one collective identity can seem like an alternative to another, yet this is not always the case. Ancestral hostility between two neighboring villages is a typical example. Depending on situational factors, villagers may or may not activate this enmity. For example, on feast days celebrating one village's identity, the rivalry between the two communities will likely be accentuated. However, if members of each village are suddenly thrown together in another setting—a distant and foreign city, for instance—then they may share an identity that contrasts with that of strangers and/or foreigners.

As such, the coherence among an individual's collective identities is produced according to each given situation. This coherence is not generic but contextual, and, of course, individuals may find themselves in situations where they feel pressured to adopt one identity at the expense of another that they do not want to renounce.

However, one must also remember the limitations of the seventh characteristic that make possessing dual identity problematic, as well as the difficulties related to the almost impossible task of controlling some features of identity (the fifth characteristic).

THE OTHERNESS OF COLLECTIVE IDENTITY

Collective identity is socially expressed (in the social behavior it informs) through reference to and comparison with other groups or collective identities. This is the "we" as opposed to the "they," the other. A collective identity is expressed, or determines behavior, only by reference to another. While it can exist in a latent state, it becomes manifest and relevant only through contact with otherness.

The relations of the members of a given social aggregate with those of another (that is, otherness) are not necessarily conflictive, although of course they can be. Relations may be complementary, competitive, or cooperative. One should also remember here that Merton envisaged reference group theory in order, among other things, to relativize what is called Sumner's syndrome, namely the belief that all groups are in-groups and always maintain a positive reference for their members (Merton, 1949). Fundamental to this issue is the problem of identification. An individual born into or forming part of a collectivity is likely to identify with it, although it is possible not to do so. If such de-identification gradually characterizes greater numbers of group members, mutual recognition undergoes de-objectification. Alternatively, a new group definition may emerge, but to achieve, performatively, both a real and objective status that new group definition must be attained through progressively neutral identifications among those so defined.

Actors experience as incompatible, at least in a situational sense, the collective identities that are the "other" to one another. However, as has been noted, this can change if the situation is modified. That said, it is worth underscoring that a certain incompatibility between (in principle) compatible collective identities is sometimes imposed on the actor from outside his or her world.

A political discourse might oblige an actor to choose between two (or more) alternatives as if they were incompatible—to the extent of making them effectively incompatible even when socially, at a previous historical moment, they were not. Consider the discontinuity created in the individual's continuum of collective identities by the political objectification of the state, which introduces an exclusionary national community. Consider other social situations, such as when an immigrant population finds itself during an election having to choose among different political options. Here, the options will necessarily imply different collective identifications. Sociologists create the same situation when they ask immigrants (in a survey, for example) to define where they feel they *belong*—their place of origin or place of residence. Perhaps this is an academic question that scarcely arises in everyday social situations, and that immigrants answer in different and even opposing ways (at least according to political or sociological discourse). It depends on who asks the question (a local or an immigrant, for example) and where (in their place of residence or origin [the latter when they are on holiday, for example]), because their reference groups and sense of belonging may vary with the situation.

Returning to the relationship between politics and collective identity, it is worth highlighting some interesting aspects of the case study presented here. It can be argued that a peripheral nationalism within a nation-state implies a certain incompatibility between it and that of the center. In an authoritarian political situation, central nationalism will impose its definition by force. In a democratic situation, each actor will have to choose through voting for a particular party, which entails the specific ratification of a collective identity. Suffice it to say, politics imposes a certain incompatibility among collective identities owing to the fact that, in the era of nationalism, identity has become political in its reference to a defined power center (one legitimated as such, although historically it may not have been so). This center therefore becomes incompatible in regard to another (the peripheral power center) that exists in either reality or the imagination. However, in nonpolitical terms the actor may also feel an incompatibility between identities that are actually politically compatible. When this is the norm in a democracy, it means that the political parties on offer have not responded to all the socially available options. However, it is well known that political discourse in modern democracies, far from being a means of channeling the problems of its citizens to those in power, is often more a mechanism to mold peoples' attitudes and claims. Furthermore, and of special interest to the present study, political discourse is also a mechanism to produce and reproduce collective political identity and transform social identity. For this reason, it should be clearly stated here that politicizing a collective identity implies making it incompatible with the claims of a similar identity from the same level.

COGNITIVE ELEMENTS OF COLLECTIVE IDENTITY

Tajfel enumerates the components that, to a greater or lesser degree, make up group membership: "a cognitive component, in the sense of the knowledge that one belongs to a group; an evaluative one, in the sense that the notion of the group and/or of one's membership of it *may* have a positive or a negative value connotation; and an emotional component in the sense that the cognitive and evaluative aspects of the group and one's membership of it may be accompanied by emotions (such as love or hatred, like or dislike) directed towards one's own group and towards others which stand in certain relations to it" (Tajfel 1981, 229).

The most immediately interesting component, the level of an identity's cognitive content, varies from one type of group to another. There are groups, such as religions, that can maintain a strong cognitive component, while in others cognitive content is reduced to a minimum, such as the mere recognition that one is a member of the group. Also, some groups within a type may have a more intense cognitive element. For example, religious groups might vary in doctrinal content and in the degree to which their members know it. Furthermore, members of the same group might vary in their understanding of these cognitive aspects. Some members or certain subgroups may specialize in the possession, development, and control of this knowledge.

Nationalism, as will be seen, projects a complex cognitive dimension, both in its European-state variant and in those movements that emerge to challenge the center. Consider, for example, the influence of nineteenth-century romanticism on some nationalist movements or the influence of social and natural science in the construction of nationalist ideas.[12] However, perhaps the most important cognitive element, as will become evident, is the political referent of the nation, necessarily possessed by all its adherents.

A basic question about certain collective identities, especially those whose most important symbolic cognitive content is constructed around an objective feature, is their potential essentialist character. We will return to this subject when we consider national consciousness, where it becomes particularly relevant. Naturally, the issue has something to do with the original arbitrary nature of human groups and with their successive objectification or naturalization by members, as discussed earlier. These issues have already been discussed. Moreover, regarding such collective identities, those who more clearly possess the said feature, or know how to operationalize it, might maintain symbolic power over those who do not.

Through theories such as those referring to in-groups or ethnocentrism, social science has treated evaluative aspects more often than emotive ones. Indeed, these latter aspects have always seemed to escape the gaze of social science.

The emotional content with which, sometimes and with different degrees of intensity, a collective identity is protected has much to do with the mechanisms and groups that inculcate it. This emotional weight is especially evident when group identity is transmitted through the family. It is even more evident during the first steps of the socialization process, when the individual does not maintain the reflexive distance necessary to separate this emotional relationship from the content transmitted within it. Consequently, in cases where a collective identity emerges that is problematic in itself, or where there is conflict between different collective identities, individuals that see either their very existence denied or their collective identity negatively valued may well express the resulting charged emotions in terms of protection of the intimacy of the family realm. Thus, their defensive actions may become violent, for they perceive their very emotive being as having been assaulted. There may also exist, although it is only insinuated here, a certain positive correlation between the emotional protection of the consciousness and the intensity of its essentialist character.

When collective group self-identification is neither problematic nor conflictive, collective identity is socially obvious. It goes unquestioned and, as such, is only of academic interest to those who are concerned with the more abstract sociological aspects—approximating what is often termed social philosophy. When, in a given social setting, collective group identity develops problems, certain profound aspects of sociality become relatively apparent. One begins to observe how sociability is suffused with ambiguity and arbitrariness, and, as always, real-world social problems, tensions, and conflict challenge theoretical investigation. Transcending any specific kind of conflict, or even identity conflict in general, collective identity is sometimes reified into an unproblematic general theoretical realm in which the existence of general theoretical collective identity is taken for granted.

The theoretical relationships between social conflict and collective identity are difficult and complex. On the one hand, all social conflicts imply a problem of collective identity. On the other hand, the concept of collective identity is unthinkable without the idea of the "other," and conflict is one of the ways of relating to this otherness. For the foregoing reasons, identities in conflict must be analytically differentiated from conflict *over* identity.

In the first instance, social conflict is polar. The more defined the conflict, the more evident the poles and the identity associated with each. The old expression "you're either with me or against me" captures perfectly this concept. Normally, the polarization and aggravation of a conflict leads to each polar collectivity defining itself with greater intensity. In reality a social conflict is a conflict between social identities. This does not necessarily mean that collective identity exists before the conflict in question. Sometimes the conflict itself is the mechanism whereby a new social identity emerges. Yet this does not imply that all relationships of otherness between two identities are conflictive but rather that all conflictive relationships imply the existence, either previously established or in the making, of two identities.

In such cases it is not a question of conflict *over* identity, but quite the opposite. It is actually a social conflict that generates, maintains, and amplifies the conflictive identities. It is therefore a question of identities *in* conflict. Conflict serves as an objectifying mechanism expressed through recognition of the adversarial group's identity. Collective identity is not problematic; what is problematic is the confrontation between two identities. Consider an example. In any given city two different ethnic groups might coexist. Their respective self-identification serves to organize and measure interpersonal (and intergroup) relations, which may vary from open warfare to a more or less "civilized" coexistence. The groups may be coequals or arrayed hierarchically. There may be open conflict along with periods of relative calm. In an extremely conflictive situation, during moments of intense strife, interpersonal relations become intergroup ones. This occurs both in the relationships among members of different groups (ethnic in this case) and, paradoxically, among members of the same group. Ultimately, in the interior of every group conflict there emerges a greater identification among group members.

Secondly, however, collective identity may be problematic in itself. That is, a group's collective identity may be socially questioned. This questioning might emerge within the group itself, it may be external to the group (coming from a larger collectivity that includes members of this first group), or it may be both internal and external. Of course, when a collective identity is problematic in itself, problematic or conflictive behavior often occurs since a group's collective identity is usually important in influencing actors that belong to the group. This identity conflict is a social one that, like any other, consists of a disagreement among social groups that compete for the possession of some social means. In this case the means are symbolic, although they have serious consequences for the political institutionalization of groups, especially the legitimizing of power. Cases in point are contemporary nationalisms that emerge within certain Western states.

The conflict comes from the politicization of collective identity (in terms of the legitimating power of the political center), which results in an incompatibility among collective identities within the same category. Defining the problem in synchronic terms, at a given time and in a given place within a particular territory that forms part of a larger state, two groups compete, each of them projecting a definition of identity for the individuals that live in this specific part of the territory. On the one hand are those that define this identity in the same way as does the state: for them the inhabitants of this territory form part of the national community corresponding to the state. On the other hand are those that subscribe to a peripheral nationalist definition of their identity. This consists of saying that those who live in this part of the territory form their own nation, meaning that they deserve a new state and thereby advocate secession from the current one. Both cases involve, to some extent, inclusive definitions: both statist and peripheral nationalists transmit an identity that not only they (those who accept the definition) but others (those who accept the alternative one) subsume.

However, the question can be more complex if each group is ethnically distinct. That said, there is not necessarily a perfect fit between peripheral nationalism and ethnic distinctiveness. In the Basque Country within the Spanish state an important part of the autochthonous population adheres to Basque peripheral nationalist positions, but there are also some Basques, as well as nonautochthonous citizens, who support Spanish nationalist postures. The relationships between the objective elements and the subjective consciousness of identity can therefore be quite complex. The Basque panorama within the French state, in politico-symbolic terms, is less complex. In the French Basque Country, because of continual emigration to northern France and the Americas, and little immigration, the ethnic composition of those that remain is pretty constant. That said, Basque nationalist political expression is less intense in France.

This first chapter attempts to construct a concept of nonessentialist collective identity that derives from a definition of identity based solely in the individual. It also seeks to foster sociological analysis that avoids questions of whether such identity is based on truth or error. This phenomenological moment must be complemented with the generative one, which concerns itself with the mechanisms by which definitions of identity are disseminated and attain social support. There is a further concern with the social actor as the source and locus of a personal identity that includes a series of collective ones. Finally, an attempt has been made to define all social conflict both as a phenomenon occurring among collective identities and as a mechanism whereby they are objectified.

The following chapter will address the political dimension by considering the specific nature of identity conflict. More specifically, it will examine nationalist conflicts where an established state centralist nationalism competes with a peripheral nationalism that is attempting to construct a new state through its definition of political identity. One such conflict, that of Basque nationalism with the Spanish state, constitutes the subject of parts II and III of this book.

Chapter Two

Nationalism as the Politicization

of Collective Identity

Peripheral nationalism means that those who inhabit a specific part of a state's territory have two coexisting social identities. Each definition of identity includes others who do not accept that identity. In effect, as in all social conflict, there is strife between identities: in our case between the identities of Basque nationalists and Spanish state nationalists who inhabit the same part of the Spanish state's territory. In a conflict over legitimacy each group struggles to impose its definition of identity.

These definitions of identity are ambiguous and uneven. Each definition of identity refers to a center of political power: one to the already existent state, the other to a state its proponents are attempting to construct. The peripheral nationalist definition of identity is inclusive since it defines as citizens all those who inhabit this partial state territory.[1] Similarly, those who maintain a centralist definition also include their adversaries, encompassing even those that support a peripheral nationalist definition of the citizenry.

However, since it is not objectified by the state, the peripheral nationalist definition of identity is generally more ambiguous. For example, it excludes totally those people who inhabit the rest of the state, while maintaining a more ambiguous relationship with those centralists who inhabit the peripheral territory. One must also remember that adherents of a centralist definition of identity can belong to the ethnic group of the territory in question. The absence of an existing peripheral state fosters ambiguity, particularly about the future. Should such a political unit come about, it would immediately confront having to create a normative classification of the citizens of the new state. The peripheral definition of identity is ambiguous, then, because different criteria may be used to establish who is included in the definition: an ethnic principle (objective and essentialist), an awareness principle (whoever considers themselves peripheral nationalists), and, finally, a territorial principle.

While the struggle might occur between two group-defined entities, it is more than simply a social conflict. Although each group possesses a general group-defined identity, in identity conflict each definition of identity additionally denies that of the other. Therefore, paradoxically, through disconnect and mutual antagonism, each definition actually reinforces the other. Here, conflict is an identity maintenance mechanism for both the centralist and peripheral nationalist groups. There is, however, another level where the two definitions of identity and groups dispute a territorial definition: each asserts a dominant definition they hope will be accepted by everyone. What makes this conflict over identity even more complex is the close relationship between these two levels. The more conflict there is between the two groups (first level), the more difficult it is for either to obtain a consensual definition of identity (second level).

Discord is naturally exacerbated when a debate over the nature of identity in general is superimposed on the conflict between state and peripheral nationalists. The conflict leads to an objectification of each entity's identity. And the stronger the objectification of each group's identity, the more difficult it is to forge a common one.

When one moves from a theoretical perspective to empirical reality, the most difficult task is to ascertain what, from among the competing social definitions, provides (at least relatively) the bases for inclusion. An inclusive dimension of identity produces the type of dual-level social conflict described herein. If each definition tries only to define the group that sustains it, then we have nonspecific social conflict: a conflict related to the control or monopoly of a specific resource. In the conflict over identity described herein, the inclusive character of the definitions stems from each one's attempt to impose itself on the other through the process of identity objectification. Nowadays this usually ultimately implies territorial political objectification.

However, in the case of conflict between a peripheral nationalism and its corresponding central nationalism, the definitions are uneven in terms of territorial political objectification. Behind central nationalists is a state that objectifies their articulation of identity. Peripheral nationalists question this objectification, but have no way of politically objectifying their own position. This means that the definitions they forge regarding their identity are generally more susceptible to change and are less coherent, since they vary according to the historical moment. Peripheral nationalism articulates a discourse that is necessarily more ambiguous, aggressive, and dramatic as a result of this lack of objectification. Moreover, state nationalist discourse characterizes itself as inclusive and peripheral nationalism as exclusive and aggressive.

Central nationalist discourse is necessarily inclusive because it includes the territory in which the conflict transpires. Peripheral nationalist discourse is necessarily exclusive because it proposes secession from the existing state and the formation of a separate territorial state. However, when proposing a new territorial configuration, it can also be inclusive regarding those who inhabit it, whether they share peripheral nationalist sentiments or not. Peripheral nationalists always criticize the assimilation and acculturation policies of state nationalism. Similarly, state nationalists who inhabit the territory in question criticize the assimilation and acculturation proposals of peripheral nationalist discourse, or even, should the case arise, the attempts at ethnic cleansing.

All nationalist discourse includes and excludes something. When a formed nation-state is monoethnic or ethnically, linguistically, or culturally homogeneous, there will be little or no discussion of whom to include or exclude. Yet in all cases there exists a potential for exclusion, however much it remains hidden by that objectification we term the state. For example, Spanish nationalism once presented itself as inclusive, but when waves of foreign immigrants began to arrive from outside the borders of the Spanish state, it changed its stance.

In sum, then, peripheral nationalism is generally more exclusive and central state nationalism more inclusive. However, as always in these types of conflict, states are multiethnic and their inclusive quality entails acculturation. The acculturating policy of multiethnic states with peripheral nationalist conflicts is clear. The acculturating nature of peripheral nationalism is rather more theoretical, as is its inclusive character, as has already been noted. For example, central state nationalists who live in the Basque Country accuse Basque nationalists of confusing Basqueness with what it means to be a nationalist. In this sense, they accuse Basque nationalists of strategic political acculturation.

In synthetic and graphic form,[2] a social conflict over identity can be represented as follows:

Conflict: between identity definitions of a territorial social reality (R).

Group A
Definition: $R = A$
Group B
Definition: $R = B$

Solution: Transformation of one of the definitions in play into the socially accepted.

$A \equiv R*$
Triumph of Group A
$* \equiv$ equals social obviousness

Here, two visions of reality compete. Their social effectiveness does not depend on their scientific objectivity but rather on each group's social strength and symbolic power. The transformation of one of the partially maintained truths into a generally shared, socially evident truth comes from the use of social diffusion mechanisms. These enable definitions that are sufficiently persuasive to transform a situation of irreconcilable conflict into a generally accepted principle of living together.

The relations between social effectiveness and scientific truth are complex. Initially, it can be argued that the social effectiveness of a definition does not depend on scientific truth. On the other hand, to be successful or credible a social definition cannot be totally arbitrary.

It has already been demonstrated that a nationalist definition of collective reality is a social one (of interest insofar as it is socially diffused), although scientists and intellectuals may play an important role in its social production (the more so when scientific and intellectual discourse enjoys great social relevance). Ultimately, defining collective reality is a performative process that might be socially successful or not. Regarding the territory of the Basque Country within the Spanish state, some subjects and groups affirm that Euskadi (the Basque Country) is a nation, while others contend that Spain is the only one. Although whether or not Euskadi is a country is relevant to the actors, this is not the question for the social scientist.

Asking whether Euskadi is a nation is a flawed question from a social scientific point of view because it supposes that there is an a priori concept of nationhood and that, through an acceptable sociological methodology, the social reality in question can be tested according to preestablished requisites. If such requisites exist, the scientific conclusion would be that Euskadi is a nation; if such requisites do not exist, there is no arguable national reality in the Basque Country. This approach, even accepting its viability, leads to a dead end. Imagine for one moment that the conclusion here was that, as Euskadi does not meet such requisites, it is not a nation. Would such sensational declarations, typically made by the media with much hype, resolve the national problem in Euskadi? All effort would be lost on not comprehending why adherents of Euskadi as a nation are so obstinate and persist in their "error." Social scientists would be accused of being in the service of central state nationalism and the conflict would continue, not only without being resolved but with this newly added divisive ingredient.[3]

Scientific truth, when feasible and sufficiently accommodating so that everyone can come to an agreement on its basic tenets, is not the only form of understanding, and, of course, there is no reason why it should provide the sole definition of a given situation (Thomas 1923) that determines individual and group behavior. Social scientists examining religion would not think of attempting to demonstrate the truth or falsity of the belief in question. Rather, they would attempt to understand the belief, how it influences behavior, or how doctrine is produced and reproduced. The belief in question, independently of its truth or falsity, exists objectively. Even supposing—and this is another problem—that such a belief could be verified, the social scientist is primarily interested in who has sufficient authority to impose what is socially accepted as truth. In other words, the real social scientific issues involve understanding through which mechanisms and processes "truths" are successful, even to what extent scientists and their own conclusions influence social behavior and through which mechanisms they potentially do so. A nation is the social definition of a collective reality that serves to legitimate an existent or imagined political state power. It is, therefore, a reading of social reality undertaken by social actors in general. As such, it is performative.

As has been established, the effectiveness of the social definition of a collective reality depends directly on the success of its diffusion among the affected social actors. The social definition is based on existent, or supposedly existent, features. However, for the observing social scientist the definition, or belief, is not a subjective projection of supposedly objective features. As in any realm of social life, definitions emanate from certain, but certainly not all, actors. Later these definitions are diffused by others, and, finally, if they are successful, they will be accepted by a growing number of social actors. A social definition's maximum symbolic effectiveness consists of attaining the level of a given, a simple matter of fact, or what might be termed social obviousness.

Looking at the problem in this way, one can argue that there can be no nation without nationalism. Consequently, one cannot speak of the nation in its full modern historical sense until the nineteenth century or, put another way, "nationalism is a doctrine invented in Europe at the beginning of the nineteenth century" (Kedourie 1966, 9).

However, there are those who affirm that the nation already existed "in the early sixteenth-century England" (Greenfeld 1992, 6) and, on the other hand, those who argue one has to wait until the eighteenth or nineteenth centuries to be able to speak about the nation (Kedourie 1966; Kohn 1967). In each case, a different aspect of the phenomenon (in the strict sense) of nationalism is being emphasized.

Some observers concentrate historically on elite consciousness and the genesis of certain elements in its perceptions that would come to constitute a widespread political identity. Greenfeld, for example, argues that "national identity preceded the formation of nations" (1992, 21). This might be interpreted as a contraposition between the idea of the nation as a social phenomenon (consciousness) and the idea of the nation as a historically created objective formation. However, and this is of principal interest to the present work, another interpretation distinguishes between a common element of understanding among elites and a consciousness eventually shared by the masses. Greenfeld notes that in analyzing each case in her study various levels were considered: political vocabulary, social relations and other structural constraints (specifically, those affecting key groups in the formation of national identity—the importance of a group always being defined as a function of its members' actual participation in the articulation and promulgation of national consciousness), and general educated sentiment. The aim is to explain the evolution of a particular set of ideas and to show how they permeate the attitudes of relevant actors (Greenfeld 1992, 24).

Other observers (those of us who think of nationalism and the nation as more recent phenomena) emphasize the widespread dissemination of such beliefs once the feeling of belonging born among social elites was transformed and acquired new political meaning. Eventually, the new political doctrine became the ultimate and exclusive symbolic source of political power for the territorial state. Therefore, as Kedourie notes: nationalism is a doctrine invented in Europe at the beginning of the nineteenth century. It seeks to determine the number of people sufficient to have their own exclusive government, for a legitimate execution of power in the state and for a just organization of international society. In short, the doctrine maintains that humanity is naturally divided into nations, that nations differ from one another according to certain characteristics that can be determined, and that the only kind of legitimate government is national self-government. Not the least of this doctrine's successes has been that such propositions have become accepted and are considered self-evident, just as the very term nation has been endowed by nationalism with a meaning and significance that it lacked until the end of the eighteenth century (Kedourie 1966, 1). Similarly, as Walker Connor contends, "nationalism is a mass, not an elite phenomenon. A nation exists only when appeal to national consciousness—appeals in the name of the nation—can effectively trigger a mass response" (1994, 352).

Kohn argues along similar lines when he states that nationalism "is no older than the second half of the eighteenth century. Its first great manifestation was the French Revolution, which gave the new movement an increased dynamic force. Nationalism had become manifest, however, at the end of the eighteenth century almost simultaneously in a number of widely separated European countries."[4] Emphasizing the importance of process in all historical development (including all events and milestones), he adds that, "although the French Revolution was one of the most powerful factors in its intensification and spread, this did not mark the date of its birth. Like all historical movements, nationalism has its roots deep in the past. The conditions which made its emergence possible had matured for centuries before they converged at its formation" (Kohn 1967, 3). For Kohn, the two spiritual forebears of nationalism, although still in utopian form, would be the Renaissance and the Reformation, since the masses continued to be dominated "by religious thought and emotion" (122). The Renaissance and humanism signified a certain liberation in regard to religion, but they were essentially "movements of aristocratic individualism, confined to a small group" (121). The Reformation once again directed attention

> to the universal concerns of religion and put an end to the brief interlude of Renaissance secularism and historical patriotism. In spite of the frequent expressions of literary nationalism in the Renaissance, the nascent nations were torn by civil war, the rival factions of magnates knew no loyalty to the nation, and the people themselves remained entirely outside the reach of nationalism. Only the rise of a strong central royal power was able to stop the internecine wars and to build or unite the future nation. In their loyalties the people still held to religion. But, like the unified political authority of the Middle Ages, the unified religious authority had been destroyed by the success of the Reformation and the victorious counteroffensive of reformed Catholicism. Although religion remained universalistic in its intentions, western Christianity was broken up into separate bodies, and the unitarian universalism was replaced by a new pluralism. At the end of the Renaissance all life was again retheologized, and religion was the dominating political issue. For political reasons no religious toleration was granted, and the "cuius regio illius religio" was accepted as

the guiding political maxim, and the new state was built around prince and religion and not around nationality. (124)

Kohn describes the seventeenth century in Europe as an era bridging the universal religious tradition and the triumph of narrow secular nationalism as a political idea. At the beginning of the seventeenth century, European states still considered themselves to be part of Christendom. As such, the royal houses of Austria and France, in their struggle to dominate Europe, claimed to still be protectors of the Church. Universalism was gradually eroded during this century, although not to the benefit of nationalities (which for Kohn were still inexistent as a conscious political factor) but rather to that of states and monarchs. Out of the disappearance of universalism (medieval fragmentation), statism, rather than nationalism, was born. Dynasties came, in a certain way, to occupy the role of religion, and loyalty gradually shifted toward the monarch. However, this monarchical state loyalty did not enjoy the same affective fervor of religious devotion, and the masses retained emotional adherence to religion. From the end of the eighteenth century onward, however, state loyalty gradually acquired such emotional appeal through the dissemination of a national idea among the masses. At this time, the progressive nationalization of religion by the new states, even those within the Catholic tradition, functioned as a bridge between the religious legitimacy of temporal political power and the secularization of the state's national legitimacy (Kohn 1967, 187 ff.).

In nineteenth-century Europe, state nationalism resulted in "the integration of the people into the nation, the awakening of the masses to political and social activism" (Kohn 1967, 581 n. 9). That said, some countries began to fall behind others in the institutionalization of the state—Italy and Germany, for example. As for Spain, despite the fact that it had been one of the first European states to delimit its territory, its nationalization mechanisms were inadequate. As a result, it was unable, as will be seen, to develop a single national consciousness throughout its territory. What was truly new (analytically speaking) during the nineteenth century was the political projection of collective identity as a legitimating function among the people of a territorially defined center of power. Collective identity, or at least cultural elements that cognitively and emotionally foreshadowed it, already existed, together with the state, of course, although in some cases this state was more a project than a reality. Consequently, the nation in its modern political shape as a form of legitimizing power makes little sense without a state. In contrast, the state not only makes sense in itself, but, in the majority of cases, exists without reference to the nation that legitimizes it. Thus, Nisbet has argued that "the nation is the offspring of the state" (1973, 164). From the European state system (McNeill 1982; Ramos 1995) determined by the Peace of Westphalia in 1648 to the European nation-state system established in the nineteenth century, the most relevant changes were not territorial but social. In particular, this entailed the gradual incorporation of the masses into political life, together with the symbolic appropriation of sovereignty by them, and the increasingly dominant economic and political role of what Marx describes as the first social class to historically possess a national character, the national bourgeoisie (Marx 1972, 71).

The culmination of this process, together with the principal elements that constituted it, has been captured perfectly by Kohn. He observes that the era of nationalism represents the first universal historical period. A long era of more or less isolated civilizations and continents preceded it; exchange among them was scant and relations were rare. Only in the eighteenth century, with the simultaneous appearance of nationalism, democracy, and industrialism, closely interconnected owing to their reciprocal origin and development, was there accelerated and wider cross-cultural economic exchange and communications. During the nineteenth and twentieth centuries every important social movement acquired a universal character. Nationalism, which emerged in western Europe in the eighteenth century, spread to the farthest corners of the world; wherever it went it shaped human thought and society in its image (Kohn 1967, 9).

The relationship between democracy and nationalism is far from clear. Greenfeld, for example, for all that she tries to differentiate the two concepts, realizes that they merge because they share many elements (1992, 10). Kohn emphasizes the contemporaneous quality of both, as well as their approximation, although he also establishes important analytical differences between them:

> Nationalism and democracy were in their origin contemporary movements, and in many respects sprung from similar conditions; but nationalism had its roots in the older group feelings and "natural" cohesion, while democracy was based on the faith in the liberty and equality of each individual—on the divine substance of each human soul which makes man in Kant's words, "an end in himself"—and on the faith in mankind as the bearer of absolute values. Natural law secularized and rationalized these religious conceptions, it did not destroy them. The rationalists of the eighteenth century did not deny the Heavenly City; they transferred it from heaven to earth, from the millennium to the present day. This City of Man, with its natural law, was as universal in its scope and message as Christianity. Democracy in its essence and scope was a universal movement; it added to the liberty of every man and to the equality of all men the fraternity of the whole of mankind. The fusion with nationalism gave it, for the time being, and under the existing possibilities of geographic conditions and organizational forms, the frame for its concrete realization; but it created an antimony which ultimately threatened to thwart the realization of democracy as soon as the technological and geographic basis of a universal society emerged. (1967, 191–92)

Nationalism, on emerging and developing simultaneously with democracy, gave the latter a practical and territorial dimension. It imposed equality and liberty at a specific level on which social reality was institutionalized and embraced, namely that of the territorial state. Furthermore, it gave symbolic territorial meaning to political power. It connected power with (at that time) the greatest possible range of collective consciousness and sentiment. However, there is an implied tension and paradox between the universalism of the democratic movement and the particularism that informs individual feeling, as always occurs when the universal becomes specific. This happens especially when this universal dimension links real emotions and sentiments to a specified territorial base.

One must also highlight the progressively political role of the so-called national bourgeoisie in an industrial age and, in particular, its socioeconomic interest in changing political legitimacy. The national bourgeoisie was the historic agent that created a new relationship between collective identity and political power in order to effect change in the territory's political structure. In different ways and with different tendencies, the national community became the symbolic repository of power from that time on. This occurred even when the national community could be framed in a variety of ways and even though that community might have employed cultural or ethnic identity in diverse fashions; or even when, in some cases, traditional cultural arrangements remained strong or, in others, when the social contract was paramount.

Of course, the foregoing typologies and distinctions are ideal cases. Although France is usually taken to be the supreme example of an enlightened, contractual, politico-civic nation, and Germany the prototypical romantic cultural one, Alain Renaut contends that "it is unjust to consign purely and simply two ideas of nation (enlightened and romantic) to the French and German traditions, respectively" (1993, 46–47). For example, the category of *Volksgeist* (spirit of the people) never explicitly appears in Herder and continues to be universal (as Isaiah Berlin demonstrates) in that it conceives of a fundamental kind of community that embraces all humankind. Further, in Fichte's work about the German nation it is unclear whether the national community precedes the state (Renaut 1993, 56; Berlin 1976, 142). On the other hand, it can also be said that the two concepts of nation existed side by side in France: the so-called nationalist one, legitimism sustained by the political right, and the republican one maintained by more progressive elements (Renaut 1993; Birnbaum 1993, 183 ff.). As Dumont (1991) has shown, all societies fall back on antagonistic principles of individualism and holism; they only differ in their measures (also Birnbaum 1993, 181). Every collective identity, and with greater reason if it has a political effect, is a changing combination of what Geertz (1973) terms primordial and civic bonds.

Anthony Smith (1994) has established a simplified typology of nationalisms that can help us to focus on the present objective, which is to demonstrate how two of the supposed fundamentals of Spanish and Basque nationalism are historically very strongly connected. Within multiethnic states the nationalism of the established state structure tends to prioritize the civic bond. When mechanisms for diffusing the civic bond fail in relation to some ethnic groups, the unwanted result is a politicization of ethnic ties and thus the birth of a contending nationalism that fosters primordial links. However, this does not mean that the nationalism of an established state must be a purely civic one (the French example, with its coexisting primordial-nationalist and civic-republican dimensions, has been noted). Nor does it mean that secessionist nationalism within an established state never advocates civic bonds; within the Spanish state the definition of who is or is not Basque is subject to fluctuation and change. Basque nationalism emerged at the end of the nineteenth century as a consequence, at least in part, of migrations into the Basque Country from other Spanish regions. However, with second- and third-generation offspring of earlier migrants, their intermarriages in some cases, and the infusion of left-wing political ideology into Basque nationalism during the Franco period, the result was a variety of definitions, dominant within certain groups and at certain moments, of who was Basque. Some emphasized Basque descent or those who spoke Euskara; others included whoever wanted to be Basque, anyone who worked in the Basque Country, everyone residing in the territory (Euskadi) that was both multicultural and multilingual, and so on.[5]

For Smith, in civic terms,

> the nation is a community of laws. It is defined by a common body of laws that encompass all citizens. This was also an important dimension of the idea of nation that republican France had. For the revolutionary patriots the nation was not only the origin of political power but also a legal arrangement; its will was law. This came about because the national will was general and sovereign to an extent that its objectives and resolutions acquired a universal validity for the citizens. Each one of these had the same rights and obligations, gathered together in the body of laws of the nation, and identical rights of representation and participation in the political and juridical community. There could be no intermediate power between the nation and its citizens. (A. Smith 1994, 7–8).

According to Smith, this civic concept of nation took root in France during the Revolution but also appeared in other Western nation-states such as Holland, Sweden, and Switzerland:

> In these countries ethnic differences and minority communities were more or less integrated (with the exception of Finland) into the dominant community whose elites controlled the fundamental state institutions. In other western states, above all Great Britain and Spain, the dominant ethnic community (or *ethnie* to say it in the French way) was not as successful in integrating ethnic minorities; Scots and Welsh, Catalans and Basques still looked at British and

Spanish civic nationalisms as if they had a predominantly English and Castilian nature, favoring an English and Castilian public culture that encroached
upon ethnic minority cultures and stateless nations. (1994, 9–10)

Ethnic nationalists, as opposed to their civic counterparts, sought a political awakening of a preexisting *ethnie*. Furthermore, as Smith observes, "their declared goal
was a return to a golden age of the said ethnie as a necessary condition of national
rebirth" (1994, 10). Some time ago, Smith (1971) himself distinguished the mythical components of ethnic nationalism, and Douglass, in an excellent analysis, applied
this outline to the case of Basque nationalism (1989, 105 ff.). As Smith recognizes,
civic nationalism implies generalization of one ethnic group's culture, which, far
from including itself alone, in fact defines both itself and all others within the state
territory as the nation. Other ethnic cultures may thus, as a result, remain relegated
to the private worlds of family and folklore (A. Smith 1994, 15 ff.).[6]

There is a third possibility, the plural nation, that basically consists of the presence of several ethnic cultures within a single state structure, each with certain recognition. This theoretical structure approximates that of those states formed by successive waves of immigration after the prior physical and political extermination of
the territory's autochthonous groups. That said, it remains difficult to conceive of a
true equality of all groups, with no acculturation of the others into one of them. In
the end, Smith recognizes that rather than a reality there is "the public recognition
of the ideal of ethnic diversity" (A. Smith 1994, 19).

Moreover, both ethnic and civic nationalism are based on a myth of a lost golden
age. This is articulated in either the supposed immemorial existence of the nation or
the formation of a new ideal public order greater than that of any one specific ethnic
group. Similarly, plural nationalism maintains the myth (melting pot) of forming a
new public culture based on diversity and equality among all of its constitutive cultures. In the example of multiethnic states, in order to achieve legitimacy in national
democratic terms, the political nationalization process always requires both the unitary production of public culture and a unitary feeling of political belonging. The
failure of this process may lead to the birth of ethnic nationalisms in the state's
peripheries.

The Basque case fits into a dual political scenario. One sector of this ethnic group
historically experienced the national project of the French state, while the other (the
majority) was immersed in corresponding Spanish state building.

In order to understand more precisely these processes of construction and nationalization within a multiethnic state (given that the case analyzed here falls within this
context), there follows a schematic explanation of the fundamental elements of the
nation-state from an analytical perspective. Later, and also in schematic form, the historical evolution of these elements will be examined. Both perspectives, the analytical
and the historical, will employ the familiar Weberian definition of the state.

An Analytical Perspective

Weber provides the most precise and concise definition of the modern state, managing to synthesize both its subjective and objective elements. Despite its brevity, the Weberian formulation contains within it many different elements and relationships: "a state is a human community that (successfully) claims the *monopoly of the legitimate use of physical force* within a given territory" (Weber 2002, 13). One can refine this definition into its several components to pinpoint the different relationships among them. The goal here is not to criticize Weber's analysis, but rather to analytically clarify and enhance it. First there is the element of "human community." In principle, Weber could take the term *community* to mean either "human association" in a general sense, or, standing by his own original definition, in a narrower one. He notes elsewhere that "a social relationship will be called 'communal' (*Vergemeinschaftung*) if and so far as the orientation of social action—whether in the individual case, on the average, or in the pure type—is based on a subjective feeling of the parties, whether affectual or traditional, that they belong together" (Weber 1978, 40). If Weber were employing the term *community* in its first, general sense, he would be using it as an imprecise way of delimiting or demarcating a social reality. The second meaning, I would argue, is more consistent with the rest of the definition precisely because the next element mentioned, territory, is the essential factor in demarcating social reality, as will be seen later. Furthermore, this narrower definition is more useful because, to put it bluntly, it allows one to introduce the problem of nation into the definition of the state and establish more deeply the relationship between the two.[7]

With the additional element, territory, Weber wants to objectively delimit the state because it objectively delimits social reality. The word "objectively" should be understood here as the contraposition of the previous subjective element, community. The territorial element is, in principle, physical, as it is defined geographically by borders defended through state violence (another element of the definition). Territory is also symbolic and significant. However, this (subjective) dimension of territory would be a dimension of the first element, namely community. Moreover, one must remember that territory is an essential element in the definition because the modern Western state abolished personalist political ties. As such, the objective delimitation of political connections is necessarily territorial (the evolution of personal rights into territorial ones in terms of their sphere of validity) (Nisbet 1975, chaps. 5, 6).

The subjective element of community and the objective one of territory are, therefore, different yet intimately related components. The relationship between them might be coincidental, for example, when, among the inhabitants of a physically defined territory, there is effectively a sense of belonging to a whole. However, such coincidence might not occur, as when within a territory smaller than the state there originates a sense of belonging that excludes the wider state dimension.

Another of the central elements in Weber's idea of the state is the "monopoly of legitimate physical coercion." This is a complex issue. Physical coercion is the prime means of state activity. "From the point of view of sociological consideration," states Weber, "a 'political' association and especially a 'state' cannot be defined by the content of what it does. In effect, there scarcely exists any task that a political association has not carried out at one time or another. Nor, on the other hand, can one say that politics has been the exclusive property of those associations that define themselves as political, today as states or those that were the historical precursors of the modern state." Citing Trotsky, Weber adds that "every state is founded on force" (2002, 13). Consequently, for Weber physical coercion is the central and specific activity of the state, and as such he speaks of its "monopoly." In other words, on the one hand, no one or nothing from without the state itself can use legitimate physical force within state boundaries, and, on the other, there is a domestic monopoly on violence in the sense that the "state apparatus" legitimates its use of force to control force emanating from any other source within the state. This, however, reveals a weakness in Weber's argument, for he does not explain the potential existence of a different internal center charged with the exercise of legitimate physical coercion and power.

It is not simply a matter of the state monopolizing physical force, but rather that the state claims the monopoly for itself and does so successfully. The latter is a positive condition in the sense that to monopolize requires being effective, which in turn initially requires political stability and then marginalizing all ethical criticism regarding this exercise of power. It is ultimately the de facto outcome, rather than a value judgment, that determines the "success."

In the same way and without value judgment, another element, namely the legitimacy of physical coercion, can be introduced. Here the issue is acceptance of this force by those people subject to it, or, in other words, "inner justification" (Weber 2002, 14). Here, once more is the subjective element. The relationship between it and "human community" is debatable. The specifically national form the state achieves in the era of nationalism is measured by the following: that the legitimacy of the center monopolizing physical force grows according to a socially diffused belief that the center of power emanates from the community inhabiting the territory, namely the nation. Consequently, another flaw in Weber's definition emerges: either what he defines is the nation-state (and not the state), and as such fails to take account of the national form of legitimacy; or what he defines is the state and thus, while his nonspecific allusion to legitimacy is correct, his use of the term *community* is not, since it would equate to a territorial demarcation or, at most, a political unit. In actuality, the communal sentiment of a people is not that which exists exclusively in a nation-state; rather, only within such a structure has this sentiment fundamental political value, since it is what legitimates the power center.

The foregoing observations can be clarified by examining briefly the problem of "success." A successful outcome, according to Weber, must become worthwhile in terms of both physical coercion and political legitimacy. However, success is not equally important in both. If there is not a minimum level of success in the monopoly of physical force, it is difficult to speak of a state, since there is no *one* center of power. However, a state may exist even if not legitimate in the eyes of some, or indeed many. This lack of legitimacy can refer to both the exercise of power and the very power center itself. In the former case, the government or a person who rules the center is illegitimate, whereas in the latter it is the state itself. In nation-states, the illegitimacy of the state stems from a lack of agreement, in a part of its territory, between the feeling of belonging to a community and the political objectification of the state reality. This is the case of peripheral nationalisms.[8]

A Historical Perspective

The multiple aspects of the preceding analytical discussion can be condensed into two key, yet complex, elements in order to explore the evolution of political structure in the West. The first of these elements is objective, namely the concentration of power in a center that dominates a specific territory. The second is subjective, since it relates to the acceptance of power by the governed; it is thus a problem of legitimacy, of how the political connection between those who rule and those who obey is socially regarded. In the nation-state, whose paradigm is the ideal—typical model of the liberal state (Künhl 1971), a totally centralized power dominates a defined territory and is legitimated by the notion that its authority emanates from the national community. One of the difficulties that the historical formation of this state runs into stems from the necessary relationship between both objective and subjective elements. This relationship consists of a certain harmony reflected in a national reality defined concurrently by territory, national frontiers, and a community of people. When there is a lack of such harmony between the territorial extent of the state and the extent of a consciousness of national belonging, peripheral nationalisms may arise within nation-states.

In the feudal era, within territories that would later become states, there existed a series of political relationships defined by the personal subordination of serfdom. That is, political power was spread among a plurality of political relations that, above all, were personal—leading to a personal legitimacy of power. The state was amorphous (Abercrombie, Hill, and Turner 1984), or, more accurately, it did not really exist in a modern sense.

The next most important historical moment was the emergence of the absolutist system. Absolutism summarizes something that at one point or another must occur in the process of consolidating the modern state—the concentration of power in a single center within a defined territory.

This power center duly emerged in royal houses, and the state took shape as a patrimonial one. For Weber, this occurs

> when the prince organizes his political power over extrapatrimonial areas and political subjects. . . . The majority of all great continental empires had a fairly strong patrimonial character until and even after the beginning of the modern times.

> Originally patrimonial administration was adapted to the satisfaction of purely personal, primarily private household needs of the master. The establishment of a "political" domination, that is, of *one* master's domination over *other masters* who are not subject to his patriarchal power implies an affiliation of authority relations which differ only in degree and content, not in structure. (1978, 1,013)

European courts in the seventeenth and eighteenth centuries, developed on the model of the Maison du Roi, were founded in the center. "In this period it was not the 'city' but the 'court' and court society which were the center with by far the most widespread influence" (Elias 1983, 54–55). This center gradually consolidated itself through imposition of its authority over the dispersed feudal domains. The court transformed into the center when aristocratic power ceased to be measured according to land possessed and instead became based on proximity to the royal house. Courtiers lived in the city, where they maintained a residence, or sometimes even resided in the monarch's palace. However, they continued to receive income from their country estates, from which they also derived their name and which they occasionally visited (Elias 1983, 45). Not belonging to the court, then, meant in a certain sense exclusion from power (17).

As for the subjective element, the legitimacy of power continued to be personal since monarchs were obeyed for who they were. Furthermore, this legitimacy developed ecclesiastically, as was to be expected in a society where the most important symbolic system continued to be the religious one.

The next most important historical moment is that marked by modern political revolutions. This era's first expression was perhaps the English Civil War, culminating in the death of Charles Stuart, who was executed for having betrayed the people as represented by the Commons (Walter 1971; Ranke 1979; Stone 1981). The era's most complete expression would be the French Revolution, when an already more modern and political language (Furet 1981), together with a certain antireligious discourse, was employed.[9] This historical moment produced fundamental change in the system of legitimating power. Importantly, the French Revolution implied both social and economic change simultaneously, as well as transformation of the symbolic universe.

The national, legal, and impersonal legitimacy of power in the nation-state probably possessed one last historical base, in the bourgeoisie's need of legal security. Bourgeois business interests required the elimination of juridical arbitrariness inherent in the exercise of all personalistic political power. As Weber observes,

> To those who had interests in the commodity market, the rationalization and systematization of the law in general and . . . the increasing calculability of the functioning of the legal process in particular, constituted one of the most important conditions for the existence of economic enterprise intended to function with stability and, especially, of capitalistic enterprise, which cannot do without legal security. Special forms of transactions and special procedures, like the bill of exchange and the special procedure for its speedy collection, serve this need for the purely formal certainty of the guarantee of legal enforcement.[10] (1978, 883)

When the bourgeoisie attempted to gain control of established power centers in specific territories, it was, moreover, interested in creating a market and abolishing political and social obstacles to the free circulation of individuals. One such obstacle was the historical link between peasants and the landowning aristocracy. Another was the linguistic and cultural diversity within these territories. It is sufficient to recall here the historical importance of central state political measures in disseminating a national-central language and culture, together with the standardization of customs and traditions (of weights and measures systems, for example), that occurred at this time. Similarly, the spread of a national educational system was also important for extending literacy and standardizing culture and language in all corners of the territory as the bases of a national spirit. To a great extent, the success or failure of disseminating national feeling in a territory depended on the strength or weakness of these processes, or, more accurately, on the strength of the bourgeois sectors that promoted these initiatives.[11]

If, in a given state, power is exercised by a central structure over a defined physical territory, and the individuals subjected to it cease to adhere by virtue of their personal political relationship to whoever exercises authority, then there is no form of legitimate symbolic representation of power other than that emanating from the subjects themselves. The nation, therefore, is the basic assumption of an impersonal legal legitimacy of the centralized state, or that found in Western countries.

A political power whose symbolic legitimacy is founded on personal feelings of dependency does not need to politicize a feeling of belonging to a territorially defined community.[12] The disappearance of political ties based on personal dependence leads, if the same center of power is maintained, to the politicization of a sense of belonging. Therefore, it becomes necessary to reduce nonpolitical sentiments of belonging to other territorially dispersed communities and generate a feeling of belonging to a new national community that equates with the territorial area controlled by the preexisting center of power. Furthermore, it is also necessary to deny the political projection of any feeling of belonging to preexisting communities. Only one sentiment of belonging is permitted in a single community that has a political identity/projection and originating, symbolically speaking, from the established center of power. Within a state territory, prior to its "nationalization," there were sentiments of belonging (but without a legitimate political dimension) to territories and communities, as well as loyalties to the nobility and, progressively, the monarch. There may even have been notions of national communities within intellectual or cultural sectors, but which did not influence the majority of the population. The state's nationalization process reduces everything to one political belonging.[13]

This, then, is the historical nature of the nation. On the one hand, in synthetic form, one can say that not all political forms or associations share a statelike dimension, nor are all state forms national (Balandier 1967, chaps. 1, 2, 6). However, more specifically it can be argued, as Nisbet does, that the nation stems from the state and not the contrary (Nisbet 1973, 164).

Historically, the nation is a form of legitimizing an established power center, in that it is occupied by social groups that tend to replace personal political connections with impersonal ones. The nation is an idea of community (mystically shared by all citizens) segregated by the state. The central functions of this idea are (1) the production of society in proportion to the state, (2) the oversight of primitive foundational violence (all states emerge out of civil wars), and (3) the cancellation of essential relationships of sociopolitical meaning of differential territories whose unification forms the state territory. Out of its own program the state produces or recreates the history of its own configuration as that of the nation, as if prior to the final statist achievement in a given historical moment it was a differentiated national community.[14] Peripheral nationalisms or collectivities that launch the idea of another nation against the state rely on the extent to which the diffusion of state nationalism was not successful.

The first structure analyzed herein is that of the state.[15] It was the first historical formation, and all other hypotheses about the nation always derive, to a certain extent, from this initial assumption.

Secondly, there are peripheral nationalisms that emerged within and against the state and imply different kinds of deficiencies in the state's nationalization process, that is, its political integration. These nationalisms experienced a decisive moment in the 1960s and 1970s in Western countries such as Great Britain, France, Switzerland, Spain, and Canada. A third type consists of Third World countries that, having emerged out of colonization, had to legitimize their state in national-community terms. In many cases, and especially in sub-Saharan Africa (A. Smith 1994, 18), this was difficult, given that in colonization a power center dominates a defined territory that in many cases does not at all coincide with an area exclusively inhabited by a specific ethnic group. In such a situation, it is difficult to create a single legitimate sense of community predicated on a center of power. This implies a paradox. The progressive globalization of the social system disseminates the pattern of the nation-state.

Edward Tiryakian describes these three cases temporally as successive waves of nationalism in human history. The first was the emergence of European nation-states and the United States in the second half of the eighteenth and beginning of the nineteenth centuries. Tiryakian also includes within this wave certain peripheral European regions that had an important level of cultural identity but lacked autonomy or political unity.[16] The second wave occurred during the interwar period of the first half of the twentieth century and principally affected Third World countries. The third wave began toward the end of the 1960s and continued into the 1970s and was a reaction against established Western nation-states (Tiryakian 1989, 143–49).

In recent times, important events have deeply affected the evolution of nationalism. First, one might cite the recrudescence of the ethnic question in the former Soviet Union[17] and the general democratization of the Eastern European countries. These changes facilitated nationalist movements. Second, the acceleration of European unification has meant important changes in peripheral nationalist expectations (regarding the nation-state), as well as for the panoply of European political identities. For example, the potential growth of a collective European identity might alter the meaning of national identity in regard to both nation-states and stateless nations. Indeed, within the stateless nation movements in Europe, the opinion has sometimes been that greater recognition is more possible within a European Union than within their own nation-states.

Part I of the present work attempts to develop a theoretical framework for an analysis of the specific case of Basque nationalism within the Spanish state. Specifically, I argue that the political identity that leads to nationalism is a collective one that, in a specific historical moment, acquires a basic political dimension by becoming the sole source of political legitimacy. This politicization of collective identity makes it incompatible with other collective identities within the same order.

The sociological character of collective identity has been established in order to focus the object of the present study. As already shown, although collective identity consciousness can be and often is essentialist—in that the actors conceive of their consciousness as stemming from objective features—all such features are social. For its connotation is never a preestablished given. In its cognitive dimension, then, collective identity is a social defining of shared reality through attributing social meaning to a feature. Collective identity is further subject to performativity, given that social definitions of collective constructs generate (if they are socially successful) the reality that they define.

Explorations of collective identities and of the processes of attributing meaning reveal that social conflict can occur among groups that try to establish different meanings or identities in regard to the same social aggregates. For this reason, a distinction has been made here between conflicts of identity (or over identity) and identities in conflict. All social conflict is a conflict among identities, and conflict is therefore a mechanism that objectifies every identity. Conflict over identity also implies a conflict between identities, since two groups advocate contradictory definitions of it. The greater the intensity of this conflict, the greater and more objectified will be the identity of each party to it.

Nationalism historically implies the politicization of collective identity when one considers that political power is the expression of a political community termed the nation. In a territorial state, only one power, and, therefore, one depository nation of it, can exist within the borders. The politicization of collective identity through nationalism implies, then, an incompatibility of this collective identity with another and different one that might be of the same nature. The de facto existence of two political identities of the same type within the same territory implies a conflict over identity. It is what happens with the so-called peripheral nationalisms of multiethnic Western states. The ability of peripheral nationalisms in such settings to take root corresponds to the degree of failure in the central nationalization process of a multiethnic state, or to the relative weakness of the mechanisms for diffusing the idea of nation.

These peripheral ethnic nationalisms, as struggles against an already established state center, were most active in western Europe during the nationalist wave of the late 1960s and 1970s (Tiryakian 1989). As such, they coincided with the rise and resurgence of what have been termed "new social movements."[18] This has prompted some of their adherents to posit that ethnic nationalist movements can also be considered one type of new social movement.

It remains unclear, for the moment at least, whether what are termed new social movements have commonalities or, at a very minimum, a certain homogeneity. Gusfield demonstrates that for understanding such diverse phenomena an overly abstract, and therefore too all-embracing, perspective is of little use in empirical research. In his opinion, a valid theory that explains all circumstances simply does not exist (Gusfield 1994, 93). Although the new social movements are not homogeneous, they still constitute a legitimate object of reflection in the same way as specific historical forms of collective action. That is what lies behind the dual approach in their study: the search for the internal dimension of a movement and its articulation with, or relation to, society in general. Touraine (1978) identifies a dual concern with (1) the generative social structural moment and (2) the analytical moment of social intervention within the movement. Melucci also speaks of using a two-tiered analysis to overcome the "myopia of the visible" in certain approaches that concentrate on the evident and measurable effects on the political level: to wit, the production of cultural codes in networks within the movement (one level) is what makes possible a tangible act within the political system (the other level) (1994, 125). Analytically, one might even speak of the threefold social effects of these new social movements. First are those direct impacts on the political system. Second are cultural effects within the population that participates more or less actively in the movement in question, or even within the population more or less identified (if but passively) with the movement's cultural agenda and codes. And third are the generative cultural effects that occur within the general populace. In order to observe and measure these impacts, some authors invoke a sense of drama (taken from Snow 1979) and the theory of mass society (Gusfield 1994, 109 ff.). I argue here that activists seek primarily to configure the cultural codes of the general population. Consequently, they often engage in attention-seeking acts or "spectacles" capable of garnering mass media attention.

Regarding the second level, militancy and individual participation in these social movements, through the very lifestyle, produces a certain sense of life purpose for the member. This can lead to a certain paradox: while the specific content of a social movement may be fixed or partisan but not totalizing (that is, in the sense of transforming the entire state and economy), for at least some of its militants there is a certain all-encompassing quality to the meaning of life that the movement establishes.

In short, the analytical field termed "new social movements" can be described as the intersection of a theory of collective action and the sociological theory of personal and collective identity at a historical juncture, namely the second half of the twentieth century, when "the forms of power that were emerging in contemporary society were founded on the capacity to inform (give form)" and when "the action of these movements occupied the same terrain and the message itself diffused by society was the same, and it transmitted symbolic forms and relationship patterns that illuminated *the dark side of the moon*"—in other words, at a time when the meanings "that the bureaucratic-technocratic apparatus tried to impose on individual and collective experience" (Melucci 1994, 120) were challenged.

One of the characteristics of social movements in this era most emphasized by analysts is their cultural character. Discussing culture is always a complex issue, because it encompasses different emotions and aspects. On the one hand, and as previously stated, these movements did not directly attack the totalizing structures of the state and the market but instead tried to alter the meaning of important constitutive elements of everyday life. As such, they were concerned more with the cultural (rather than political or economic) contents of society, understanding politics to be the logic of state institutions or the state itself. Indeed, they often tried to avoid economic and politico-state determination of social phenomena. They conceived of culture as an independent variable, falling short of positing so-called objective determinations. However, their objectives were not utopian for a number of reasons. First, they tried not so much to change economic and political decisions as to raise people's consciousness about culturally established meanings. Second, the members of these movements attempted at the time to live according to these new cultural meanings by acting them out. It was a kind of presentism (attributing priority to the moment) that was often viewed from without as illusory and marginal. Their objectives were cultural, an attempt to influence the rest of society through media-hyped drama (Edelman 1988). They were attempting to launch something akin to social contagion.

Among the new social movements, two kinds of relationship were established regarding identity.[19] One form was generative, whereby the members possessed a more or less widespread identity structured in various levels of belonging to a more or less diffuse community. As all movements have complex compositions in their internal subgroups, logically the degree of feeling varied according to greater or lesser proximity to the movement's core structure and values, and also according to the degree of agitation within, and opposition from without, at a particular moment. This solidarity could even, according to such conditions, become supranational or international. However, some social movements possessed another kind of more specific relationship with personal and social identity. They attempted to change the very cultural meaning of elements on which the identity was based, such as gender or age. Their members worked within the public sphere to further an agenda that affected their private identity, thereby blurring the boundaries between the private and the public (referred to as "life politics" by Giddens 1991).

However, not all cultural content of the new social movements could be reduced to organizational elements of personal identity. In some cases they were elements of the public sphere that became organizing principles of private identity. The ecology, pacifism, and antinuclear movements, for example, worked with public content. The shape of these groups structured a belonging that became the organizing principle of intimate identity.

If politics affects social dynamics and synthesis (Balandier 1967, 58), in general new social movements are political in a new way: namely, they do politics in another style, beyond the institution of the state, and thereby transform the cultural meanings that hold together our societies.

In light of the foregoing reflections, peripheral nationalisms cannot be placed within these new social movements, since their primary focus is the state and its disappearance within the peripheral territory, to be replaced by a new independent state. Their logic is therefore oriented toward the state, and their activity is directly political in the most classic and conventional sense of the term. These nationalisms share a close relationship with culture, but in a slightly different way from the new social movements that seek to transform existent cultural codes related to age, sex, nature, and so on. Nationalist movements legitimize their political activity by arguing for the persistence of traditional languages and cultures. They see peoples as needing their own states in order not to perish. Therefore, the goal is to regain cultural forms or revalidate existing patterns, not produce new ones. Moreover, their reference is a physical territorial unity more or less circumscribed by political boundaries, whereas the new social movements attempt to transform mentalities in general.

However, under authoritarian political regimes a nationalist movement acquires very specific characteristics. Let us say, for example, that an authoritarian regime is that which prohibits public expression of ideas and feelings contrary to the official truth. This obviously proscribes both the political and general expression of peripheral nationalist ideas. On the one hand, this means that nationalist parties cannot be formed and that those that are created or already exist cannot participate in the political process. (In the extreme case, political violence can be used against the state, although more likely there is clandestine activity that emerges in the public sphere on specific occasions without warning.) This situation, in which public activity by nationalist parties is impossible, means that what unites different opposition groups is more important than what divides them. As such, the general movement, through a kind of broad unanimity, is more important than its individual parties and other components. However, given its ultimate goal, peripheral nationalism is still a political movement of the classic kind.

On the other hand, official control of public expression implies that over time the public sphere's social mechanisms which might serve to produce and maintain a political identity. This is especially true of both the classic essential mechanism of the national education system and of the mass media.

As will be seen in chapter 4, during the most brutal years of the Franco regime, from the end of the Spanish Civil War (1939) until the mid-1960s, the reproduction of Basque nationalist consciousness withdrew into the private sphere. That is to say, it retreated to the world of family and friends, and even more to the hidden back rooms of private cultural and folkloric associations or the clandestine activity of certain parish churches. Therefore, in large measure, nationalism, under such strong authoritarian conditions, centered on the family world where nationalist consciousness was overlain with a large dose of emotion. Politics shaped personal identity and experience so that the relationships between the public or political and private spheres acquired a specific character.

As will be seen in chapter 6, this structuring of the private realm from a political perspective led, during the change to democracy (or the so-called Spanish Transition), to a very specific relationship between the private and public spheres. The intersubjective and associative private networks continued to be dynamic in a world where new political parties were emerging. With the creation of political parties, the previous consensus within the movement as a whole was lost. However, each party claimed as much as it could of that associative and intersubjective network. All nationalist organizations implicitly embraced a cross-class, communitarian national message in which social plausibility rested on the intersubjectivity of the classless notion. However, this would create problems when it came to organizing the instrumental agendas and bureaucratic structures of political parties.

The intersubjective associative component of nationalism impedes democratization because it entails progressively incorporating new institutions and professional politicians into its own realm, one that remains apart from everyday social life. Consequently, a strong tension arises between the institutions seeking the dismantling and restructuring of the collectivity's quotidian life and those favoring its persistence. This tension leads to a progressive condensing or confining of the movement and its support to more and more reduced social spaces. First it was the anti-Franco consensus, then a pro-Basque one, followed by the division between the moderate Right and the radical Left within Basque nationalism. Most recently, there is political isolation of the Herri Batasuna (Popular Unity) party, a last reduct in which the movement and its intersubjective dimensions are more salient than the organizational one. The use of force and, above all, emotional and rational attitudes toward the violence, have been key factors in this process.

With the progressive liberalization of public expression that came with democracy and with the progressive political dedramatization of politics by the younger generations (for whom the dictatorship was already a narrated rather than experienced history), more conventional new social movements emerged. All of them, and especially the antinuclear and antimilitarist movements, have found in the more movement-centered and less party-oriented sector of nationalism a cause célèbre for those who believe all conflict to be good, since it seeks the breakup of the state (Jaureguiberry 1983).

Just as the new social movements constitute a culturally approved relief from contemporary society's dearth of social meaning and appeal, nationalism (the more movement centered and less party oriented it is) also fulfills this need. It produces in those who join a feeling of partaking in a meaningful existence. And just as in the new social movements, there is a breaking down of the barriers separating the political/public from the private spheres. The public/private barrier characterizes contemporary democracies and contributes to the individual's sense of a lack of social meaning and personal purpose. Consequently, while new social movements and nationalist ones are not the same, they have certain affinities based on the search for meaning by actors in advanced societies. Both, then, possess important symbolic capital, which in turn makes them attractive to those who engage in the quest.[20]

In this chapter nationalism in general has been defined as a sociohistorical movement that promotes the idea of a specific relationship between collective identity and political legitimacy. Peripheral nationalism has been defined as a conflict over identity. Two definitions of the same social and territorial (referring to an internal part of a territory in the state) reality thus compete in asserting their ideas as socially correct. The outcome of this competition will ultimately depend on their credibility and the efficiency of their diffusion mechanisms. Peripheral nationalism has been described here as the perverse effect, from the state's perspective, of the state's

failure to performatively diffuse a supraethnic national concept within a multiethnic reality. From this perspective an attempt has been made to understand the historical meaning and specific nature of the so-called nation-state. This has been undertaken from an analytical point of view that traced the historical evolution of the
foregoing elements. The chapter considered the different waves of central state and
peripheral nationalisms that emerged historically, with particular emphasis on European peripheral nationalisms of the 1960s and 1970s. This wave coincided with the
emergence or resurgence of the so-called new social movements. Finally, examination of the differences and similarities between these new social movements and
peripheral nationalisms led to the conclusion that the similarities are greater when
the nationalist movements emerged under authoritarian political regimes.

Basque nationalism, as will now be seen, is a prime example. It is a conflict between a peripheral ethnic nationalism and a central state. Multiethnic Spain has
been territorially determined since the late fifteenth century, but its central state
nationalization process is far from complete (Linz 1973). Within its territory are
various peripheral nationalisms, of which the most virulent and problematic for the
legitimacy of Spanish democracy is that of the Basque Country. Basque nationalism
emerged at the end of the nineteenth century with a definition of Basque political
identity that was incompatible with the Spanish national idea. Within the ensuing
conflict over political identity, Basque nationalism's definition of Basque identity (as
is true of the opposing definition) has been subject to performativity. As such, the
central goal of the remaining analysis is to focus on the social mechanisms of maintaining and, where possible, extending and changing political identity as transmitted
by Basque nationalism.

PART TWO

Reproduction and Radicalization

of the Nationalist Consciousness

During the Franco Years

Chapter Three

The Problematic Legitimization

of the Spanish State in the Basque Country

Symbolic Capital: The Origins of Basque Nationalism

The present work will not address the entire history of Basque nationalism, which is over one hundred years old. To clarify, this work is not about the production but rather the reproduction of nationalism, following Marx's important methodological distinction between an explanatory model of a social phenomenon's historical production and the subsequent performance model of its (possibly expansive) reproduction.

In volume one of *Capital*, Marx, from a different theoretical perspective and after analyzing capital's reproduction process, addresses the problem of "so-called primitive accumulation." He observes that

> we have seen how money is transformed into capital; how surplus-value is made through capital and how more capital is made from surplus-value. But the accumulation of capital presupposes surplus-value; surplus-value presupposes capitalist production; capitalist production presupposes the availability of considerable masses of capital and labor-power in the hands of commodity producers. The whole movement, therefore, seems to turn around in a never-ending circle, which we can only get out of by assuming a primitive accumulation (the "previous accumulation" of Adam Smith) which precedes capitalist accumulation; an accumulation which is not the result of the capitalist mode of production but its point of departure. (Marx 1977, 873)

Within the political economy that Marx criticized, this primitive accumulation presumably resulted in the historical conditions of capitalist production, thereby erasing the original problem instead of resolving it. For Marx, the question was the origins of those conditions that allowed for and defined the performance model of capital reproduction. It was, therefore, a historical question, because primitive accumulation "assumes different aspects in different countries, and runs through its various phases in different orders of succession, and at different historical epochs" (Marx 1977, 876). But questions about primitive accumulation involved more than the socioeconomic accumulation of the first great quantity of money. They also included the origins of social conditions constituting the assumptions about capitalist production. Marx believed that his reproduction model explained capitalist performance, but he could not explain what he took for granted: capital and work. Why and how these came about he would have to explain in another way.

The present work does not ignore the historical roots of the so-called Basque problem. Indeed, throughout it are numerous historical references (namely, prior to 1939). However, these roots are not systematically analyzed. They are then more specifically considered through a theoretical-methodological framework that regards the situation in 1939 as a departure point for a primitive accumulation of nationalist symbolic capital. As such, this year marks a break between the first primitive accumulation, governed by certain specific sociohistorical laws, and the social performance and reproduction that grew out of this initial symbolic capital. The latter naturally was governed by significantly different laws and mechanisms. The Basque problem has a clearly political projection. It might be defined as a political response to the shape the Spanish state assumed through its modern formative process. From 1939 (or even 1937, when the Basque Country came under the insurrectionary rule of Franco) onward, a new form of state came into being. After military victory in the Spanish Civil War, this new state instituted a period of harsh political persecution of (among other things) peripheral nationalisms. This would have the undesired direct effect of multiplying and broadening the social mechanisms of nationalist reproduction. Consequently, Basque nationalism took root among new social sectors but also became more radical. This radicalization occurred in a more general political sense (as Basque nationalism became more left wing) and also in a more specifically nationalist sphere (in that it became more separatist). Similarly, Basque nationalism became more radical in embracing militant violence with a strong political protagonism and ample social acceptance.

The central goal of this part of the book is to identify the elements and mechanisms that supported the reproduction and diffusion of Basque nationalism at this time (chap. 4). However, after Franco's death in 1975, and as dictatorship gave way to a democratic state, the mechanisms of the previous regime transformed as a result of the new democratic imperatives. These transformations will be analyzed in the third part of the book (chaps. 5 and 6). The present chapter, however, will first summarize the origins of the Basque conflict and nationalism.

Caro Baroja dramatically describes the continual role throughout Basque history of a strange protagonist—violence or warfare. According to him, it is war—or more accurately a series of wars over a short period—that produced the specific character of the Basque people today. It was, then, a combination of violence, warfare, and invasion, together with the very personal misery experienced by numerous families that—more than juridical, sociological, or economic problems—shaped these characteristics. These wars coincided not only with great technical and economic catastrophes (the decline of pre-modern Basque industries such as wooden shipbuilding and iron foundries, along with the fall of the Spanish empire in the Americas), but with the destruction of Europe's Old Regime societies (Caro Baroja 1980, 69).

Political violence continues to be one of the most important features of life in the Basque Country today. Violence—like politics in general—forms part of everyday life, and so is an important force in the socialization of youth from the Franco years to the present. Collective disapproval of state violence has been accompanied by a certain legitimizing of violence in the Basque Country, which the state classifies as terrorism. This process began in the late 1950s and, in somewhat different form and dimension, continues to the present day.

For two centuries, Basque society has found itself divided between two social and political definitions of social reality. The fall of the Old Regime was plagued by difficulties and tensions in the Basque Country, where violence and social change emerged and occurred hand in hand. The Carlist wars (1833–39 and 1873–76) were the most important expression of this division, although the problem was equally evident between the conflicts.[1] Social scientists and politicians have frequently asked whether these conflicts offer the first glimmer of a Basque national consciousness. As a result, they have sought testimonies from these times that might be considered separatist, nationalist, or even the opposite. However, social reality is always more ambiguous and complicated. To be sure, within the Carlist/Liberal disputes of the nineteenth century there were economic interests at play, as well as social classes in conflict, but political and ideological differences also confronted one another.

The Carlist wars can be interpreted as a conflict between progressive liberalism and conservative traditionalism, between modernity and tradition, and between city and countryside. However, these dichotomies are laced with ambiguity, not only because the conflict was localized but because it was defined as a local struggle. In other words, the ideal of a unitary Spain was pitted against a local ideal of a unitary Basque Country. This happened because within Spain the social and economic conditions of the Basque peasantry were specific unto themselves. What was presented as progress and social reform in other places was not most important in the Basque case.

One territorial dimension of the ideological conflict and the ambiguity of the dichotomy was that the social base of the secessionist movement in Gipuzkoa during the War of the Convention (1793–95) was formed by a group of Liberals, whereas in Madrid Liberals were the bedrock of Spanish state centralism. This ambiguity held right down to the birth of the Basque Nationalist Party (PNV) in the 1890s, and even within the inner circle of the great industrial and financial bourgeoisie of Bilbao that emerged in the latter half of the nineteenth century. Specifically, this sector defined itself as simultaneously liberal (theoretically supporting the creation of a modern

TABLE 3.1 *Population of Spanish Basque Country, 1857*

Province	Population	Capital	Population
Araba	96,398	Vitoria/Gasteiz	18,710
Gipuzkoa	156,493	San Sebastián/Donostia	15,911
Navarre	297,422	Pamplona/Iruña	22,702
Bizkaia	160,892	Bilbao/Bilbo	19,923
Total	711,205		

Source: Author's calculation based on the census records of the National Institute of Statistics.

TABLE 3.2 *Use of Basque Language, 1867*

Province	Inhabitants	Basque Speakers	%
Araba	123,000	80,000	65
Gipuzkoa	176,000	170,000	96
Navarre	300,000	60,000	20
Bizkaia	180,000	149,000	83

Source: Núñez 1977a.

state) and foralist (in favor of maintaining the *fueros,* or specific local rights associated with Old Regime Spain). Furthermore, it came to defend a specifically centralist state position only after ascendant Basque nationalists, as well as socialists, began to co-opt Bizkaia's local institutions, the ones previously controlled by the bourgeoisie.

At the beginning of the nineteenth century, the Basque Country was a small, mainly rural society composed of a dispersed population and a few important towns. The Basque language was most common in those areas with greatest population dispersal.

In regard to political administration, the fueros gave most autonomy to the management of internal affairs. In the Basque Country this foral autonomy was defended by the local petty aristocracy and the peasantry against liberal centralism, but without furthering a specific ideology or elaborating a political project. The petty aristocracy and peasantry, whose interests may seem contradictory, fought alongside one another in the Carlist Wars. This was because liberal agrarian politics—above all, the disentailment of village commons—did not benefit the peasantry. Furthermore, there were intimate social relations between peasants and nobles, since, unlike in other areas of Spain, the Basque nobility was not of an absentee type.

Carlism was the fierce defense of a form of life. This system was threatened by the twin processes of urbanization and industrialization, as well as by political and administrative centralism. The cities were principal enclaves of liberalism (theoretically favoring a strong unitary Spanish state), yet the new nineteenth-century urban middle classes also played an important role in the emergence of nationalism. This irony has been highlighted by Beltza in his examination of the twin late-nineteenth-century Basque cultural and political renaissance movements out of which nationalism emerged (1974, 68).

Ultimately, the triumph of the liberal state, the abolition of the foral system, and rapid industrial growth combined to condition the birth of nationalism in the strictest sense: namely, as a political project (the acquisition of a Basque state, to be known as Euskadi, governed by one political party, the PNV [Partido Nacionalista Vasco, or Basque Nationalist Party]). This political movement was preceded by an intellectual and cultural renaissance that sought to identify the common bases (through linguistic and anthropological studies) of Basque life that differed from Spanish historico-juridical ones (Beltza 1974, 68).

Bilbao's industrialization would transform the Basque Country's class structure. A small group of (mostly related) families, having accumulated their capital mainly through the exploitation of iron deposits, embarked on a process of industrialization while establishing extremely important financial institutions.[2] At the end of the nineteenth century, this bourgeoisie attempted to dominate both the market and the state. At the time, the Spanish state was weak. It was governed by a monarchy based on traditional aristocratic relations and in chronic fiscal crisis. Therefore, the political solution to the problem of creating a state adapted to the needs of the Spanish market was to ennoble the industrial and financial bourgeoisie: "one might say that, in terms of the growth of a new dominant class, all socio-historical development between 1865 and 1950 can be understood, in our society [Spain], as the progressive reconstruction of the old aristocracy through the incorporation into its ranks of the elite bourgeoisie of our economy" (Moya 1975, 66).

Furthermore, this new financial aristocracy emerged out of a dual market (in the sociological sense of the term): the financial and the matrimonial.[3] As a result of these class developments, the lack of a bourgeois revolution—an often referenced historical characteristic of modern Spanish society—became even more pronounced. Such a revolution (had it occurred) would have legitimized, indeed would have to have legitimized, a state that was both middle class and Spanish at the same time. This "revolution" (not necessarily in the strongest sense of the word) would have furnished the critical means for the cohesion of Spanish society, its important symbolic capital. Instead, the state, rather than relinquishing the concept of ascribed status (Old Regime) and reconstituting itself as the national state of the Spanish bourgeoisie, came under the control of a financial aristocracy that in turn co-opted the means of political, economic, and administrative power (Moya 1975, 50, 80).

Bilbao's industrial and financial elites remained ambiguous on the question of Basque autonomy. On the one hand, they were interested in the development of the Spanish state; on the other, they wanted to preserve some local institutions that were under their authority. When they eventually lost this control to the middle class in 1916, they moved toward consolidation of the state. From that year onward two political forces began to dominate local institutions: Basque nationalists and socialists.

Basque nationalism was politically strong in those areas where industrial development was particularly evident: Bizkaia and, somewhat later, Gipuzkoa. According to López Adán, for Basque nationalism—that is, the response of a differentiated ethnic group to an external threat through politics whose objective is the formation of a nation-state—to emerge, rapid social change is not enough. Rather, within the group, modern classes, linked to industrial and urban development, must also appear and be prepared to create a new nation-state around their interests. During the nineteenth and early twentieth centuries, the industrial high bourgeoisie was the class most capable of lending political strength to this process. As will become apparent, a section of this class did indeed embrace the Basque nationalist project. The petty bourgeoisie was another important class in this project, for Basque nationalism's ideologues and intermediate cadre emerged out of this sector. Both bourgeois social sectors tried to imbue Basque nationalism with a response to the problems of the entire citizenry (all Basques) in order to also attract working-class support (López Adán 1977, 128–35).

In Araba and Navarre the industrial and petty bourgeoisie were of little importance. Indeed, these two provinces would not significantly industrialize until the middle of the twentieth century.

According to Elorza, for the outside observer "Basque history during the last one hundred and fifty years appears as a succession of paradoxes. Basque nationalism itself presents not the least contradiction in its ideology. It emerged in urban areas and only later extended into the rural environment, although it was precisely this latter sector that gave it its theoretical underpinning. It did so even to the point of concocting a myth that survived through changes in its collective consciousness: the archetype made up of rural images in a more and more urban society where the traditional countryside found itself on the road to extinction" (Elorza 1978, 69).

However, obviously it was in cities that people experienced most intensely the social changes associated with industrialization. Here, the mechanisms of the symbolic production of meaning were controlled by specific social groups. Older forms of life were disappearing, and new ones were being imposed. The nationalism of Sabino Arana, founder of Basque nationalism, was fundamentalist. It was even racist in that it appeared as a response to the great wave of migrants that came to Bilbao as a result of industrialization and *endangered* both Basque culture and traditional ways of life. Nationalism was ultimately the negation of everything that had happened to that point, proposing the substitution of a different totality: the creation of an autoch-thonous Basque state that would assume control of the social process, eventually shaping a society anchored in the *essence* of the Basque people and governed by traditional political methods (a form of populist democracy rooted in the munici-palities).[4]

When the Spanish Civil War broke out in 1936, Bizkaia and Gipuzkoa were al-ready at the height of their industrial development and Basque nationalism was an established political force (principally in Bizkaia). Nationalism's general alignment with the Spanish Republic took place despite the weakness in the Basque Country of the pro-Republican Left and the loyalty of Basque nationalists to Catholicism, the church, and the Vatican (generally allied with Franco's rebellion).

Prior to the civil war, two general political models for shaping the Spanish market contended for the attention of the Basque industrial bourgeoisie. One was supported by the vast majority of Bilbao's great industrial and financial high bourgeoisie. It was opposed to Basque nationalism and therefore supportive of Franco's *revolt*. It also attempted to create a unitary Spanish bourgeoisie (through financial and matri-monial alliances), together with a strongly centralized and standardizing state. The other bourgeois sector sought to forge a political alliance between an autonomous Basque territory and the central state. As such, it attempted to establish, within the Basque Country itself, a cross-class coalition (including the creation of Basque na-tionalist labor unions in league with the bosses) through nationalist ideology. This latter model was supported by the less economically powerful industrial bourgeoisie (upper middle class) of Gipuzkoa and Bizkaia, as well as the odd prominent member of the industrial elite.[5]

From 1939 onward, after the civil war, nationalism's symbolic primitive capital found itself in a different sociopolitical context—Franco's Spain. These new circum-stances would lead to a complex process of geographical dissemination of the nation-alist message and its social expansion and intensification.

After the Spanish Civil War: The Two Bourgeoisies

The end of the Spanish Civil War implied a clear defeat for the pro-Basque national-ist structural model with respect to the trinity of class-market-state. Moreover, with the emergence of the new state, the role and influence of every social group was effected and affected by previous affiliation with one of the two sides, the victors or the vanquished.

The industrial and financial high bourgeoisie gradually came to transfer decision-making power over its capital to Madrid (the central circuit of executives, the seat of head offices, the source of political appointment of high-ranking executives, and so on). As a social group, it would continue conducting political affairs (within busi-

TABLE 3.3 *The Press in the Basque Country During the Franco Years*

Province	Sale Time	Name	Print Run		%	Controlled by
Bizkaia	Morning	El Correo Español	86,32	(a)	50.5	Bourgeoisie (right wing)
		Gaceta del Norte	84,777	(a)	49.5	Bourgeoisie (right wing)
		Total	171,106		100	
	Afternoon	Hierro	11,510	(c)		The "Movement" (right wing)
	Monday	Hoja del Lunes	96,039	(a)		Press association (variable ideology within pro-Franco limits)
Gipuzkoa	Morning	Voz de España	38,130	(b)	55	The "Movement" (right wing)
		Diario Vasco	31,229	(b)	45	More right wing than Voz de España
		Total	69,359	(a)	100	
	Afternoon	Unidad	10,409	(b)		Right wing (sports)
	Monday	Hoja del Lunes	70,234	(b)		Press association
Navarre	Morning	Diario de Navarra	37,925	(b)	77.5	Right-wing antinationalist
		Pensamiento Navarro	11,000	(c)	22.5	Right-wing antinationalist
		Total	48,926		100	
	Monday	Hoja de Lunes	19,484	(b)		Press association
Araba	Morning	Norte-Expres	7,000	(c)		Local/oligarchic bourgeoisie (right wing)

Sources: Núñez 1977a; Unzueta 1979.
(a) April 1976, (b) January 1976, (c) 1971.

nesses in their relations with the state, as well as in local institutions and in the state apparatus) and financial speculation within Bilbao's greater metropolitan area (Pérez-Agote 1979a,b). Thereafter, the slow process of transferring financial and industrial decision making into the hands of specialists, directors, and executives, and the increased tempo of urban real estate speculation (without planning or even taking into account aspects related to the productive activity of the city), would soon produce an industrial and urban impasse in Bilbao. The city came to be characterized by a large concentration of industry based on an aging infrastructure and mindless and uneconomic urban sprawl.

This social class, the industrial and financial high bourgeoisie, constituted a pillar of Franco's new state and clearly came to be defined in two ways. On the one hand, both in public and private, it was anti-Basquist (that is, hostile to Basque cultural expressions). On the other, it displayed little cultural leadership. This was most apparent in the distancing of itself from both the popular press and the university. During the Franco dictatorship, Bilbao, finding itself subject to direct control by this high financial bourgeoisie, was paradigmatically lacking in cultural initiatives (in relation to its size, level of development, and affluence). The ostentatious wealth, the evidence of its economic and political power, its anti-Basquist nature, and its notorious incapacity for leadership made this extremely compact (territorially and socially speaking) social group a symbolic center of Francoist oppression.

Under Francoism, the Basque press was totally and openly antinationalist.[6] Furthermore, in the majority of cases this antinationalism was aggressive and militant (see table 3.3). A large part of the press was controlled by the industrial and financial high bourgeoisie, while the rest belonged to a chain of control spearheaded by the "Movement" (the name of the official state ideological apparatus).[7]

As for other forms of mass media in the Basque Country during the Franco years, most radio stations adopted a right-wing, anti-Basque nationalist position.[8] There were, however, some exceptions, such as the station belonging to the church (Radio Popular). Television remained the state's *private property*.

In terms of education, one must remember that the Basque Country had no public university until 1968 when the University of Bilbao was established. Before then, students in the Basque Country had access only to a School of Industrial Engineering and, from 1955 onward, one university division: Economic Sciences, which officially operated through the University of Valladolid in Castile. One must, therefore, highlight the absence of a humanities faculty in the Basque Country during the Franco era and, consequently, the pervasive cultural and linguistic repression, especially given the potential importance of such a faculty in preparing primary and secondary school teachers. After the death of Franco, a university system was created within the Basque Autonomous Community (Araba, Bizkaia, and Gipuzkoa) in 1978.

That said, there has been a private university in the Bilbao for more than a century: the Jesuit-run University of Deusto. Until comparatively recently, this university had only two schools: law and economics. In 1868, the School of Law was created with the elitist intention of attracting members of the aristocracy and high bourgeoisie. It was a time when the high bourgeoisie of Bilbao, in the process of establishing itself socially, needed a means of contact with other bourgeois groups and the aristocracy.[9] The School of Economics was established in 1916, at a time when the major European powers were involved in World War I and Bilbao's industrial growth was becoming increasingly independent of foreign capital. This school thus came to serve the arbiters of economic rationalization, and so selected students on the basis of intellectual ability rather than social standing. Grants were established to facilitate entry of those capable students who could not afford a university education.[10] Consequently, the two schools—law and economics—emerged and operated under quite different, but equally important, historical imperatives for the dominant social class.

This class, in creating standards and models of behavior, presented "all things Basque" (behavioral forms, dress, language, style, and the like) as bad taste, provincial, rustic (the term *casero,* literally "farmer" or "farmlike," came to be used in reference to Basque culture, implying the ordinary or unrefined), and, ultimately, lacking elegance. Unfortunately, there is no research on this subject. Nor has there been any sociological investigation of the interesting social changes in the bourgeois sectors after Franco's death. In particular, that part of the high bourgeoisie that maintained relations with the PNV attempted to co-opt the highest social positions, from where it could mold forms of social behavior. However, one must not overlook the fact that during the final years of the Franco regime, Basque nationalism began to enjoy, as will be seen, increasing social acceptance, though not political dominance. As a result of this gradual shift, behavioral forms underwent important transformations.

The less socially and economically important industrial bourgeoisie,[11] mostly found in Gipuzkoa but also in some areas of Bizkaia, was predominantly Basquist and nationalist. Thus it constituted a pillar of the Basque Nationalist Party. Disenfranchised from the end of the civil war (1939) until the general legislative elections of 1977, this social group was relatively politically inactive during the Franco years.[12] This bourgeoisie's economic performance is another matter, since it made important financial gains during the dictatorship. One might conclude that this sector created an industrial structure that entailed a specific means of developing and sustaining industrial relations. Within these (highly ambiguous) arrangements, this social group—which might be termed the nationalist bourgeoisie—never came to be defined as a source of national-cultural oppression, since it was, after all, Basque nationalist, nor as a source of social oppression, particularly regarding other Basque nationalist groups. This ambiguity shaped both its general social relations and those more specific relations between the working-class and nationalist movements. One episode illustrates these ambiguous relations perfectly. Towards the end of 1971, "one event that absorbed the front pages of the state's newspapers, that summed up ETA's new activity, and that symbolized its intention of coordinating its activism with the working-class movement, was the kidnapping of the industrialist Zabala. . . . The target had been carefully selected: he was not only a boss who had assumed a hard-line stance in a conflict with his workers, he happened to be Basque. Criticism of ETA-V regarding its pact with the Basque bourgeoisie was no longer accurate" (Ortzi 1975, 384–85). Number 63 of ETA's journal *Zutik* offered the following explanation: "All bosses are the same for us . . . whether they have Basque surnames or not changes nothing . . . all of them exploit us. They say Zabala is Basque, but he exploits the workers with the same cruelty as any other boss, independent of his nationality" (cited in Ortzi 1975, 385). The kidnapping, which had tremendous symbolic reverberations at the time, demonstrates another ambiguous relationship: that of the Basque nationalist bourgeoisie and the PNV with ETA.

This ambiguity of class, and especially industrial relations, was framed, at least in part, by the process of industrial and urban development specific to Gipuzkoa and Bizkaia (with the exception of the metropolitan area of Bilbao). A widespread and high level of industrialization occurred in Gipuzkoa, but it was dispersed throughout the province. One must, therefore, speak of Gipuzkoan multipolarity when defining this particular industrializing and urbanizing process (see tables 3.4 and 3.5).

The distribution of population and industry throughout the social space had important consequences for relations among Gipuzkoan social classes. In particular, different social groups lived and interacted with one another in a highly compressed social space. As such, these classes maintained direct, continuous, and daily interaction. The nationalist bourgeoisie found itself subject to direct social control from the other social classes. It had to adopt attitudes and behavioral forms similar to those of the other social groups. For the industrialist or businessman it was important to not parade one's superior economic or social status, given the existing industrial relations (friendly and paternal) within the province's factories. This was also true of political relations, since face-to-face interaction with constituents was common for political leaders. In Gipuzkoa, social and political relations were manifestly both keenly localized and personal.

The cases of Bizkaia and Araba, whose populations were highly concentrated in their respective capitals (Bilbao and Gasteiz), stood in contrast to Gipuzkoan dispersal. Navarre constituted an intermediate category. Although it did not formerly possess an urban center as did Bizkaia or Araba, from the 1960s onward Pamplona in particular grew through industrialization. Industrialization in Araba began in the 1950s (tables 3.4 and 3.5).

In conclusion, what should be highlighted is that Bilbao's industrial and financial high bourgeoisie dominated the public sphere: both politically, through their open

TABLE 3.4 *Population Growth by Province and Autonomous Community*

Province	1857	1877	1887	1897	1900	1910	1920
Araba	96,398	93,538	92,893	94,622	96,385	97,181	98,668
Gipuzkoa	156,493	167,207	181,856	191,822	195,850	226,684	258,557
Bizkaia	160,579	189,054	235,659	290,222	311,361	349,923	409,550
Basque Autonomous Community (a)	413,470	449,799	510,408	576,666	603,596	673,788	766,775
Navarre (b)	297,422	304,187	304,051	302,978	307,699	312,235	329,875
BAC + Navarre	710,892	753,986	814,459	879,644	911,295	986,023	1,096,650

Province	1930	1940	1950	1960	1970	1975	1981
Araba	104,178	112,876	118,012	138,934	204,323	238,233	260,530
Gipuzkoa	302,339	331,753	374,040	478,337	631,003	682,507	693,786
Bizkaia	485,205	511,135	569,188	754,383	1,043,310	1,151,485	1,181,389
Basque Autonomous Community[a]	891,720	955,764	1,061,240	1,371,654	1,878,636	2,072,225	2,135,705
Navarre[b]	345,883	369,618	382,932	402,042	464,874	483,667	506,062
BAC + Navarre	1,237,603	1,325,382	1,444,172	1,773,696	2,343,510	2,556,092	2,641,767

Source: Gurrutxaga, Pérez-Agote, and Unceta 1991.

[a]Corresponds to the current Basque Autonomous Community.

[b]Corresponds to the current Foral Community of Navarra.

TABLE 3.5 *Percentage of Total Provincial Population Represented by Capital City*

Capital City	1900	1930	1940	1950	1960	1970	1975	1981	1986
Vitoria/Gasteiz	45.63	54.43	56.12	56.32	62.38	73.06	76.37	78.30	78.39
San Sebastián/Donostia	32.31	40.64	44.98	43.94	42.71	44.86	45.72	46.10	45.81
Bilbao/Bilbo	57.36	67.62	69.23	71.22	76.13	78.28	78.97	78.90	78.30
Pamplona/Iruñea	17.00	19.20	23.55	25.42	31.00	42.15	45.54	49.00	—

Sources: Gurrutxaga, Pérez-Agote, and Unceta 1991; Pérez-Agote 1989.

Note: The greater metropolitan area of the capitals has been used rather than just the city itself. If not, for example, the figure for Bilbao would be misleading given that the municipality of the capital merges seamlessly with other large municipalities into a single urban sprawl.

alliance with the Franco regime, and socially, given the visibility of their wealth and power throughout the Basque Country during the Franco years. This permitted and socially reinforced the political pressure the state exerted on the language, culture, and ideology of Basque nationalists.

The Radicalization of Basque Nationalism During the Franco Regime

Table 3.6 details the effects of the Franco regime on support for Basque nationalism. Here the percentages of the nationalist vote, both within each of the four provinces and as a whole in the Basque Country, are outlined at two key junctures: immediately prior to the Spanish Civil War and shortly after Franco's death. Of course, during the Franco years there were no free elections. In this table we discern a general increase in the Basque nationalist vote. One might tentatively argue that, before the civil war, even moderate (in political and Catholic terms) Basque nationalism outside the framework of the Basque Nationalist Party (PNV)—let alone more radical varieties—was practically nonexistent. However, from the beginning of the political transition after 1975, radical (left wing and separatist) nationalism became important.

First, though, we must consider a crucial factor in the profound changes that occurred between these two points. There was increased migration from various Spanish provinces into the Basque Country during the interim. Table 3.7 shows a rapid increase in the population of Bizkaia and Gipuzkoa during the 1950s and 1960s, as well as the overall population change roughly corresponding to the era of Franco's rule (1939–75). The direct demographic effects of the civil war are minimized, since the baseline statistics are from 1940. There was, then, enormous population growth throughout the Basque Country in the thirty-five years between 1940 and Franco's death.

An approximate calculation of the population trends in the Basque Country during the first seven decades of the twentieth century, formulated by a Basque institution, appears in table 3.8. Generally speaking, Bizkaia and Gipuzkoa received most of the new arrivals, a continuation of a process already discernible toward the end of the nineteenth century.[13] However, it is also evident that during the decades 1951–60 and 1961–70, that is, at the zenith of the Franco regime, these same provinces received the greatest number of migrants. Araba and Navarre would reverse their strong tradition of out-migration only in the 1950s and 1960s, respectively, during which time they began to show a positive migratory balance. Clearly, the general industrialization process in Bizkaia and Gipuzkoa one hundred years earlier began to penetrate the other two provinces at this time.[14]

Being a local or a migrant came to be one of the most discriminating variables

TABLE 3.6 *Percentage of Nationalist Vote Prior to Spanish Civil War and in First General Legislative Elections After Franco's Death*

Region	1933	1936	1977	1979
Araba	27.33	20.2	21.1	37.7
Gipuzkoa	34	29.9	46.1	54
Bizkaia	46.4	56.1	39.8	48
Navarre	9.1	2	7	17.3
Total	30.8	24.4	36	49.9

Sources: Linz et al. 1981; Fusi 1984; Gurrutxaga, Pérez-Agote, and Unceta 1991.

TABLE 3.7 *Basque Population Growth During Franco Dictatorship, 1940–1975*

Area	1975 Population as % of 1940 Population
Araba	211%
Gipuzkoa	206%
Bizkaia	225%
Navarre	131%
Total	193%

Source: Table 3.4.

(Llera 1984, 315) with which to explain the voting patterns of the various Basque nationalist and Spanish centralist partisans. If one takes into account the general tendency of migrants to vote for centralist options, then Basque nationalism's electoral gains (reflected in table 3.6) are surprisingly large.

A comparison of the electoral scene prior to the Spanish Civil War in the 1930s with that of the 1970s after the death of Franco (see Linz et al. 1981) shows significant change. In the forty years that separate these two moments, adherence to Basque nationalist ideology clearly grew. Moreover, an extremely radical nationalism emerged on the political scene. The radical variant of Basque nationalism manifested a dual character: on the one hand, it promulgated the extreme nationalist position (supporting separatism and independence); on the other, it legitimized the armed violence of the separatist military movement ETA (Euskadi ta Askatasuna, or

TABLE 3.8 *Midcensus Migratory Balances, 1901–1970*

Decades	Araba	Gipuzkoa	Navarre	Bizkaia
1901–1910	-9,203	6,157	-25,957	-2,959
1911–1920	-7,239	8,174	-12,486	18,997
1921–1930	-5,210	12,729	-21,185	18,290
1931–1940	2,650	9,964	-2,305	-1,344
1941–1950	-3,797	10,568	-19,833	18,987
1951–1960	7,703	48,754	-20,499	96,399
1961–1970	42,547	64,845	18,127	148,804

Source: *Dinámica de la población y del empleo en el País Vasco*
(Bilbao: Cámara de Comercio, 1978), 56.

Euskadi and Freedom). The extension and intensification of nationalism introduced new complexity into the general political situation. One might argue, for example, that at certain moments of political tension with the center all Basque nationalists remained relatively united; however, in the day-to-day interactions of local Basque politics (and given the existing political autonomy) serious conflict emerged within Basque nationalism.

Political Identity, Violence, and Legitimacy in the Basque Country

Throughout the nineteenth century central political power suffered a crisis of legitimacy in the Basque Country. At certain times, the competition between centralists and regionalists resulted in the military violence of the century's several wars. Even during peacetime, however, Basque society experienced tremendous tension linked to the memory of war and the fear of future conflict.

Thus, two visions of political identity competed in the Basque Country during the nineteenth century: one involving the legitimizing of the central state, the other involving its delegitimization, which came to characterize Basque nationalism. The PNV interjected the tension between these competing visions into the new working-class movement that emerged during industrialization, and at the same time provoked tension with its leftist or socialist branch. Both groups, Basque nationalist and leftist, while contesting the loyalty of the working class, were in conflict with the central state. It was this shared opposition that produced specific political pacts and an alliance during the Spanish Civil War against the Francoist rebels who were attempting to assume control of the state.

After the hostilities were over, the political repression of the Franco dictatorship would provoke the creation of an armed organization by a segment of the first post-war Basque nationalist generation. This group could not perpetrate the same level of violence as the state, although its actions had enormous symbolic resonance. However, during the Franco years, within certain sectors of the Basque population, there was a gradual legitimizing of, and affective identification with, ETA's violence. Concomitantly, state violence and the state itself were progressively delegitimized. After Franco's death, with a new democracy in place, ETA continued its violence, but the symbolic value of its actions changed dramatically. In particular, ETA lost the affective support of many Basques, although an important part of the population was sympathetic enough to keep ETA going.[15] The social division produced by ETA's violence provoked internal conflict within the Basque Country and profound division among nationalists themselves.

During the last two centuries, political violence has been a feature of social life in the Basque Country. In widespread social sectors, to different degrees, there has been a strong questioning of the state in general, and the state's monopoly on legitimizing violence in particular. In other words, the very existence of a national Spanish community has been called into question and its social obviousness made nearly impossible. Therefore, Basque nationalism was, at the root, not a simple crisis of legitimacy, but a questioning of the very foundational moment of the state. In theoretical terms, this moment could be defined as when effective control over everyone (namely, all the members of the two groups in the aftermath of a civil war) was established. In other words, the state held a monopoly on physical coercion, but without establishing its clear legitimacy as reflected in its general acceptance. The moment was defined by the establishment of effective, but not legitimate (for everyone at least), power. As Moya observes, in Spain during the nineteenth and twentieth centuries and up to the outbreak of the Spanish Civil War in 1936, there was a latent civil war (Moya 1975, 65). Without a doubt, one of the key elements nourishing this dynamic was the political identity of the Basque Country.

The most socially important dimension of Basque political violence was not its capacity to crush the state apparatus. This is why several Marxist analyses of Basque nationalism are unsatisfactory given their preoccupation with the state apparatus itself. However, though local violence has been, above all, symbolic or subjective, still it has been effective. It has managed to impede the gradual establishment of a social obviousness that within the Spanish state territory there exists a single national community. Throughout the whole process of state formation, an alternative form of violence existed within the Basque Country that was instrumentally far inferior to that of the state. Consequently, Basques have lost all their battles with the state. However, they have been able to upset it and, at the same time, managed to prevent the state apparatus from ever becoming legitimized as a nation.

Within the period covered by the present work, three moments, or stages, can be established regarding the relationship between political identity, violence, and the state. These three stages correspond to the Spanish Civil War (1936–39), the Franco dictatorship (1939–75), and the post-Franco years (after 1975).

During the first of these stages, the Spanish Civil War, two visions or definitions of collective reality competed with one another: a central nationalist and a Basque nationalist perspective. They were maintained by different social bases of support. Franco's rebel forces rose up against a republican government that attempted to integrate both peripheral nationalisms and the Left. Therefore, the democratic forces of the Left and the peripheral nationalists united against the rebels. However, on the Basque question there was not such a clear division. Within the rebel group, the Catholic and Fascist Right clearly opposed any separate Basque political identity. Among those defending the Spanish Republic against Franco's uprising, however, there was some political acceptance of Basque nationalism along with a certain ambivalence that was never completely resolved. In any case, the war interrupted attempts to seek a solution to the question in the 1930s based on the concession of a Basque Statute of Autonomy and the entry of Basque nationalists into the Spanish government. This attempt to resolve one of the latent causes of the civil war was also one of the elements that unleashed the conflict in 1936.

Once the war was over, with the rebels victorious, a new state was created. This marks the second stage, in which a unitary central power was established with a monopoly on the use of violence. Once more, two irreconcilable visions of Basque political identity competed with each other. However, the state imposed its centralist vision as the official and only acceptable version. While some citizens agreed, others did not. The dissenters, of course, could not publicly express their disagreement. The authoritarian state controlled, or at least attempted to control, all public mechanisms of ideological reproduction: the educational system, the mass media, political association, public rituals, and so on.

The Basque nationalist vision had to fall back on private mechanisms to maintain its existence. The contexts included the family and groups of friends; the means consisted of the daily ritual encounters in intimate settings imbued with a collective spell of silence. Similar activities were systematically covered up by the church, or its lower clergy, as well as by cultural and sporting clubs. In short, there were hidden mechanisms, the unstated objectives of certain public associations, and the systematic public concealment of certain political activities within religious life. At the end of the day, it all added up to clandestine activity. Within this context, the public appearance of ETA's transgressing violence gradually gained the affective support of certain sectors of the population. During the Franco dictatorship, therefore, the Spanish state continued to be in a foundational stage. It possessed a monopoly on physical violence, but did not possess a monopoly on legitimacy, as demonstrated by the growing affective support for violent protests and confrontation.

The third stage corresponds to the political transition that began after the death of Franco. In the Basque Country, it coincides with an attempt by those who had struggled to impose their differing visions of the political future to reach some form of agreement. They sought an agreement on the practical methods each group might use to impose its vision, ultimately through democratically elected institutions. As will be seen, this pact on the use of peaceful methods was accepted by one part of Basque nationalism. ETA's military violence continued however, with the acquiescence of a relatively important segment of the entire population. Yet those who had accepted the new situation, democratic Basque nationalists, did not reach agreement with the other democratic forces on a unified definition of Basque political identity. As a result, the political status of Euskadi continued to be a problematic issue within the Basque Country, as well as within Spain as a whole.

This chapter has sought to give an overview of Basque nationalism's historical trajectory. Then, and in a general way, it has examined the political consequences of the Spanish Civil War in Basque society. These included the unintended consequences of the Franco regime's political persecution of the Basque language and culture, as well as of Basque nationalist organizations and ideology. One of the unintended consequences was the radicalization of Basque nationalist consciousness at the core of the first postwar generation. In the following chapter, the specific social mechanisms that maintained and radicalized Basque nationalism during this time will be examined.

Chapter Four

Basque Nationalism

During the Franco Dictatorship

The Basic Mechanisms for Reproducing Consciousness

The arguments here about the reproduction of Basque nationalism during the Franco years have much in common with the work of Hank Johnston in his study of Catalan nationalism under the same regime. Johnston asks how certain nationalisms (in the Baltic states, in Georgia, Armenia, and Moldavia, and, of course, in Catalonia) survive in the face of severe repression. The answer, in the Catalan case, forms the nucleus of his work: "Regarding the Catalan movement, the chapters that follow present evidence that the extraordinary redefinition of friend, foe, and shared symbols that characterizes the success of the movement was fundamentally accomplished not as a result of changing political opportunities, nor by strategic calculations of power and resources, but rather by cultural processes located at the level of participant interaction" (1991b, xiii).

The present work also acknowledges the arguments of James C. Scott (1990, chap. 5) in his discussion of the resistance, and even subcultural dissidence, of social groups and sectors subjected to relationships of dominance. Restricted to playing an acquiescent role in public life, they elaborate a series of practices, gestures, and even a counterideology (118). These elements coincide in what Scott terms a hidden transcript. This develops in various "places," either physically or nonphysically specific, and at a safe distance from the watchful eye of dominant groups that control the public transcript. Scott's model is especially useful when considering resistance that is barely structured and fleeting. To his general question, "How cohesive is the hidden transcript?" (134), one might respond, in regard to the Basque case during the Franco dictatorship, that dissident nationalist culture was relatively cohesive, especially until the mid-1950s when a radicalization of the first post–civil war nationalist generation became apparent.[1] Moreover, in the Basque context the dominated social sector had very structured social relations, as will be seen.

Three of Johnston's theoretical perspectives will be used here to explain Basque nationalism during the Franco regime: his concept of a subculture of opposition,[2] as applied to the Catalan case (1991b, chap. 4); the notion of a religious-oppositional

74

subculture, which he uses to discuss Poland and Catalonia (Johnston 1989); and the concept of a religious-nationalist subculture, which, borrowing from one of my works,[3] he uses to define nationalism in the Basque Country during the Franco era (Johnston 1991a). Together, these interchangeable ideas refer to a subculture of political opposition against an authoritarian regime. This subculture was laced with religious belief and sentiment, maintained (at least in part) through a system of close familial and friendship relations, and systematically attempted to elude the scrutiny of central political authority. According to Johnston, this subculture consists of three key elements. The first is cultural content, composed of a blend of political, national, and religious symbols. The second "includes the processes by which the cultural content is passed and refined between generations. A key aspect is the primary socialization that occurs in the family. Because oppositional attitudes are acquired as part of social, psychological, and moral development, it follows that the imprint of an oppositional subculture on the individual can be quite enduring." The third element "is the social organization of culture. Here too the family is the primary structure. Within the subculture, families are linked through friendship and common membership in the secondary organizations. . . . In this respect, church organizations provide an important forum for interaction" (Johnston 1991b, 50).

Additional elements can be added, especially having to do with the relational nature of the subculture. After all, if the subculture in question were not immersed in a political system that was attempting to persecute it, there would be little sense in constructing such an analytical framework. Thus, a fourth element would be the authoritarian political system that, as will be discussed below, tried to hinder the reproduction of the ideology and the subculture in general. Indeed, it was the very existence of the authoritarian political system that made religious organizations important as contexts for interaction free from state scrutiny (third element). There was also the symbolic importance of religion itself (first element).

A fifth element emerges out of the authoritarian nature of the political system: the closed and secret nature of the subculture, given its obvious need to remain hidden. Here, any examination of subculture encounters a paradox. On the one hand, the subculture in question is very apparent, with clearly demarcated social boundaries. On the other, it is quite difficult to access. Basque nationalism during the Franco dictatorship, explored in this chapter, presents a prime example of such collective clandestineness.

A sixth element can be added to the concept of nationalist oppositional subculture, deriving from the relationship between politics and religion within the subculture itself. It is argued here that, in every example of this kind, a secularization of the subculture takes place. For example, such analysis has been applied to political situations in both the Franco dictatorship and the Soviet Union. In both cases the subcultures of opposition included a strong religious tradition. However, while the

Soviet regime systematically persecuted religion, the Franco dictatorship invoked Catholicism and the church as sources of political legitimacy.[4] Whereas subcultures in communist regimes generally tended to unite the general population, the religious clergy, and the church hierarchy, this was not entirely the case with the nationalist subcultures during the Franco regime. In fact, there were disagreements within each of these groups as a consequence of the Franco regime's close connections with the Spanish church. Indeed, not for nothing was the official state ideology described as national Catholicism. This was one result of the ideological weakness of Franco's movement: the regime sought religious underpinning for its political legitimacy (Johnston 1991b 214 n. 1).

Therefore, the sixth common element to note is that, in every case, and in addition to the differences mentioned above, within the subculture a certain ethnic solidarity or collective identity was formed. Unable to attain political objectification,[5] this identity turned instead toward a religious objectification of the kind described by Durkheim in *The Elementary Forms of the Religious Life* (1915). In this work, he establishes religion—or the church, understood as a community of believers—as the mortar of society: "Thus there is something eternal in religion which is destined to survive all the particular symbols in which religious thought has successively enveloped itself. There can be no society which does not feel the need of upholding and reaffirming at regular intervals the collective sentiments and the collective ideas which make its unity and its personality." He adds: "What essential difference is there between an assembly of Christians celebrating the principal dates of the life of Christ, or Jews remembering the exodus from Egypt or the promulgation of the decalogue, and a reunion of citizens commemorating the promulgation of a new moral or legal system or some great event in the national life?" (Durkheim 1915, 427).[6]

This religious objectification of collective identity implies a certain intrareligious secularization, as religion undertakes a task that is not exactly religious. Furthermore, when authoritarian power loses its validity, secularization occurs as well. A certain democratic and national construction emerges from a part of the population that previously confined political value to its own subculture, without needing to refer to religion or the church for its reproduction.[7]

In order to understand why, in the Basque case, certain mechanisms of political socialization—the family, religion and the church,[8] groups of friends (*cuadrillas*), as well as leisure-time rituals, such as going from bar to bar (*poteo*), and the associative world—became important and not others, one must take into account the kind of regime constructed by Franco. Without debating in detail its precise nature, there's no doubt it was authoritarian (Linz 1976).[9] In this sense, then, it was characterized (a) by the establishment of an *official truth* regarding political reality, and (b) by effective political control of the public mechanisms for producing and disseminating ideas, above all during the initial years of the regime.

In regard to the first characteristic, it can be argued that the official truth directly affected political identity, given that well-defined peripheral nationalisms (including the Basque version) had been on the losing side in the Spanish Civil War. According to the official Spanish line, the Basque Country, or, more accurately, the Basque Provinces (Provincias Vascongadas), as Bizkaia, Araba, and Gipuzkoa were termed by the Franco regime, were part of Spain. As such, *Basque separatism*, as Basque nationalism was called in the official jargon of the day, was strictly outlawed.

Naturally, to disseminate this official truth the regime used all of the available public mechanisms, especially public education at all levels, as well as the media. The extent of its success is open to debate. "Public mechanisms" refers not to actual ownership or effective possession (of an educational center or a newspaper, for example), but rather to the climate in which the mechanism operated, its social visibility, and its degree of administrative institutionalization. Franco's regime attempted to control, with increasingly less success from the end of the 1960s onward, all mechanisms of symbolic reproduction in Spanish society. However, this was only effective when these mechanisms, and social deviations from the official line, were visible enough to be accessible to social control. Therefore, reproduction of truths that contradicted the official version was confined to the private realm and to the microsocial dimension of certain public institutions. Contexts beyond official control included the family and some forms of intersubjective relations within cuadrillas, relations among cuadrillas during poteo, and voluntary associations functioning secretly as forums of political socialization. The church could also facilitate activities that contributed to Basque nationalism's reproduction, although over time its credibility with the Franco regime and its impunity declined.

Since 1979, when the first five interviews (I-1 to I-5) were conducted with the heuristic goal of ascertaining the nature of relevant political socialization, it has been clear that such religious and associational commitments were quite effective in reproducing Basque nationalism. Moreover, the possibility of effecting them during the Franco years was confirmed in most of the interviews. Indeed, as will be seen in this chapter, in the most radical sphere, ETA's own initial internal documentation reveals that great importance was accorded the role of religion. Furthermore, ETA members continually referred to the important role of priests in organizing activities with a strong element of political socialization and which tended to be of the radical nationalist variety.

The key difficulty in studying development and change within Basque nationalist consciousness stems from one characteristic: its main reproduction mechanisms were not directed, in the period under examination, by political or intellectual leaders.[10] If such leaders had existed, they would have catalyzed these mechanisms, thereby attracting the attention of social scientists. In turn, these observers could have more easily analyzed the production of this ideology through concrete written sources.[11] Of course, such analysis alone would be insufficient for fully understanding any social movement. However, the difficulty is worsened by the fact that in the

Basque Country during the Franco years there was no specific professional intellectual group. To be sure, certain clergymen and lay persons had some degree of influence, particularly within intimate associational circles. But in the interviews undertaken, no mention is made of any crucial role played by either texts or political leaders as transmitters of Basque nationalist consciousness. On the contrary, those who mentioned reading habits during time spent in jail or exile cite more general texts (see interviews with I-9, I-11, I-20, I-21, and I-28). For example, there is I-19's description of the activities of imprisoned activists: "As far as I know, they spend their time studying and learning Euskara (Basque). And normally in studying Marxist theory through some specific books. And precisely because the people in power allowed them free access to certain kinds of books, the problem of independence, the national problem, remained vaguer. So there was exposure to a pure form of Marxism, which neither recognized nor eradicated the problem of nations. I think this was one of the reasons that important changes took place within the group between ETA-V and ETA-VI" (I-19).[12]

The distrustful way in which this former ETA member refers to pure Marxist political literature reveals the limits of Marxism for understanding the national problem. It also raises the question of how contact with Marxist literature in jail or exile influenced these activists. However, one thing is certain: the general reading habits of these activists had certain consequences for the violent organization's attempts to create working-class fronts.

The lack of references within these individual social biographies to political or scientific literature, or indeed to specific Basque nationalist intellectuals or political leaders, underscores the intimacy between politics and daily life. Indeed, one might argue that there was no real differentiation between collective life (intersubjective relationships, social interaction) and political life for important sectors of the population.

Nor did politics during this era produce any ideological leadership. This was because the two most important nationalist organizations during the Franco years, the Basque Nationalist Party (PNV) and ETA (in its different versions), were not essentially centers of ideological production. Rather, the PNV, owing to the conditions of daily life enforced by the Franco regime that prohibited it from functioning as a political organization, remained a kind of symbolic repository of nationalist consciousness. As for ETA, although some of its original or historic members attempted to carry out acts of direct consciousness-raising among the people (I-18), the dynamic of the movement was moving in a different direction—toward recruitment of activists. Ultimately, it should be noted, such popular consciousness-raising occurred in a more indirect way—through a process, analyzed below, of affective identification with violence rather than through activities specifically directed at producing such consciousness-raising per se.

Dense social solidarity, in the sense of both tremendously intense intersubjective relations and strong commitment within the associative world, was an essential feature of Basque society and is perhaps one of the key reasons political and intellectual leadership did not emerge during this time.[13] Indeed, explaining why a type of behavior more commonly associated with very traditional societies continued to be important in a highly industrialized one continues to be a problem for sociological analysis. Effectively, these characteristics were separate, albeit strongly rooted, elements pertaining to a society whose social system had been challenged by the twin processes of industrialization and urbanization. These processes were very rapid and traumatic and quite specific to certain areas. Such was the case with Gipuzkoa (and certain areas of Bizkaia that were relatively industrialized, though not Bilbao, which experienced a different process), where there was a heterogeneous pattern of urbanization and industrialization. This resulted in a social space reduced enough to allow for the persistence of social relations, as well as intimate social control more resonant of traditional society.[14] Indeed, in varying degrees this social climate is characteristic of the entire Basque Country.

One result of the extension and modification of Basque nationalist consciousness during the Franco years was that politics and violence became typical elements of daily life. Moreover, the increased reproduction of the nationalist code was linked to specific social means and institutions that constituted its breeding ground. This ideological breeding ground was in turn intimately linked to the everyday social life of intersubjective and associative relationships.

The complex interdependence among individual personal life, collective life, and political life in the Basque Country during the Franco years is essential for understanding how nationalist consciousness, and the sense it imparted, developed during this time. In schematic terms, the problem can be framed as follows:

In part, one must focus attention on primitive symbolic capital's development, which, together with the birth of ETA, formed the future axis of affective identification for new generations. Another critical dimension is that a general awareness of a nationalist problem gradually transformed from acknowledgment of to identification with the problem. This principally occurred through affective identification with ETA's violence and through dissemination of consciousness from fairly limited social circles to significantly wider ones. The national question, in cultural, political, and violent ways, penetrated a world of strong interpersonal relationships and a highly active associative way of life. This dual focus naturally leads one to consider the principal social mediums and institutions through which such national consciousness was reproduced. One must also consider the complex phenomenon of sympathy for the use of violence.

In examining each social medium and institution, the focus here will not be on their general function or mode of operation, but rather their contribution to repro-

TABLE 4.1 *Physical Repression During the Franco Years*

Year	Numbers Arrested	Numbers Exiled or Escaped	Numbers Imprisoned	Numbers Wounded and/or Killed by Security Forces
1968	434	38	—	—
1969	1,953	342	862	—
1970	831	128	396	416
1972	616	—	328	216
1973	572	—	316	178
1974	1,116	320	315	105
1975	4,625	518	632	—

Source: Núñez 1977a, 21. (The data for 1971 are missing.)

duction of the nationalist code. In other words, attention will be paid to the specific ways in which they provided mechanisms to further that reproduction. Consequently, the emphasis here is not on a sociology of the family or religion, for example, but more on a sociology of nationalist consciousness. The analysis will focus on qualitative and more profound aspects of the phenomenon rather than on simple causal relationships among different variables.

FAMILY AND RELIGION

The main features of the nationalist familial universe during the initial years of the Franco regime are apparent in the interviews with I-25, I-26, I-27, I-29, and I-30.

The defeat in the Spanish Civil War was still very recent and had left a tremendous frustration among the vanquished. The end of the war meant a return to everyday life, but not necessarily the disappearance of physical threat. Postwar life was, naturally, very hard on everyone. Within nationalist families there remained both frustration over the defeat and fear of both physical[15] (see table 4.1) and cultural repression.[16] Use of the Basque language was completely prohibited, as was use of any Basque symbol. With different degrees of resignation, Basque speakers stopped employing the language outside of the private realm. Furthermore, aside from using (or not using) the language within the family circle, many families were ambivalent about transmitting to their children Basque nationalist sentiment in general and the culture and language in particular.

On the one hand, families were interested in maintaining their Basque nationalist symbolic universe and ideology through their children's education. On the other, they were consumed by a physical fear and social concern with what that might imply for their offspring. It is therefore hardly surprising that the practical solution to this dilemma or conflict of interests was often a kind of familial silence. Opting for either of the two options—namely, support for, or denial of, this symbolic universe within the family—came with a high cost. In the interviews with 1-25 to 1-30 one can see clearly the ambivalence about Basqueness in children's education; the practical approach was to simply refuse to speak of such matters. These six nationalists, between sixty-five and seventy years of age, recall that they could communicate their political or cultural doubts and questions only within limited and intimate contexts. It might well be away from everything, "in the mountains," where every Sunday morning they would go with their friends; in bars; or in their own homes or the houses of relatives, chatting with their parents or siblings. However, when it came to their children, silence became the most feasible resolution to their dilemma.

The same dilemma emerged within nationalist families when it came to transmitting the Basque language. Although parents knew that speaking Euskara might cause problems for their children, they also wanted to keep the language alive. The dilemma was felt most keenly in families where Basque was the maternal language, and was even more pronounced when knowledge of Spanish was limited. These families took different approaches to their children's education, ranging from those that encouraged, and even forced, their children to speak Euskara at home (and, by the same token, not do so in public) (1-2) to those who decided not to transmit the language.

The reverse situation was that of children who, for all their families' ambivalence, were educated in an environment that negated the symbolic familial universe that their own parents were trying to deny. Testimonies of the following type are typical: "My problem with Basque is that until I was six or seven years old I couldn't speak Spanish, and then I spoke it very badly. I remember, when I was at my first nuns' school, the taunts and humiliation I received when the teacher laughed at the way I spoke Spanish. This was a normal situation. Everything Basque was completely ridiculed. This is where those typical Basque characters, the ones that appear in the theater speaking Spanish badly for everyone to laugh at, come from" (1-18, a man of between forty and fifty years of age, son of a Basque-speaking nationalist family).

This public rejection of the symbolic familial universe and the language, together with evident parental frustration and even fear, shaped the feelings of children of nationalist families about being Basque as well as their attitudes toward Basque culture and its symbols.

The Basque language was most subject to political repression in the public and educational spheres. This was the result of a general prolonging of wartime and postwar legislation that attempted to erase Euskara from all spheres of public life. For example, as the Order of May 18, 1938, from the *Boletín Oficial* of May 21, 1938, stated: "The unhealthy provocation, emanating from some provinces, of regionalist sentiment must be highlighted as the source of certain registered anomalies. This brought a good number of names to certain registers that were not only written in a language different from the official Spanish, but contained a meaning contrary to the Unity of the Fatherland. Such cases occur in the Basque Provinces [Vascongadas], for example, with the names Iñaki, Kepa, and Koldobika and others that betray an unquestionable separatist meaning. . . . Accordingly, it is ordered that: Article 1 . . . in all cases involving Spaniards, names must be registered in Spanish." Similarly, the Order of May 16, 1940, from the *Boletín Oficial* of May 30, 1940, prohibited "the use in designating brands, commercial names, signs of establishments, and any other class of industrial property of all languages other than Spanish" (Núñez 1977a, 14–17).

This public linguistic persecution naturally had certain effects on both the functional and symbolic dimensions of the Basque language. From a functional point of view, there was an obvious decline in the number and proportion of Basque speakers. Moreover, the language withdrew from specific social spaces, which in turn accelerated its stagnation. Clark, after examining data from a number of sources, outlines the general process of this quantitative loss of Euskara during the Franco years in the following terms:

> In 1934, out of a total population slightly larger than 1.2 million, about 570,000 were judged capable of speaking Euskara. In the early 1970s, although the population had nearly doubled to 2.3 million, the number of Basque-speaking persons had declined to slightly more than 450,000. It would clearly be conjectural for me to assess precisely the reasons for this decline, and the degree to which an influx of non-Basques into the region was causing the use of Euskara to diminish. But on the basis of the above findings, it seems incontrovertible that use of the language among ethnic Basques has declined during the Franco years from causes quite apart from whatever impact there may have been from the rest of Spain. (Clark 1979, 144)

This decline in the functionality of the language was clearly traumatic—that is, it became a self-conscious process. In addition to the general historical trend of language decline prior to the Franco regime—when the functional value of Basque diminished under the twin pressures of industrialization and urbanization and resultant language contact led gradually to a diglossic situation—there was now overt political repression of the language. This repression accelerated the loss of Basque's functional value, but also, from a more symbolic point of view, the language came to be overvalued as a nationalist emblem. This traumatic self-conscious decline in Euskara's functionality lay at the heart of a number of symbolic overvaluations. First, the language's predicament became a key factor in the political radicalization of young members of the PNV during the 1950s. Second, Euskara assumed a central role in the gradual expansion of nationalist consciousness during this time. Indeed, it even managed to galvanize a strong social movement promoting the language—one that exists to this day. This latter development indicates that imbuing symbolic value can affect a language's functionality, encouraging both acquisition and use. For example, Tejerina offers a glimpse into the magnitude of language recovery that began in the early 1960s. In Gipuzkoa there were eight *ikastolas*[17] in 1963, but seventy-one in 1975; in Bizkaia during the same period the figures rose from two to forty-five; in Araba from one to six; and in Navarre from none to twenty-two. The growth in the number of pupils attending these ikastolas was similarly spectacular, above all in Gipuzkoa and Bizkaia. In the former the number of pupils grew from 520 during the 1964–65 academic year to 17,971 during 1974–75; in Bizkaia the figures rose from 54 to 5,822; in Araba from 22 to 1,026; and in Navarre from none to 1,892 (Tejerina 1992, 130, 133).

However, the principal concern here is to explore the symbolic universe of nationalist families during the post–Spanish Civil War era. Analyzing the meaning of generational relationships in these families during this time is crucial. The biggest change in this regard was framed by a tension, continuous throughout the 1950s, within the Basque Nationalist Party between its elder leaders and young followers. More specifically, this tension resulted in the creation of an organization (ETA) that would soon take up an armed struggle.

The symbolic universe of these families was obviously Basque nationalist in sentiment as well as culturally and politically. Such families were also deeply religious. ETA's radicalization affected three key areas: political behavior, language and culture, and religion. Modification of political activity and behavior is the most obvious. The political passivity imposed on the PNV by the Franco regime had been, to a certain extent, acquiesced to and therefore legitimized by this party. Specifically, the PNV hoped that through lobbying for the assistance of the Western democracies it would achieve the destruction of the Franco regime. By the late 1950s, or after two decades of dictatorship and with no end in sight, this strategy seemed more and more illogical, especially to the younger generation. The embargo of Spain by the United Nations had been lifted, and Franco had managed to establish diplomatic relations with the United States in 1951. Consequently, any hope that the world's democracies would help destroy Spanish "fascism" no longer seemed reasonable.

As for the other two elements, language (also culture, although it is vaguer) and religion,[18] the following discussion attempts to trace their connections. It is impossible to understand the birth of ETA during the 1950s without reference to the value, declared by all the group's founders, of the Basque language. These founding figures all came from nationalist families (in general, adherents of the PNV) and attempted to radicalize nationalism's cultural and political policies. "In 1952, a group of students in Bilbao—who would later form the leadership nucleus of ETA in its first incarnation—met to publish an internal bulletin called *Ekin,* whose translation, significantly, means 'to do.' . . . At the time, their ideological tactics did not differ from those of classic nationalism; for a number of years their textbooks would be the works of Sabino Arana, Eleizalde, and Aranzadi [historical figures in the Basque political and cultural world]. But they were united by a living consciousness of national oppression, a tremendous interest in the Basque language—most of them had overlooked it and had to learn it, becoming *euskaldunberris* [literally 'new Basque speakers,' or adult learners]—and an ethnic concept of Euskadi [the Basque Country]" (Ortzi 1975, 279). In the interview with 1-18, a founding member of ETA, the feeling of humiliation provoked by linguistic problems was evident. The same was true for 1-19, another early (though not original) member, when he described those founders. He talked about the sons of Basque-speaking families and the petty bourgeoisie (using words like "small workshop" and "store"): "Euskara was generally spoken within the family, at least by those with whom I was in contact; Euskara was an everyday family reality." Despite the apparent contradiction among these founders and first members in terms of knowledge of the language, such differences could be justified because the recruitment of activists took place in different, and very defined, social realms. "The main circles in which activism developed would be rural ones such as in Gernika and the Gipuzkoan Gohierri [a highland region of Gipuzkoa]" (1-19).

Further, within this sociogeographic realm the specific recruitment of individuals took place within closed circles, the only contexts in which Basque nationalist sentiment and ideology could operate freely. For example, one of the organization's manuals, dating from 1960 and designed for both members and sympathizers, though especially aimed at the former, warned:

> Basque-language classes, dances, and folkloric activities in general are tolerated, although not promoted. Precisely, then, it is important not to introduce markedly nationalist elements into the said classes. It is the obligation of every activist to promote all these activities, but by carefully trying not to appear as an "instigator," given that said activities in *españolista* [pro-regime] circles are attacked for being separatist. However, the activist must work to win over people from these groups, as often it is in this area where such effort tends to be the most straightforward. During excursions it is especially important to avoid any subversive statements, above all in the company of strangers. In the same way, photographs are dangerous and must be carefully avoided. (*Documentos Y* 1979, 1:155)

On the other hand, the same manual dedicates a whole chapter to one's "personal position regarding Euskara." Here the Basque language is treated as an essential differentiating element, and as an *ethnic, affective,* and *patriotic* value. Among the various obligations of the *abertzale* (Basque patriot) is guaranteeing "an Euskaldun

[Basque-speaking] family with Euskara as the normal language" (*Documentos Y* 1979, 1:253 ff.). As previously stated, space precludes a systematic analysis of the various ideas associated with the Basque language and its evolution. It is enough to observe that support for the language was an essential link to the beginnings of political radicalization, emerging as both a personal and a familial obligation.

Despite the nondenominational definitions by both the above-mentioned Ekin group and ETA, and despite the charges made by PNV activist Juan Ajuriaguerra that the leaders of Euzko Gaztedi (Basque Youth) were "communists, flamboyant, and smugglers" (Ortzi 1975, 279, 298),[19] the truth is that ETA's ideology in its formative years was immersed in a religious universe. In the above-mentioned 1960 manual, religion appears in numerous sections. First, there is a chapter dedicated to "Our Responsibility" (*Documentos Y* 1979, 1:161 ff.), written in ethical terms, with a section titled "Responsibility Before God and Before the Fatherland" (162). In this section's "Summary" the conclusion is framed in the following terms: "Christianity has taken firm root in Euskadi; but it is an undisputed principle of our people, freedom of conscience" (168). Second, at times religion and nationalism appear as one and the same: "A logical premise of our activity must be a tremendous concern with responsibility for our behavior; this behavior is consistent with an ideal, with the vocation of a nationalist faith, because we must understand that, as the apostle demonstrated regarding his Christian faith that without labor such faith was lifeless, so must we also with our nationalist faith. And we need a great deal of living faith, for he who fights with faith deserves victory" (165). Third, among those differentiating characteristics related to national consciousness, the first one listed is religious:

> As regards the religious question, the Basques have always followed a conceptual Christianity, far removed from earthly points of view. Ideas and beliefs have never been confused with cultish material elements or external manifestations, nor the priestly ministry with the person who holds this title, nor ecclesiastical with civil jurisdiction. Clericalism has never been a native plant among our people, although on occasion it has managed to take root, either through the influence of outsiders or a confusion of ideas on the part of our own people. . . . As opposed to Spain, oscillating between clericalism and antichurch ideas, between these two opposing intransigent positions in religious matters, our people have always maintained an intermediate position, traditionally anticlerical and profoundly religious. (192)

Fourth, curiously, ideas concerning "methods of action" (171 ff.) are taken both from communist and JOC (Juventud Obrera Católica; Catholic Workers' Youth—a church organization dedicated to recruiting young people to undertake various social projects) models, interpreting them "beyond" their respective doctrines. However, the document does observe of the communist model that, "for the Communist Party, nationalists are only a means of gaining acceptance among a whole people for communist politics. This is hardly surprising. Communism is essentially stateless and antipatriotic" (182).

Without doubt, the most striking element of these observations is the mythological character of the discourse on the differentiating religious nature of the Basque people—specifically, their "intermediate position," that is, both their anticlerical and profoundly religious sides. This is, in effect, a legitimizing discourse (in mythological terms) of ETA's own ideological position. In other words, through these arguments ETA activists were attempting to contrast their position with the traditional PNV clericalism of their parents. There are references to the fact that, on occasion, clericalism had gained support through the "confusion of ideas on the part of our own people."

According to the observations in interviews with I-25, I-26, I-27, I-28, I-29, and I-30, during the 1940s there were as yet no associations or social institutions beyond those of the National Movement (Franco's official state organization). The one exception, of course, was the church. Indeed, it continued to be an important point of reference among nationalist families. As for everyday parish life, in those parishes where, as a political consequence of the Spanish Civil War, there had been a change of priest, an apostolic vacuum existed that was only filled during Sunday mass. In other parishes, where life remained the same, the image of both parish and priest continued to be important. People typically went to him in search of material help, to find work, and to request information about Basque nationalist family members being held in jail. This all took place outside the typical *spiritual* relations, associated, for example, with the religious indoctrination of children. Furthermore, it was quite normal to see the priest in a bar, and one could speak with him about politics because there was general agreement on the main issues.

It was therefore logical that the symbolic universe of the next generation, young people at this time, was profoundly religious. Similarly, it made sense that the generational revolt or radicalization against the cultural humiliation and acquiescence of their elders was also a rebellion against the institutional world of the church that paralleled that of their families. In the interview with I-18, that need to break free of the inactivity was perfectly expressed:

> One must remember that, between the ages of eighteen and twenty, and from then until I was twenty-three, I was in the thick of everything in Euskadi. At that time, when we got involved in the problem of ETA, we belonged to the PNV and, within it, to EGI [the youth wing]. It really was a serious moment, because we were a group that thought things, as the PNV saw them, couldn't go on like that. In the first place, because we were young people who had more radical and sentimental ideas, and we even had a set of social questions too . . . , during that initial time those of us who were part of the more radical wing of EGI assumed

a strategy of dialogue with the PNV, with its leaders and especially with José Antonio Aguirre [party leader and *lehendakari,* or Basque president in exile], who, at the time, was still alive. . . . [But] they rejected us, that is, a rumor had already spread among them that a part of EGI was communist, of this and that, that we were too progressive . . . and they weren't interested. And this was exactly the spark that encouraged us to maintain our position, adopt some specific approaches; and then came the split with EGI. . . . We formed a group apart. It was the beginning of ETA.

At that time I was a Christian, or I tried to be, ever since the moment that I opted to carry out consciousness-raising work, because my own personal morality as a Christian told me that the freedom of my people was a just cause. Within the movement, three fronts were created: political, armed, and cultural. As you can see, a social front wasn't even considered. It would be a year later when the need to form one arose. At the time, my work was very underground; of course all relationships were completely clandestine, nobody knew ETA existed; we carried on for three years without anyone knowing anything about us. . . . They were the best years . . . and it was extremely positive work, that is, consciousness-raising work carried out by groups. . . . During this time, no armed actions were carried out, the only thing that the armed front did was to beat up some teacher that crossed the line a bit with his ideas. . . . There were also people ready to paint slogans on walls and things like that. . . . Thus, simple things were carried out much more focused on tasks of consciousness-raising. . . . Every three months one or more [activists] used to leave, and this is when I began to clash with my comrades because I didn't think this implied any failure, while they said that it called for an urgent response to the situation. . . . I was under pressure from the so-called leaders and their obsession with militancy and the activist . . . so that I couldn't keep on working. (1-18)

In the words of another historical activist:

The first activities included painting slogans on walls, circulating pamphlets, and things like that. Precisely during these activities the question of the compatibility of violence with the Christian religion emerged, because many of those involved came from a religious background. As such, they used to ask themselves that if, while carrying out one of these initial activities, they had been seen by, for example, the municipal policeman who knew them, should they kill him or face prison or death? (1-19)

It seems clear that during the Franco years the general content of national consciousness became more and more secular. In part, this secularization came about as that traditional church-centered religion (Luckmann 1967) declined, as will be seen later. In part, also, it appears that the central role of religion within Basque nationalism was gradually replaced by politics. Gradually, then, the church was judged from a political perspective, and this would become a central part of nationalist discourse. Therefore, *aranista* nationalism (namely that original form of Basque nationalism associated with the PNV's founder, Sabino Arana), created in defense of the Basque people's culture, religion, and morality, was gradually replaced by a profoundly political nationalism. In other words, politics became sacred.

In the interviews carried out with individuals of subsequent generations, a gradual disinterest in religion and the church is apparent. Yet this does not necessarily mean that these individuals completely abandoned their religious ties. Normally, they talk about a Christian family and the personal renunciation of religious practice at a certain age, but they make no mention of a traumatic loss of faith. Therefore there seems to have been a gradual growing disinterest in religion. In effect, politics slowly became, during the 1960s and especially in the 1970s, the basic symbolic element of these new generations. Involvement in politics, then, through its implications for both one's personal and social routines, would reinforce, through specific mechanisms, the mechanisms of social solidarity.

Thus, within the nationalist family there was rapid socialization of both Basque nationalist sentiment and certain religious ideas. As the nationalist dimension became more radical among the children of the immediate postwar generation, there was no corresponding intensification of religious commitment. It was quite normal to lose interest in religion without any traumatic effects. Indeed, generational tension seems to have come more from political radicalization than from the youths' abandonment of religion.

If one considers the interviews with I-9 to I-17, all members of a cuadrilla[20] that was very radical in its politico-nationalist ideology, one sees that they all came from religious backgrounds. Indeed, the majority of them came from very religious families. However, only one of them assesses politics in religious terms. Speaking about ETA, he said, "as an abertzale [Basque patriot], I see that what they do is fine, and I think that it's one way to achieve something, but then there's my conscience, and I see that, as a person, the last thing one should do is take another person's life, as I believe that God gave us life and we should value it" (I-17). He is the only informant to declare himself a believer and practicing Christian, and the only one who retains doubts about violent methods. The others invert this relationship, making politics the value from which one should judge and assess all remaining human activity, including religion.

It also appears that the nationalist family felt the impact of generational radicalization, in the form of generational tension, at its very core. This is evident in the interviews. However, one must remember the specific situation: young people radicalized during the 1960s and 1970s, who suffered tremendous repression by

Franco's state. What impact did this have on the families of those imprisoned or exiled? The campaigns in favor of prisoners and exiles, calls for political amnesty, and the like had a clear familial element during the 1970s. And, within these campaigns, the role of women—wives, girlfriends, sisters, and, above all, mothers of prisoners—stands out.

Some of the questions directed to both the earlier and recent activists were designed with the role of women in mind, in order to understand how families reacted to finding out about their activism and perhaps later imprisonment or exile. The first family reaction seemed to be fear ("what if they get you, what if the police come here to the house") and was more emotional than logical: "Parents didn't take on the responsibility, they didn't understand," but they did sympathize, assist, and so on. One could do more with an emotional response than an ideological one, or with political or religious principles. One of the earlier activists argues that there was a significant difference between the early days and the late 1970s/early 1980s: "I don't see that problem [fear] now when I'm with many of their parents, but more that they're proud, glad, and the first to offer help" (1-18). What seems certain is that, as more and more people were affected by these developments during the 1960s and 1970s (above all in Basque nationalist social circles), prison and exile lost their social stigma and reprobation.

In conclusion, the basic role of the family, in regard to the subject of this work, was to rapidly instill Basque nationalist sentiment among the children. However, and above all during the post–Spanish Civil War years, this socialization was conducted in silence or, in some cases, with a warning about not using the Basque language in public. This resulted from fear and choosing "to raise the children through ignoring politics." However, some children would interpret parental frustration, the denial of their culture and language, and their parents' ambivalence in transmitting a code—the culture and language—as a need to do something. Thus, they gradually became more radical in their political activity and nationalist sentiment.

However, all this took place in terms of a familial, nationalist, and religious code:

> But those who created ETA were radicalized people who understood what losing the war meant and began to see their parents totally exploited by the defeat, left without a cent; therefore I had to respond to this, although my father couldn't; he was impotent, because, with a war that he lost and then the struggle to raise his children, he had enough to face. So I found myself obliged to sentimentally react to this situation, the situation in Euskadi. As I said before, this was partly due to the stance of the PNV; that's why I find it very funny when they say they've always been involved in the struggle and this and that, when, at the decisive moment, [the PNV] couldn't respond in any way. (1-18)

This statement sums up the earlier argument and ultimately highlights the ambivalent nature of the relationship: his father "had enough to face . . . with a war that he lost," and later, the PNV "couldn't respond in any way." The emotional quality of familial relations explains a lot about the ambivalent relationship of the PNV and ETA during the Franco era. It also explains how the PNV's ambivalence about violence was less and less sustainable in the period after Franco's death.

The creation of ETA at the end of the 1950s was, then, an expression of generational radicalization within nationalist families. It came at a time when the first post–Spanish Civil War generation appeared on the public stage. At the time, there was general radicalization in nationalist families and at the heart of the PNV, which brought with it a certain tension between generations. For the youth, there were two sources of this generational conflict (of which ETA was the most visible manifestation). One, it was a reaction against the Spanish political system, against its persecution of all things Basque and its capacity to humiliate and frustrate their parents. Two, it was an ambivalent reaction against their parents. In part, the young identified emotionally with their parents; but they also perceived their parents as passive accepters of the situation.

This kind of ambivalent relationship, involving both identification with and rejection of their parents, was relatively common in intrafamilial generational relations. It can be attributed to an emotional link between parents and children as well as an adolescent need to break free of these ties. And it was facilitated by new social structural conditions, to which young people are always more willing to adapt than are their elders. This ambivalent relationship underscores the complexity of generational politics (Mannheim 1952). The relationship has micro and macro dimensions. As Johnston argues, "studies of generational politics tend to focus on macrosociological social determinants such as urbanization, industrialization, economic and technological change, or the common experience of a historical event, to the detriment of the processes by which generational perspectives are individually acquired" (1991b, 52). In particular, a central aspect of the microsocial dimension is intrafamilial generational relations,[21] which introduces a specifically emotional element. For this reason, youthful opposition to the previous generation can be reinforced by opposition to parents or, on the contrary and under certain conditions, softened by it. In this oppositional subculture, relationships are in no way simple, nor do they necessarily derive from the same source. The youths of this subculture, like the previous generation, oppose the state. Furthermore, they identify with their parents insofar as they perceive them to be mistreated by the state. However, they oppose their parents insofar as they believe them to have been insufficiently active in rejecting this dominance. Resisting both the dominant regime and their parents reinforces in the young their generational sense of a dual mission (Mannheim 1952).

Returning to the case under consideration, children reacted ambivalently to their parents' reluctance to transmit the Basque language and nationalist ideology. They identified even more intensely with Euskara and nationalism, while at same time accusing their parents of inactivity and indifference. Consequently, the youth advocated activism in the political realm, specifically regarding the language, and this activism sometimes involved armed violence.

As has been noted, parents themselves responded ambivalently to the political repression by the state against those youths involved in activism. This ambivalence was defined by an affective identification with the problem that was accompanied by a politico-ideological rejection of their children's position.

THE ASSOCIATIVE WORLD AND THE CUADRILLA

Interviews with I-18 to I-23 were more focused than others on an investigation of familial relationships in relation to politics. They were carried out with individuals who had been activists. Time and time again these interviews show that the main avenue through which one joined ETA was one's immediate neighborhood. Individual 22 explained this most clearly:

> I'd say that one didn't join ETA basically through student channels; one joined through neighborhood contacts. One joined through other groups like those of the parish or the scouts; in the neighborhoods, wherever there was a dance group, *ochotes*,[22] choirs, etc.; these were more likely channels into ETA than the university. So most of the people I know that have been in ETA didn't enter through high school or university, but the neighborhood. There would also have been people that joined ETA through factories, but not necessarily because of this as much as because their families would have been nationalists, their general surroundings too, and, of course, also they themselves. But the main channel into ETA was not the factory or the university, although people are a little mistaken about this; it was mainly the neighborhoods. (I-22)

A little later he offered a key insight into why the university (and at the same time the factory) could never be a breeding ground for militancy in ETA: "While I was at the university, because I was already active in ETA and the clandestine nature of this activity was extremely closed, I didn't even publicly participate in the student movement, not because I was against it but because the clandestine nature of my life continually prevented me from doing so" (I-22).

ETA's real breeding ground, then, was the "neighborhood." "Neighborhood," however, refers to the larger social setting: specifically, the social environment and neighborhood associations. Recruitment into ETA could only occur within a homogeneous medium. The foregoing recollection is interesting in that it comes from the son of migrants living in a neighborhood that he himself describes as a migrant one. Until the age of seventeen, when he joined ETA, this individual was involved in many associations and youth groups, both church related and secular, connected with music, dance, sports, and so on.

Other individuals also spoke about the social medium of recruitment, although in less direct ways. For example, individual 21 remembered that "there were no student or work circles, only popular or neighborhood ones" (1-21). Earlier he commented that "at the neighborhood level, before, there used to be talks given by the parish priests in which they didn't speak only about religious subjects but also social ones, perhaps not political ones, but well . . . subjects that were close to the concerns we might have had" (1-21). Similarly, individual 20 recalled that "from the age of fourteen, right after getting out of nuns' school, some friends and I organized study and discussion groups on what we thought were the most important questions. Another older friend was the one who advised us in our work. Additionally, at a more popular level, we worked quite intensely on behalf of libraries, cultural development, literacy, children's recreation, etc." (1-20).

The neighborhood and town made up a close-knit social milieu composed of an associative network in which, under openly declared functional objectives, there was intense socialization of young people. It is evident from other interviews just how many people passed through this network and how many of them define this step as their initial introduction to politics, social questions, and the national cause. This was the case with 1-1. He joined a dance group in a Bizkaian town, formally operated by the PNV but really controlled by the Movimiento Socialista de Euskadi (the Socialist Movement of Euskadi). There were talks, meetings were held, and some people were selected for "formation." This individual considers his relationship with the dance group as essential for his national and social initiation, as well as for the link between the two. Similarly, 1-2 joined an extracurricular parish group, where he became interested in social and political matters. His Basque nationalist consciousness surfaced later, after he lived through the violence associated with the last official state of exception declared by the Franco dictatorship. Similar stories emerged in the interviews with individuals 6, 8, 9, 10, 11, and 17.

On the other hand, the interview with individuals 24A and 24B was an attempt to penetrate what made up the nonofficial, or socially hidden, dimensions of this associational world. It was carried out with two leaders who experienced intimately the social life of several large associations. This interview reveals some of the most important areas in the life of these associations: the division between stated and hidden objectives; interest in the survival of the association itself as a way of life; the close relationships with other associations; political questions and the problem of legality; the multifaceted relations with political organizations, including ETA; the problems associated with attempts by political organizations to control these associations, especially in the period immediately following Franco's death; and the direct and continuous contact with state repression.

The cuadrilla of friends was another key element in youth socialization in neighborhoods or towns. It is difficult to provide a precise or detailed sketch of this most informal of social institutions, even from a general viewpoint. From the interviews it appears that, in terms of social stratification, their composition was not homogeneous, although there were certain boundaries. In neighborhoods of important population centers, boundaries were mostly imposed by the social makeup of the neighborhood itself or the behavior of the cuadrilla in question. Social heterogeneity was more common in smaller towns. Within the youth cuadrilla, membership normally included both those who studied and those who worked. Indeed, any potential prestige derived from educational levels was balanced by the fact that those who worked enjoyed more economic advantages. Engagements and marriages were obstacles to the cuadrilla's permanence. However, it was quite normal for the basic structure to continue intact, though with diminished activity as its members began to "go their own way"—that is, when they formally began an adult life associated with work and starting a family. A general characteristic of the cuadrilla is that, when regular interaction becomes difficult, meetings between members become more ritualized and formal.

The cuadrilla met intermittently: during vacations, weekends, and free time at the end of the day. For certain age groups, the cuadrilla could be mixed in gender. For example, a female might join a male cuadrilla. However, the most typical form has always been the male cuadrilla whose central daily activity is the poteo, *chiquiteo* (or *txikiteo*).[23] In the interview with individual 11 (interviews with individual 9 through 17 refer to a cuadrilla), the interviewee affirmed that "the principal pastime [of the cuadrilla] is doing the classic txikiteo," adding that, "whether Saturday or Sunday evening, the group goes to Arrasate, Bergara, or another nearby town to spend the afternoon going from bar to bar or to have a snack" (I-11). The way that individual 11 himself defined this activity is very revealing: "the cuadrilla began very early to do the ancient Basque sport of txikiteo. This encouraged all of us to do it a little more" (I-11). Besides the ironic use of the words "ancient" and "sport," what is highly revealing here is the Basque nature of his definition, together with the concept of "doing" the txikiteo.

What this definition shows is that the txikiteo transcends a mere pastime. Indeed, it is a highly important activity not only personally but from a national, and, in extreme cases, a political point of view. The parallels between this activity and that of hiking, as explained in the interview with 24-B, are also striking: "In the Franco era the mountain became like the *mendigoizales* [hiking clubs that doubled as youth sections of the PNV] or *gudaris* [Basque nationalist soldiers during the Spanish Civil War]—it became a form of struggle. One of the strongest ways of protesting at that time was a mountain celebration, the Bizkargi [mountain] picnics, etc. They were completely banned by the Civil Guard because it was the place where the Basque spirit was really preserved" (24-B).

The camaraderie associated with leisure pursued within the cuadrilla and in hiking and mountaineering clubs belonged to the transgressive realm. The complete prohibition of all things Basque[24] meant that any expression of Basqueness inevitably involved transgression. Public expression of Basqueness was forbidden, so transmission, communication, and participation in the prohibited symbols had to take place within the intimacy of the family; in the narrow circles of the cuadrilla; in the back rooms of cultural, dance, and hiking associations;[25] and in the daily round of the poteo. As this extremely tight-knit social life had no channels of public expression, there was pent-up internal pressure. Many young people who grew up in this collective clandestine social milieu during the 1960s and 1970s gradually came to feel emotionally tied to the violence of ETA. Individuals 9 to 17 (all supporters of Herri Batasuna, HB, or Popular Unity, the radical Basque nationalist political party) refer to ETA in the following terms: "necessary and transcendental" (I-9), "children of the Basque people," "for the good of everyone" (I-10), "it seems strange to think that this simple acronym [ETA] can mean so much for a people," "rooted in everyone" (I-11), "we're tired already of injustice and lies" (I-12), "it emerged out of the people and that's why they support it" (I-13), and so forth. On the other hand, individual 22 thoughtfully explained this support: "In a Bilbao neighborhood among young people in parish groups, the center of attraction was ETA. ETA thrived at that time, in my opinion, because of this" (I-22).

The cuadrilla's political connection made possible, one supposes, a direct experiencing of political repression during the 1960s and 1970s. During these decades, cuadrillas took charge of organizing assistance for prisoners held by the Spanish state.[26] From about 1970 onward, this collective life became less clandestine, principally in the form of large-scale demonstrations that were more and more common until immediately following Franco's death. The tight-knit collective life became public, especially after the 1970 Burgos trial in which sixteen people were tried militarily for ETA activity (the event drew international attention). Increasingly, the clandestine lifestyle was replaced by the growing public use of Basque symbols. "All things Basque" began to occupy a dominant public social place, although obviously not in a political or economic sense.

It should be emphasized, then, that during the 1960s and 1970s the Basque Country experienced both the violence of ETA (leading, for some, to a feeling of emotional attachment) and, among many sectors of the population, repressive state violence. The large number of political prisoners (Núñez 1977b, 119–35) in a society as small as the Basque one meant that the repression (in different ways and to different degrees) was a generalized personal experience. This was even the case for those who were not personally affected, nor affected through their families or friends, since everyone lived through the states of exception. Although they did not directly experience any repression, individuals 2, 3, and 5 recounted vivid memories of life during the last state of exception.

In chapter 6 we will revisit these intersubjective and associative relations by exploring the differences in the form and function of these factors in the Francoist and post-Francoist contexts.

The Franco Regime: A Time Line of the Reproduction Process

One of the key characteristics of a nationalist movement inside a state is that it configures itself as a conflict over the political objectification of "we." This means that it defines itself in terms of a conflict over what constitutes the society's focal point, in both Parsons's (1974) and Shils's (1975) sense, as well as from the different perspective offered by Eliade (1992) in his treatment of society's sacred center. I would argue that the common denominator of this social dimension is a Durkheimian understanding of religion (Durkheim 1915; Pérez-Agote 1984a). The centrality issue is most appropriately framed by Shils:

> Society has a center. There is a central area within the structure of society. This central area implicates, in various ways, those who live inside the ecological domain in which society exists. The personality of a member of society, in a wider sense than merely an ecological one . . . is made up by their relationship to this central area. This central area is not, as such, a spatially located phenomenon. It always has a location more or less defined within the territory that the society lives in. Its centrality, however, has nothing to do with geometry and little to do with geography. The center, or the central area, is a phenomenon that belongs to the world of values and beliefs. (Shils 1975, 3)

The issue of a society's symbolic center is important in those societies where the foundational social dimension is open to debate, where there may be (essentially political) orientations toward different centers. This in turn raises the problem, even for social scientists, that a particular behavior can be analyzed and evaluated (in terms of its rationality) from a perspective other than its own, as when peripheral nationalism is interpreted from the state's centralist point of view.

In the Basque case, outlining events in the reproduction process of nationalist consciousness requires identifying critical moments that are important from the perspective of the Basque Country itself.[27] These key events were specific to the Basque Country during the Franco years. Only after Franco's death, and the subsequent attempt to come to an agreement over "complex centrality" (in which the political order was the State of the Autonomies, defined through the relationship of constitution-statute, and the new legitimacy problems in the psychosocial sense of the term), did a state event also constitute a key moment inside the Basque Country. I'm departing here from a concern with the reproduction of Basque nationalist consciousness. However, one can also establish different periods, from different points of view, based on key moments in the development of the Spanish sociopolitical system.

The new state that emerged with Franco was based on victory in the Spanish Civil War. The legitimizing of the war itself and then the new state acquired a religious tone. It could not have happened differently, given that the war was nothing more than the bloody outcome of a profound social tension that marked the whole historical trajectory of Spain's awkward modernization process—that is, the political rationalization of a state solidly based on status differences (in the Weberian sense).

As Carlos Moya points out, the gradual establishment of capitalism during the nineteenth century precipitated a crisis in Old Regime assumptions on which the Spanish state was based. This was not an episodic revolutionary crisis, but rather a long and conflictive political dynamic. It manifested itself in latent civil war that produced successive *restauraciones* (restorations). Each one sought to recuperate an impossible and mythical Old Regime order through social legitimizing of a religious nature.

The conflict that best demonstrated this crisis was that which led to nineteenth-century wars between liberals and Carlists. This was the political expression of the rural-urban conflict, or the struggle between a traditional agricultural economy and an emergent capitalist one that erupted on religious estates and communal land; a conflict between a church structured according to an Old Regime model and a state that was trying to modernize. Later, the restoration era associated with the politician Antonio Cánovas del Castillo (after 1874) would result in reconciliation between liberals and Carlists, a foretaste of similar compromises between the church and state and between landowning interests and financial capitalism. During this reconciliation process the financial aristocracy,[28] functioning simultaneously as outcome and decisive agent, would assume the form it would later take as an essential protagonist of the 1936–39 Spanish Civil War. The final restauración was that undertaken by Franco after his victory in this war (Moya 1975, 65–66). But what Franco left pending, without which there could not be authentic restoration, was the *nationalization* of the state. Franco's regime was incapable of promoting (as had been the case with previous state incarnations) the necessary social mechanisms—especially a sound *national* education system—by which the idea of Spain could be disseminated. In other words, he failed to define Spain as a social group to which people would adhere irrespective of all other social divisions and differences.

Once more in Spanish history religion was employed politically, this time to justify the civil war[29] and the new state formed out of the conflict. Indeed, it could not have transpired in any other way, given a military victory and the traditional "Spanish confusion between the right and Catholicism" (Jutglar 1973, 1:119 ff.).

Not only did the new state propose legitimizing its power in religious terms, it made the church its basic institution in the development and control of the ideological realm in Spain. "The official consecration of the civil war as a Crusade implied that, in terms of a potential Falangist [or fascist] ideology, the ultimate ideological key to the system would be one of a traditionalist-Catholic religious kind" (Moya 1975, 96). Furthermore, this latest restoration brought about by the civil war would augment, as did that of the Cánovas restoration era after 1874 (Vicens Vives 1970, 157), the already decisive importance of the church within the educational system.

The religious legitimizing of the new state created a number of problems in the Basque Country, where, in large part, religion and the church were on the defeated side. The new state could not present the war as a *crusade* of good against evil, of Christianity against atheism and communism, because a large section of the clergy came from the defeated Basque nationalist side and because one of the ideological underpinnings of nationalism was a thorough commitment to Catholicism.[30]

On capturing Bilbao in 1937, Franco's first decree regarding the Basque Country was to abolish the Conciertos Económicos (Economic Accords), agreements between Madrid and Bizkaia and Gipuzkoa that established their tax remittances to the central government. These were the two provinces where Basque nationalism was most active. Furthermore, in the explanation of the decree, Bizkaia and Gipuzkoa were classified as "traitorous" provinces and therefore subject to punishment. Of course, the intent was not to punish the traitors of the provinces but rather the provinces as a whole.

The classification of these provinces as "traitorous" demonstrated that the state was already prepared to exercise political power without a clearly defined legitimacy. From this moment on, the state imposed a series of measures designed to completely persecute Basque culture and its symbols, along with Basque nationalism and all forms of expression of social discontent. These measures were implemented according to both a warlike code (treason) and foundational violence, with the states of exception functioning as periodic rituals of symbolic maintenance.[31] These decrees were principally designed to allow for indiscriminate persecution in a given area. As such they came to mark, discriminate against, and socially define the area itself. Within this process, indiscriminate state violence[32] had the effect of integrating all those who, not accepting the legitimacy of the state, inhabited that area.

From the end of the civil war onward, Basque nationalist families, like others on the losing side, were plunged by their defeat into a state of frustration. Additionally, the heavy symbolic repression of Basque language and culture produced within these families an ambivalence toward the socialization of their children in terms of language, culture, and the symbolic nationalist universe in general. This ambivalence ranged from those families who obliged their children to speak Euskara at home but warned of the dangers of doing so in public to those who refused to speak of the war or anything to do with Basque issues.

In many cases, silence enveloped the history of the civil war, nationalist ideas, language, and memories. Still, a pattern developed within the family whereby, through osmosis, what was silenced was transmitted and even magnified by virtue of such silence. It lent a magical, sacred, mysterious, and mythical character to the secret intimacy of the familial universe and (especially) use of the mother tongue—all underscored by parental fear, frustration, and parental ambivalence regarding their children's socialization. These elements had important consequences for the image their children developed of the Basque language, culture, and symbolism. Specifically, among the youth there emerged a generational radicalization of Basque nationalist consciousness.

The Basque Nationalist Party (PNV), which had assumed practically all nationalist political aspirations prior to the Spanish Civil War, was thereafter forced either underground or into exile. This obviously hindered its day-to-day political activity, limiting its instrumental capacity to partial and specific action. Furthermore, during the postwar era, the PNV maintained the belief that the Western democracies would defeat Franco. This became more and more unlikely, especially after an alliance began in 1951 between the Franco regime and the United States and the United Nations ended its international embargo of Spain.

It was at this time, toward the mid-1950s, that a new wave of radicalized youth emerged within the PNV. Ultimately, they would form ETA as a response to the political and linguistic inactivity of the PNV.[33] Thus, within Basque nationalism the previous generation's basic ideological elements were radicalized. Furthermore, as has been discussed, religion came to be an important factor in the new generation's (and especially ETA's) ideological design. At the outset, ETA was no more than the tip of the iceberg of generational radicalization within Basque nationalism in general and within nationalist families in particular. As noted, this generational radicalization was ambivalent: it opposed parents for their inactivity, while empathizing with their frustration and humiliation. Within nationalist families this affected every sentiment; only the emotional pain provoked by linguistic, cultural, and political repression can explain the virulence of the response. Later, throughout the 1960s, and in response to important economic growth and large-scale immigration, there would be a significant social and political radicalization of ETA consciousness; and this would bring with it important consequences for Basque nationalist consciousness in general.

PUBLIC SILENCE AND VIOLENCE AS AN EXPRESSIVE LANGUAGE:
FROM THE BIRTH OF ETA TO THE BURGOS TRIBUNAL (1970)

The state's ban (supported by certain social sectors) on using the Basque language during the Franco era had several important social consequences.[34] Both geographically and socially, it reinforced the gradual loss in Euskara's communicative function. Some Basque-speaking families did not teach the language to their children. And in all cases its use withdrew into the most intimate realm of interpersonal relations. This meant that the language retreated from public social spaces—the exception being limited use in some churches. At the same time, however, the vigorous political pressure exerted against the language gradually caused a traumatic awareness of the loss of Euskara. Consciousness of the loss led initially to an increasing social and political valuation of the language. Then there arose a language-recovery movement, whose principal manifestation was the ikastola, or Basque-language school. These schools began operating clandestinely in 1960 and remained underground for the next ten years. Subsequently, they multiplied rapidly and today constitute a formidable educational network.

Symbolic state violence was not waged against the Basque language and culture alone; it completely limited all forms of cultural expression other than the official Spanish one. All expressions of social discontent or disagreement with this official line were likewise prohibited. The symbolic violence perpetrated by the state imposed public silence on a society intimately layered with intersubjective and associative relationships. Indeed, the only public appearance of Basque nationalist symbolism up to 1970, with a few specific noninstitutionalized exceptions,[35] was ETA's utopian and transgressive violence. This violence became the language of silence and was experienced as the public expression of an imposed social silence. As such, it gained a great deal of emotional support from social actors through the complex interpersonal and associative network. Furthermore, the symbolic (and of course physical) violence of the state imbued ETA's physical violence with social meaning. Finally, the gradual incorporation of young people from all the neighborhoods and towns into the associative world and the interpersonal network led to affective support by these generations for ETA's military violence.

States of exception were instituted as a ritual exacerbation of the day-to-day violence—in other words, as indiscriminate violence inside the affected territory itself.[36] Whether of the day-to-day or the ritual kind, this state violence took place in a small (in demographic terms) and compact (in terms of interpersonal and associative relations) society. Therefore, important sectors of the population experienced official violence daily.

Practically all those interviewed that came from a Basque nationalist background had some experience with state violence, either personally through a death, imprisonment, persecution, or exile or through the physical harm of someone close to them. Moreover, they all had unforgettable memories of the above-mentioned states of exception.

The social experience of this repression permeates both their individual and collective lives (collective memory). Politics and violence belonged to everyday life, constituting the subject matter in interpersonal communication and associative relationships; and was subsequently expressed in the context of the multitudinous popular demonstrations that grew more frequent after 1970.

During the 1970s, ETA gradually became immersed in armed violence. It was a political phenomenon that cannot be understood in political party terms. Rather, one should understand ETA as a social movement that was not organized into a single framework. It was irregular and ramified. From time to time it split into factions, but there always existed a kind of continuity based on a core military group defined by a radical Basque nationalist ideology. Its members attempted to understand a changing social reality from this basic ideological subject position, namely, the industrialization of the Basque Country that, in the 1950s and 1960s, created a proletariat out of the remaining Basque peasantry. Furthermore, the Basque Country attracted an influx of people from different parts of Spain. Then, too, the workers' movement was revitalized to a certain extent. Occasionally, the radical Basque nationalist nucleus of the movement, its most dynamic sector, would organize a *workers' front*. This facilitated the entry of (generally Marxist) politico-theoretical elements into its ranks and ideology. Consequently, the leftist stance within one sector of the movement would provoke a virulent reaction from radical Basque nationalist quarters. There emerged a theoretical debate over what to prioritize in both theory and practice: the class struggle or national liberation.

The consequences of these sporadic tensions were twofold. One, a schism led to the formation of a new group and the movement of members to organizations linked to the traditional Left. Two, there was an ideological transformation within the radical nationalist group itself. This implied the acceptance of generic Marxist ideas within the radical nationalist group and acceptance of the national question within more leftist groups. For leftist sectors that periodically split off from the most nationalist sector, class struggle was accepted as the central theoretical and practical component of ideology. They therefore either abandoned the armed struggle altogether or submitted it to strict political control. Conversely, the nationalist sector privileged violence as its central tactic and was more motivated by idealistic ethics and sensitivity. In this regard, the Basque nationalist sector more closely resembled Weberian models of affective social action or social action motivated by values. Thus, one can conclude that Basque nationalism during the Franco era, sensing the changing reality, generated a left wing, whereas one cannot say that the Left generated a degree of Basque nationalism.

This is precisely the reverse of what would happen in Navarre during its pronounced industrial development of the 1950s and 1960s, and especially after the presentation of an Industrial Promotion Plan by the Navarrese *diputación* (regional government) in 1964. As has been pointed out in another study,

> what emerged first in Navarre was a political radicalization (in leftist terms), and this is what led to the gradual assumption of nationalist hypotheses. This, and nothing else, is why throughout Navarre (in elections corresponding to the democratic era) the radical Basque nationalist vote count was higher than the moderate one. The sequence of basic mechanisms that explains the mediation between, on the one hand, the process of industrialization and urbanization

and, on the other, the adherence of radical nationalism in Navarre would be, schematically speaking, the following: a flow of Navarrese peasants, traditionally subject to the ideological control of the church (Carlism), to Pamplona, and other regional capitals; a sudden change in their way of life; a profound ideological switch toward leftist positions within the church, among those priests and seminarians in contact with new realities; the birth and development of certain radical workers' organizations that, owing to the above-mentioned circumstances, took root in the church; the provisional embracing, on the part of these organizations, of the most radical workers' movement model, which was at the time that of the nationalist sector within the workers' movement in Bizkaia and, above all, in Gipuzkoa. (Pérez-Agote 1989b, 13)

In the 1950s and especially in the 1960s, intersubjective and associative relations became stronger and stronger. This intensity did not correspond to the high levels of industrial development and urbanization that had emerged. But in general, the daily collective rituals undertaken by cuadrillas between the ages of eighteen and sixty-five became increasingly important. At the same time, there was a tremendous upsurge in the group activity of youth, gastronomic, cultural, hiking, and dance associations.[37] The close-knit social realms of the neighborhood and town made up this associative and interpersonal network. In the associative world, under openly declared and functionally specific objectives, a strong degree of youth socialization took place. Through such activity, interest was stimulated in social and political questions. As a result, those involved joined a generically nationalist symbolic universe that was reproduced daily through the activity of the cuadrilla and poteo.

This whole collective life had no public expression; rather, it was a form of collective secrecy. It was maintained in the intimate realm of family, in the cuadrilla, in the back rooms of associations, and in the poteo ritual. Critical nationalist forms of consciousness were shaped through such channels, and, gradually, a collective emotional attachment to ETA's violence, as the only possible expression of the enforced silence, was forged. At the same time, a (similarly emotional) rejection of state violence, as represented by the security forces, took shape within this collectivity.

The confrontation between state and ETA violence in a demographically confined and highly socially compact society meant that both violence and politics became normal features of everyday life, both individually and collectively. As a result, those symbols socially identified as Basque were gradually perceived and evaluated as symbolic transgressions of the rules of Franco's regime.

THE STREET AS A POLITICAL SPACE: FROM THE BURGOS TRIBUNAL (1970) TO FRANCO'S DEATH (1975)

The twin social processes of confrontation (between state and ETA violence) and reinforcement (between ETA's violence and the collective emotional attachment to it) rapidly increased the pressure exerted by the earlier mentioned intersubjective framework of silence.[38] The situation changed, however, in 1970 when this collective life found a public expression. From 1970 onward, it took more and more to the street at crucial social moments. Despite happening only intermittently, this taking to the street signified the beginning of a process by which Basque symbols came out of the private realm and into the social arena: Basque nationalism and its symbols became public. Basque nationalism gradually came to dominate both the street and all public spaces, excepting political institutions.

The public expression of collective life intervened in the processes of confrontation and reinforcement. The taking to (and of) the street and ETA's violence became mutually reinforcing and constituted a serious confrontation of state violence. This complex social dynamic culminated in the first years after Franco's death, complicating the reform associated with political rationalization in Basque society. *Rationalization* is not used here in an evaluative sense (that is, neither in a positive nor a negative way). Rather, the point is that the political space of this dynamic was, from 1970 onward, the street. Therefore, it became difficult to separate politics from collective life and the street and situate it in a different sphere of social life where representatives (both in the sense of a political delegation and in a theatrical sense) of the people—professional politicians—assumed center stage. Ultimately, this was Spain's attempt to adapt the Western political model through the so-called political reform or democratization of society.[39]

The Role of the Church in the Reproduction of the Basque Language, Culture, and Nationalism

CHURCH, LANGUAGE, CULTURE

The important role of religion and the church in the Basque nationalist familial world of the post–civil war era has already been discussed. Likewise, the difficulties that the Franco regime encountered in trying to legitimize both the civil war and the new state in the Basque Country, owing to the close relationship between the Catholic Church and Basque nationalism, have also been examined. However, these events cannot be fully understood without comprehending the historical and profound relationship between the Basque clergy and certain popular social and cultural sectors in the Basque Country.

Luis Michelena argues that "the real Basque enigma is that which explains the preservation, not the origin, of the language." This author ascribes an important role in the maintenance of the Basque language, mainly from the seventeenth century onward, to both the church and clergymen, in particular those of the French Basque Country:

In addition to documents of great worth for the history of the language, we owe to them, along with a great deal of verse, a model of literary prose that even today retains an inspirational vigor. . . . This model greatly influenced authors on this side of the [French-Spanish] border, mainly Gipuzkoans and Bizkaians, in the eighteenth and early nineteenth centuries. . . . What should be underscored is that at that time a religious form (dogma, morality, rites, discipline) that we have come to know took root, tied to the identification of a good part of the secular and ordinary clergy with the people. This identification was especially close in the matter of language, where the criteria of religious content, together with preaching [in the Basque language], for a long time constituted practically Euskara's only prose standard. To tell the truth, one might suspect that the clergy were not quite so attached to the language of the country in Araba and parts of High Navarra [as opposed to Basse Navarre in France]. (Michelena 1977, 19–20).[40]

From this statement, by an eminent expert in the Basque language and its history, the supreme importance of two relationships can be deduced. First, there is the close relationship between religion and the clergy and the language, indicated by the prevalence of religious literature and the participation of the clergy in literary production (both of which are clear from tables 4.2 and 4.3). Second, there is the close relationship between the clergy and the people, which is related to the first point. Furthermore, it can be confirmed that Michelena's analysis is valid mainly for Bizkaia and Gipuzkoa. These were provinces in which Basque nationalism later became most important and where there remained higher percentages of Basque speakers, both before and after the civil war.

If one considers tables 4.4 and 4.5, certain interesting conclusions emerge. First, the growth of both literature and writers in Euskara should be highlighted. Second, if one compares the 1934–35 figures with those of 1972–73, the profound secularization of both literature and writers in Basque is apparent. However, the process was not linear, as the statistics corresponding to the height of the Franco regime (1962–63) reveal. For during this time the percentage of clerical writers in Euskara grew. The reason for this, of course, was that the repression of the Basque language and culture after the civil war of 1936–39 once more forced them into the refuge of the church.

The church, in every aspect, could provide refuge to all opponents and critics of the Franco regime, owing to an organizational framework that was intimately tied to broad social sectors and to its possession of premises (throughout Spain). This latter fact was important in a society where the right of assembly was completely denied. In the same way, the church in the Basque Country, which was linked strongly to the Basque nationalist universe, provided refuge for both the Basque language and culture.[41] This caused a great deal of tension within the church itself, mainly between a hierarchy closely linked to the political leadership of the Franco regime and the lower

TABLE 4.2 *Production of Books in Euskara by Era*

Production Type	16th Century 2nd half	17th Century 1st half	17th Century 2nd half	18th Century 1st half	18th Century 2nd half	19th Century 1st half	19th Century 2nd half
Total production	1	6	6	5	24	26	33
Nonreligious production	1	—	1	1	1	1	4

Source: Sarasola 1976, 183.

TABLE 4.3 *Estates to Which French and Basque Writers of the 16th–18th Centuries Belonged*

Estate	France	Basque Country
Nobility	28%	—
Clergy	6%	90%
Third Estate	66%	10%

Source: "The French Book Trade in the Ancient Regime," cited by Sarasola 1976, 53.

clergy that, more in contact with basic social reality, quickly changed both its ideas and its activities. Of course, the changing focus of the clergy came about because of the tensions produced by industrialization, immigration, and political repression.

The church fulfilled another important role during the Franco era regarding two key aspects of the reproduction process: namely, the extension and intensification of Basque nationalist consciousness described earlier.

First, one should note the general role of the church in the educational system, especially in those centers dedicated to training the clergy—the seminaries and novitiates of different religious orders. It might be argued that these centers constituted, during the 1950s and 1960s, the only possible spaces in which to maintain and develop a cultivated Basque language. In this respect, the collaboration of seminary and novitiate students (Franciscans, Benedictines, Jesuits, Carmelites, and so forth) in Basque-language journals was particularly important. In these pages, authors representative of the several Basque dialects encountered one another's forms of expression and began institutionalizing and standardizing the written language.

This was important, as heretofore Euskara was essentially transmitted orally. During the 1950s and 1960s these religious centers offered the only means by which Basque speakers could learn to read and write in the language.[42]

These observations do not contradict those made earlier regarding the secularization of Basque literature. In table 4.5 one can observe how, in 1972–73, the number of lay writers (constituting 53.1 percent of all writers in Basque) outnumbered their religious counterparts. However, of these lay writers 20.6 percent (Sarasola 1976, 21) had been to either a seminary or novitiate, later experiencing a *secularizing* transformation. On the other hand, it should be noted that fostering a cultivated Euskara had importance that transcended linguistic and literary concerns. These centers constituted real social means of cultivating a Basque nationalist consciousness. From the end of the civil war onward, and especially in rural areas, the only opportunity to pursue an education beyond the most basic level for those from families of low or medium social levels was offered by either schools attached to novitiates or by the novitiates and seminaries themselves. Consequently, it is easy to see why those centers affiliated with religious orders and seminaries were so important for reproducing Basque nationalist consciousness.

One must not overlook the importance of the church in education.[43] If its peda-

TABLE 4.4 *Publication in Euskara (Production, Reprinting, and Translation)*

Time Period	Total	Essays and Social Science	Religion
1934–35	19	5.8%	20%
1962–63	42	—	—
1972–73	101	36.6%	3%

Source: Sarasola 1976, 18–19.

TABLE 4.5 *Writers in Euskara*

Time Period	Total Number	Lay Writers	Religious Writers
1934–35	12	41.6%	58.4%
1962–63	20	25%	75%
1972–73	65	53.1%	46.9%

Source: Sarasola 1976, 20.

TABLE 4.6 *Percentage of Students in Church Centers Out of Total Number of Students in Same Grade in the Province*

Location	Primary Education 1968–69	High School Education 1967–68	Advanced Education 1974–75
1. Araba	18.1	55.7	—
2. Gipuzkoa	12.1	46.3	65.8
3. Bizkaia	24.3	41.6	30.8
4. Navarra	28.1	48.1	100.0
1+2+3+4	21.5	45.4	49.0
Spain	14.7	32.2	3.7

Source: Núñez 1977a.

gogical role was, indeed, critical in Spain in general, then it was even more so in the Basque Country, as one can clearly see from table 4.6.

Second, an important role devolved to the church in what has been referred to here as the associative world. The church's relative political immunity, together with its network of centers, meant that it came to serve as an instrument and frequent channel of many clandestine activities for both the workers' and nationalist movements. Indeed, the church not only lent its premises to these activities, but also served as an originator, an instigator, and a maintainer of a large part of this associative world, especially in youth circles. In the interviews carried out with important members of a range of associations (cultural, hiking, dance, and so forth),[44] it became apparent that during the Franco years a good number of them were linked to the church in many ways (as official parish organizations or simply through the involvement of a particular priest, for example). One should remember the importance, already discussed, of this associative world as both a producing and reproducing mechanism of a Basque nationalist consciousness that was gradually becoming more politically and socially radical.

The intense social and political involvement by the clergy, parishes, and religious orders led during the Franco years to a growing tension between these clergymen and both the church hierarchy and political authorities. This was reflected in a series of documents in which the clergy criticized both the political and religious hierarchies.[45] Increasingly, and still during the Franco era, this protest evolved from political criticism based on ethnic differences in the Basque Country to a debate on broader ethnic and social questions, with a noticeable tendency to deny the legitimacy and violence of the state and a corresponding inclination to legitimize, as a necessity, antistate violence.[46]

ACCELERATION OF THE SECULARIZATION PROCESS IN THE 1970S

In terms of a traditional religiosity (Luckmann 1967), and compared with Spanish levels of religious belief, the Basque Country has been until recently extremely religious. This was the case despite greater industrialization and development there than in the Spanish state as a whole. However, this traditional religiosity in respect to the church is now closer to Spanish averages (at least as reflected in the available statistics). This is because the Basque Country experienced a more concentrated secularization process (which accelerated specifically in the 1970s) than did Spanish society as a whole.

The fact that, until quite recently, religiosity in the Basque Country[47] was appreciably greater than the Spanish average is evident from a number of sources.[48] Table 4.7 shows the percentage of Basque-born bishops. In 1960, the Basque Country provided a quarter of all Spanish bishops; this, despite the fact that at the time the area only accounted for 5 percent of Spain's population. However, a gradual decline in this percentage is also discernible. Similarly, in 1960 the number of churches per one thousand inhabitants in the Basque Country was 2.3, while in Spain it was 1.4 (Núñez 1977a, 57). Table 4.8, showing the number of priests per one thousand in-

TABLE 4.7 *Percentage of Bishops Born in the Basque Autonomous Community and Navarre*

Area	1960	1975	1990
Basque Autonomous Community and Navarra	27	18	15
Spain	100	100	100

Sources: Núñez 1977a, 56; *Anuario de la Iglesia en España 1990* 1990, 213.

TABLE 4.8 *Number of Priests per 1,000 Inhabitants*

Area	1960	1975
Basque Autonomous Community and Navarra	1.8	1.1
Spain	0.8	0.7

Source: Núñez 1977a, 82.

TABLE 4.9 *Evolution of the Number and Proportion of Senior Seminarians*

Area	1960 Number	%	1968 Number	%	1975 Number	%	1990 Number	%
Basque Autonomous Community and Navarra	754	9.4	855	12.2	140	5.9	89	4.4
Spain	8,021	100	6,995	100	2,371	100	1,999	100

Sources: Núñez 1977b, 86); *Anuario de la Iglesia en España 1990* 1990, 129–75.

TABLE 4.10 *Number and Proportion of Priest Ordinations*

Area	1955 Number	%	1963 Number	%	1975 Number	%
Basque Autonomous Community and Navarra	106	—	75	12.1	18	5.6
Spain	—	—	616	100	321	100

Source: Núñez 1977b, 90.
Note: In the *Anuario de la Iglesia en España 1990* there are no statistics on ordinations.

habitants, uncovers a similar pattern. In table 4.9 one can observe how (also in 1960) senior seminarians from the Basque Country represented 9.4 percent of the Spanish total and that this proportion continued to rise until 1968 when it reached 12.2 percent. This was owing to the fact that, while in the rest of Spain the number of senior seminarians fell between 1960 and 1968, the number actually rose in the Basque Country. Thereafter, around 1970, the fall in both number and share was incredibly abrupt. This would seem to indicate that the aforementioned religiosity oriented toward the church was still strong during the 1960s. However, one should also recall that during the 1950s and 1960s the seminary was an important avenue of study for many young people. This seems to have been the principal reason for the high attendance, if one takes into account that, although the number of senior seminarians grew throughout the 1960s, the number of ordinations of priests did not (as is evident from table 4.10).

TABLE 4.11 *Sunday Mass Attendance, 1972 as %*
of Population Over Age Seven

Andalusia	22.4
Aragón	61.2
Balearic Islands	58.3
Basque Autonomous Community and Navarra	71.3
Canary Islands	22.4
Catalonia	21.7
Extremadura	26.7
Galicia and Asturias	40.8
New Castile	17.6
Old Castile and León	65.3
Valencia and Murcia	30.2
Spain	34.6

Source: Núñez 1977b, 68.

Duocastella was the first person to seriously examine religious practice at a Spanish national level. In 1967, he mapped religious practice in Spain and notes "an intense and homogeneous religious experience in the Basque-Navarrese region" (Duocastella et al. 1967, 46). In general, he calculates Sunday mass attendance for the region at somewhere between 75 and 100 percent, while illustrating the "crack in the industrial area of Bilbao" with a percentage of 53.6. Duocastella attributes this latter figure to a strong migration into the area of people from regions in the south of Spain where religious practice was lower (Duocastella et al. 1967, 52). Table 4.11, also based on the data of Duocastella (cited by Núñez 1977a), demonstrates how, in 1972, the percentage of people attending Sunday mass in the Basque Country was still much higher than in Spain. In fact, for this year the percentage was higher than in any other region.

There is some data about religiosity and religious practice for 1987, but it is certainly not wholly compatible with that of 1972. However, using this data, it is possible to deduce that, by 1987, levels of religiosity and religious practice in the Basque Autonomous Community were close to Spanish levels. Table 4.12 demonstrates how religious self-definition is likewise similar in the Basque Autonomous Community and Spain as a whole. And table 4.13 highlights the fact that, in terms of religious practice, levels for the Basque Autonomous Community are a little lower

TABLE 4.12 *Religious Self-Definition in Spain and Basque Autonomous Community in 1987, Expressed as %*

Religion	Spain	Basque Autonomous Community
Practicing Catholic	42	43
Nonpracticing Catholic	41	38
Non-Catholic Christian	3	4
Other religions	1	1
Believer, but without any specific religious affiliation	4	3
Agnostic	3	3
Nonbeliever	5	7
No response	1	1
Total	100	100

Source: Pérez-Agote 1990.

than in Spain. All this would seem to indicate that between 1972 and 1987, there was a more intense process of secularization in the Basque Country than in Spain as a whole. Finally, by way of demonstrating this, table 4.14 shows that the Basques who say they practice religion less often than the Spanish average recall that their parents reported Basque religiosity as being more intense than in Spain as a whole.

GENERATIONS, RELIGION, AND POLITICS

The previous sections have dealt with the fact that apart from the general secularization process during the Franco era, there was also a secularization of Basque national consciousness. Consequently, Basque nationalism evolved from being a religiously centered movement at the end of the Spanish Civil War into a politically focused one. In other words, where once nationalism judged politics from a religious perspective, it later began to judge the church from a political viewpoint. Lest one underestimate the importance of this change, remember that, from the outset, Basque nationalism's spiritual basis was so important that even early members of ETA laced their political theories with religious content.

Judging from the interviews with those individuals born into nationalist families between 1945 and 1960, it would appear that politics became more and more important just as religion ceased to be significant. It was quite normal to abandon religious

TABLE 4.13 *Frequency of Mass Attendance in Spain and Basque Autonomous Community in 1987, Expressed as %*

Attendance	Spain	Basque Autonomous Community
Never	27	30
Several times a year	30	23
Once a month	11	12
Almost every Sunday	14	16
Every Sunday and on holidays and/or several times a week	17	19
No response	1	—
Total	100	100

Source: Pérez-Agote 1990.

TABLE 4.14 *Memory of Parental Mass Attendance in Spain and the Basque Autonomous Community, Expressed as %*

Attendance	Spain		Basque Autonomous Community	
	Mother	Father	Mother	Father
Never	17	10	13	17
Several times a year	22	17	14	9
Once a month	10	11	13	14
Almost every Sunday	16	20	21	26
Every Sunday and on holidays	19	25	25	30
Several times a week	2	4	2	3
Don't know	11	9	11	10
No response	3	4	1	1
Total	100	100	100	100

Source: Pérez-Agote 1990.

practice without experiencing excessive trauma, and family conflict arose more as a result of political radicalization than religious indifference. In general, therefore, those young people who began to take an interest in social and political issues during the 1960s and 1970s appear to have gradually become more secular while, at the same time, experiencing a profound and increasing sacralization of everything political. Politics became the central focus of their lives and the basic yardstick by which they made most of their important judgments.

However, the following generation, those born after 1960, experienced a different process. Their interest in social life and awareness of social problems began in the 1970s, or when Basque nationalism began to dominate the public realm. This is key to understanding why a clear dedramatization of the Franco era occurred, as an essential general element of this new generation's political consciousness. This new generation experienced the Franco regime as a crisis-ridden system and Basque nationalism as an ideology that increasingly dominated public spaces. For these young people, the "horror of the Franco years" belonged to an a posteriori mode of explanation, or objectified history, instead of a lived historical experience. As a logical consequence, they came to demystify politics as the means for making sense of the world.

Furthermore, in a long series of interviews that demonstrate the value of describing this generation in such terms, another of their basic characteristics emerged. These same young people generally tended to shy away from the great global political and religious idealism of previous generations. Instead, they were more interested in pursuing personal or individual goals and values, along with interpersonal communication in and of itself. There was no denial, as such, of religion or politics; rather, political and religious questions began to be addressed more at the small-group level of interpersonal communication than in terms of all-embracing ideologies. In other words, involvement in politics and religion came to constitute options, among others, through which this new generation found its intimate community of meaning.[49]

By the end of the 1990s, a new generation was coming onto the social and political stage. In general, it seemed to be following in the footsteps of the previous generation, particularly through its dedramatizing of the Franco era. However, toward the end of the century it was also evident that a very specific sector of this generation was engaging in violent street activity at the behest of more radical adult mentors and the proponents of violence. We will consider this problem in greater detail in the next chapter.

Finally, it is possible, through the interviews, to trace the relationship (at the end of the 1980s) between age, religion, and voting habits. Voting habit was the only variable that was associated with religious practice among all age groups. The most religious people were PNV (Basque Nationalist Party) voters. The next most religious group was the voters of two Spanish right-wing parties—Alianza Popular (AP; Popular Alliance) and Centro Democrático Social (CDS; Social Democratic Center)— along with those of other parties and Eusko Alkartasuna (EA; Basque Solidarity), the latter being a splinter party of the PNV. These were then followed, at some distance, by voters of the Partido Socialista Obrero Español (PSOE; Spanish Socialist Workers' Party), Euskadiko Ezkerra (EE; Euskadi Left), and Herri Batasuna (HB; Popular Unity). In all cases there was a considerable difference in religious practice among age groups, especially if one takes into account voting habits. Specifically, among the youngest people (15–30 years old and PNV) 30 percent took part frequently in religious services. Among those in the second oldest age group (31–40 and PNV), this rose to 44 percent. Finally, in the oldest age group (41–51 PNV), the percentage was 67. For the same age groups, but among those who voted for HB, the percentages were 2, 17, and 25, respectively (Pérez-Agote 1990).

Forms of Violence and Their Role in the Reproduction of Basque Nationalism

Throughout this exploration of the different socialization mechanisms involved in nationalism's reproduction, it has been clear that forms of social violence in Basque society have been important in shaping Basque nationalist perceptions of political reality. Similarly, violence has also played an important role in legitimizing and delegitimizing nationalist behavior. Indeed, as we have seen, the fact of symbolic and physical violence pervades all the aforementioned political socialization mechanisms and contexts.

The previous sections have dealt with the general meaning and importance of political violence during the Franco era. We can now consider different factors in the violent situation. For the objective here is to discover the changes that occurred in the post-Franco era.

During the Franco years there were two opposing forms of physical violence in the Basque Country: an original state violence and the violence of ETA. These were experienced as oppositional forms both by social actors and by members of the state's police and military apparatus. However, this violent situation came about through a critical massing of other kinds of physical and symbolic violence. Sometimes symbolic violence was inseparable from the physical kind. This was the case, for example, in the violence exerted against certain symbols and accompanied by a physical violence against those who displayed them. Similarly, physical violence itself had a high symbolic element.

The symbolic violence of the state (Factor A) had two main axes of activity. The first of these was more important during the initial years of the Franco regime after the Spanish Civil War and entailed a physical rejection of the individual and familial Basque nationalist symbolic universe. It was especially important to ban the Basque language in all public spaces, particularly in the schools. The symbolic family universe was obviously affected. This might explain, in part, the virulent reaction.

This explicit assault on the language had two quite distinct consequences. On the one hand, as an intentional political act, it reinforced the language's decline by further restricting its use, both geographically and socially. This occurred because some families did not transmit the language to their children or because the language withdrew into the most intimate spheres of personal relations. In addition, it ceased to be used in genuine public social spaces, with the exception of the churches. However, this political pressure on the language (and culture), and the attitude of groups of high social status who treated Basque culture with scorn, resulted in a gradual awareness that Euskara was losing its communicative efficacy. Unintentionally, the political persecution led to a gradual positive symbolic valuing of the language. In other words, more speakers began to make a point of using Euskara, which enhanced its capacity to symbolize both social solidarity and ethnic difference. Therefore, this tremendous social and political pressure transformed Euskara's decline as communicative vehicle into a cause célèbre; and this consciousness-raising, it should be noted, was experienced traumatically. A further consequence, even less predictable and intentional, was the recovery of the language's communicative function through the gradual creation of ikastolas, or Basque-language schools.

The second main axis of state violence was the *absolute* impossibility of publicly expressing any cultural form that differed from the official one. This generally went hand-in-hand with a prohibition against any form of dissatisfaction or disagreement with the official version. The absolute or extreme proscription of all forms of local expression is particularly noteworthy, since it meant that any such expression, or any action, however small, located an activity within the same order of possibility-impossibility. The prohibition was absolute, but, through resistance, everything became possible with the same degree of possibility (*everything is impossible, so everything is possible*).

Thus, Factor A meant, in general terms, that public silence was imposed on a society that was solidly layered with intersubjective and associative relationships. The only public appearance of the nationalist symbolic universe for many years (until 1970) was the transgressing and utopian violence of ETA. This violence came about through the language of silence and as a public expression of the imposed silence. It therefore achieved strong emotional support from social actors through the complex interpersonal and associative network of the Basque Country. Thus, the symbolic violence of the state gave social meaning to the physical violence of ETA.

The attitude of the social groups that dominated the Basque Country during the Franco years toward the Basque language and culture reinforced the symbolic violence exercised by the state. This was especially true of those families linked to the financial and industrial elite and the high bourgeoisie of Bilbao, along with those of Donostia (although possibly in a different manner). Unfortunately, the generation of this attitude and its dominant place in society cannot be examined in more detail owing to an absence of research on the subject. What is evident, however, is that to political pressure on the Basque language during the post–civil war era, one should add the pressure of the leading social groups. They considered Euskara a rural, coarse, rustic, and uncivilized language. No doubt this contributed to its withdrawal from social life (giving way to what the dominant generation defined as *correct, educated,* and *civilized* models of behavior), especially in certain sectors of the industrial bourgeoisie. In particular, these were people from middle-level and family-run industrial concerns, mostly from Gipuzkoa and that part of Bizkaia outside Greater Bilbao. However, gradually, from the 1970s onward, this social definition of all things Basque as simple or rustic came to compete increasingly with the social prestige (though not politically or economically reinforced) of things associated with Basqueness.

The second factor, Factor B, worth differentiating analytically is the physical violence exercised by the state. At the outset it is worth remembering that, with the occupation of Bilbao by Franco's troops in 1937, the new state classified Bizkaia and Gipuzkoa as "traitorous provinces" according to a code of war rather than the terms of peace. The state imposed its authority without any attempt to legitimize its power in communitarian or consensual terms.

The state's violent activity during the Franco era had two social consequences. First, Factor B emerges as socially indiscriminate state violence, especially in Gipuzkoa and Bizkaia, where the vast majority of states of exception were imposed. The ritual appearance of these states of exception in a specific area, without discriminating between social actors or taking into account the internal differentiation and hierarchical nature of these social spaces, meant a general social proscription of the area in question. At the same time, the states of exception gave inhabitants a sense of shared purpose. That is, because they were singled out for state violence, the inhabitants felt communally and collectively under assault.

Secondly, because Factor B took place in a small society (demographically speaking) layered with strong networks of interpersonal relations, important sectors of the population experienced this factor personally, every day. The state's physical violence was not theoretical or abstract for these people; it was a lived experience.

Experiencing the repression fused individual and collective lives into a shared social experience. As politics and violence became everyday factors of life, constituting the symbolic bases for popular action (popular in the sociological sense, as real cross-class relations in reaction to a perceived threat from an *external* agent), they gained increasing support from 1970 onward.

The previous sections of this chapter have shown that practically all those interviewed experienced Factor B, through a death, imprisonment, persecution, exile, or the physical pain of someone close or even pain to themselves. Furthermore, they could all recall the events of the states of exception. The overlapping of individual and collective experience made politics an interpersonal realm. Imprisonment or exile ceased to be degrading; rather, the stigma was transferred to the state, especially to its security forces as the practical, palpable, and daily agents of Factor B. The *original arbitrariness* with which Franco's state operated entered into each individual's personal life, which then emotionally shaped and changed the collective drama. Everyday life became less prosaic, just as politics became more run of the mill. At the same time, state oppression reinforced the network of interpersonal relations that converted this violence into one subject of interpersonal communication. When, in 1970, this closely knit social network used the streets as an expressive public space, the unifying central theme was opposition to state violence (Factor B) and support of the other physical violence (Factor C, ETA violence).

As already stated, the focus here is not on Factor C's process or its social mechanisms. Rather, my interest is in the social meaning that ETA's violence acquired for social actors in general, as well as the attitudes it awoke in them.

Armed struggle and the use of violent methods in political life was not a subject of social debate during the Franco era, at least not in political rhetoric. Rather, it was an experience that people lived as a daily norm. This, in turn, nurtured social attitudes that led to acceptance or rejection of armed violence. Its gradual acceptance during the period in question, as a response to symbolic state violence (Factor A), has been discussed in previous sections. ETA's specific activity was symbolically framed by the public silence imposed by the state on the close-knit network of intersubjective life. ETA thus came to represent an antistate phantom perpetrating a just violence. Many of the actors knew some of violent activists, or someone who was thinking about taking part or who was intimate with those involved. ETA's violence (Factor C) became a means of communication or social interaction, thereby reinforcing the close-knit network of social relations.

Within Basque nationalist families during the 1960s and 1970s it was difficult to completely reject Factor C, even if one ideologically repudiated (above all on religious grounds) violent methods and feared the state's reaction. Either a family member belonged to the ETA, or the family knew people from other families who had been persecuted, exiled, or imprisoned or who had died in the struggle. Violence could be criticized most from an ethical point of view or out of fear, but the response was always emotionally determined. The PNV, as the symbolic repository of Basque nationalism, maintained ambiguous relations with armed groups during the Franco years, configured precisely by such emotional ties. Indeed, the very emergence of ETA cannot be understood without understanding the generational tension discussed earlier.

As a political phenomenon, ETA should be seen not as a unitary political organization, but rather as a social movement, albeit one without a single orthodoxy or praxis. Historically, ETA has operated in diverse and irregular ways, resulting in many internal schisms and the desertion of many of its members to other traditional political organizations. In spite of this, as has been demonstrated, most of those who emotionally identify with the group, conceive of ETA monolithically as both a symbol of unity and the armed struggle of the Basque people. This came about, during the mid-1970s, when different factions of ETA began to evolve into purely political organizations, in a situation where no one specific branch managed to control the different strains of popular mobilization. This popular base continued to endorse, most likely affectively, the unitary image of the armed movement. This is why actors involved in antiestablishment political activity have only paltry levels of affiliation with those purely political organizations.

The social consequences of the different violent factors can be summed up as follows:

The denial of a public space of expression in interactive life, along with the emergence of a physical violence from the Basque nationalist realm (Factor C), produced among these social actors a gradual identification with, or affective support for, physical violence as a response to the absolute denial of expression of all forms of social discontent.

As a result, more and more social sectors came to share a certain emotional connection to Basque nationalism. Basque symbols gradually enveloped society in general as transgressions of Franco's norms.

The physical violence of ETA (Factor C), that of the state (Factor B), the state's symbolic violence (Factor A), and the consequent social discontent and transgression came increasingly to form the core content of social interaction.

The delegitimizing of any expression of Basqueness therefore led social actors to associate all things Basque with prohibition and potential transgression. Because this prohibition and denial was absolute, it unified all things Basque. Consequently, any disagreement about a specific dimension of Basqueness (culture or the language, for example) became secondary. All things Basque and their transgressing prohibited nature (impossible = possible) became *tout court* symbolically relevant.

Thus, ETA's physical violence was legitimized politically as the defense against the illegitimacy of the state's physical violence and, more generally, of the state itself.

Another basic political consequence (mostly noteworthy during the final moments of the Franco era) of the behavior associated with the mechanism previously described as *the impossible is possible* was the difficulty in completely redirecting political life toward a political realm differentiated by parties. This would become most pronounced during the era of political reform in post-Franco Spain.

This chapter has analyzed the mechanisms, private or hidden, associated with reproducing Basque nationalist consciousness. It has also explored the role different types of violence played in this process. Both of these issues were considered in the context of the Franco regime. In this historical era, reproduction was in part based on the emergence of an oppositional subculture (Johnston 1989, 1991b) whose mechanisms of reproduction were activated beyond the direct control of the state: the family, the cuadrilla, the poteo, private associations with clandestine functions, and the church. On the other hand, the reproduction of Basque nationalist consciousness was also based on the social production of a political violence that achieved gradual affective support within this oppositional subculture and that recruited new followers.

The next part of the work, part III, seeks to understand the period after the death of Franco in 1975. Specifically, it addresses what happened to the above-mentioned elements—political violence along with the support it achieved (chap. 5) and the oppositional subculture (chap. 6)—after the Spanish political system was democratized.

PART THREE

Transformations of Nationalist

Consciousness in the Post-Franco Era

Chapter Five

Transformations Within Forms of Violence

During the Post-Franco Era

The specific aim of this chapter is to analyze what happened within the forms of physical and symbolic violence that made up part of the political process during the Franco era. The state's symbolic violence, exercised through repression of Basque language, culture, and ideology, would form a symbolic framework for legitimizing ETA's violence and concomitantly delegitimizing state violence.

In the Basque Country, violence was normal or expected behavior. That is, the call for armed conflict did not occur just in politico-intellectual rhetoric. Rather, it was a socially accepted means (in at least some sectors of the population) of achieving legitimate (if relative) objectives such as political independence.

Violence during the Franco years was real and direct. Numerous individual and collective lives became interwoven through this shared experience, particularly as experienced through the already mentioned complex network of social relations.

A range of social attitudes about violence existed— from unconditional support to rational rejection—shaped by more or less subtle forms of a relatively conscious division between reason and sentiment. Within the Basque nationalist world there were two extreme points of view about the violence. There were those who accepted ETA's actions both rationally and emotionally. Others could not justify the violence on rational grounds, yet supported it affectively. The latter, therefore, experienced a compartmentalization of reason and sentiment, as well as the tensions caused by their ambivalent attitude. The distinction between the two forms of support of the violence (and the tension within the ambivalent one) is not merely rhetorical. It corresponds to lived experience. Consequently, individual, as well as generational, support of violence could vary dramatically over time according to the social and political circumstances.

An essential part of Basque nationalist culture was the image of the varied and specialized social bodies that controlled the means of legal violence. Particularly interesting in this regard were the changes brought about by the overhaul of the state police's image and by the creation of the new Basque autonomous police force—the Ertzaintza.

Initially, this chapter will explore symbolic state violence toward the Basque language and culture (Factor A), followed by a similar examination of the different forms of physical violence—that of the state (Factor B) and that of ETA (Factor C).

Transformation of the Symbolic Violence of the State (Factor A)

When Franco died, the general situation of the Basque language changed profoundly.[1] It was first possible to use Euskara openly, and then over time it became institutionalized and actively promoted by a Department of Linguistic Policy (Secretaría de la Política Lingüística) of the Basque Autonomous Government and an official institution dedicated to language development known as HABE (Helduen Alfabetatze Berreuskalduntzerako Erakundea; the Association to Reestablish Basque Literacy Among Adults). The autonomous Basque polity had a certain legislative capacity to make Euskara official in public administration and to earmark funding for linguistic development. Educational institutions, groups, and courses promoting Euskara literacy flourished; the ikastolas were legalized and institutionalized, and an important number of them were integrated into the public educational system. Finally, Euskara also entered, though slowly and with great difficulty, into the public university and the new autonomous administrative system.

The creation of institutions specifically concerned with linguistic development was especially relevant: "In HABE in 1979, that was when we got this under way. We began with a 16 million-peseta budget. The 1984 budget was a billion. That . . . says something! Because money wasn't poured down the drain; it was invested in specific things" (I-33).

However, while some viewed the appearance of new institutions to promote Euskara as essential, other more radical people at the polar extremes considered it either insufficient or nonessential:

> I suppose you know what Euskal Herrian Euskaraz [The Basque Country in Basque, a very radical linguistic social movement] said: that there was no planning, that there was no arrangement regarding Euskara in the Vascongado ["Basque Area," used here in a derogatory sense; the word refers to three of the four Spanish Basque provinces] government. This meant that Euskara was not official anywhere, not in city halls, the judicial and economic system, or in any system where we had to make official contact. It was not official anywhere because they didn't want to impose Euskara. The problem was that if one didn't impose the language, it tended to disappear.
>
> If the Vascongado, or Vasco [Basque], as they call it, government was incapable of subsidizing the ikastolas and promoting Euskara throughout the whole Basque nation, if it couldn't introduce it into the public educational system, if this Vascongado government couldn't make all the kids, either from here or

immigrants, use our national unified language, if it couldn't even introduce it into the economic system, or the political or judicial system, for us that government was illegitimate as far as finding a coherent solution for our national language. (I-32)

On the other hand, within the institutional spectrum were "parallel institutions." As I-34 observed, within the linguistic field "there is no institution that doesn't have a parallel." Yet the problem was not as simple as an institution and its parallel belonging to sectors differentiated by the degree of their political radicalness within the Basque nationalist world. Sometimes this was not the case. For example, I-33, a member of the PNV and a high-ranking official within linguistic policy making, when speaking about the attempts to normalize the language, recognized that "there was a model defined by one academy and a parallel academy—nobody knew what it did but it was there. . . . There was a majority party in government [the PNV] that supported the two academies, that experienced this linguistic problem in its own jurisdiction, within its own party. . . . The measures that we were taking in the government provoked a counterreaction within the party itself that supported us; though this didn't reach the government because, although it financed the two academies, it gave only one tenth [of the funding] to the parallel one" (I-33).

Sometimes the substratum of political support for an institution and its parallel was vastly different according to their degree of radicalism. This was the case in the conflict between AEK (as previously noted, a movement dedicated to teaching and developing Euskara that historically preceded HABE and was close to Herri Batasuna) and HABE. Most radicals, politically and linguistically speaking, considered the Basque Government's HABE to be the real parallel institution: "If, for example, AEK operated with twenty something thousand students and extended throughout Euskal Herria, how could that Vascongado government—Vascongado because it didn't include Navarre and even less the northern Basque Country, thus it can't be termed Basque—decide to create HABE, thereby dumping twenty something thousand students and exchanging them for the six or seven thousand that HABE had? This was incomprehensible" (I-32).

These transformations in the institutional and organizational structure led to profound changes in the system through which people socially and politically valued the Basque language. In the first place, a consensus about the need for a linguistic and cultural recovery of the Basque Country was shattered. This unified view, which dominated during the Franco years, was characterized by politicized voluntarism—which meant that in the linguistic field there was little professionalism. A transformation was taking place, from an age in which there was political consensus about the positive worth of the Basque language and culture, but with scant opportunity to promote them openly, to, in the post-Franco years, a shattering of the unified front owing to the need to revalue Euskara and Basque culture in general. In this new context a professional approach was urgently needed to replace the former "feel good," but largely ineffectual and impotent, consensus that had been inherited by the political parties (and which provoked and exacerbated their divisions):

> Party politics is awful for the cultural and linguistic world. For all parties, language and culture are a screen. Language, for example. For HB, it's a weapon to be launched against both the state and, importantly, the autonomous institutions.
>
> In general, we've moved from one era, the Franco years, when we all agreed in principle with Euskara and Basque culture, and which was governed by voluntary will and politicization that implied a certain lack of professionalism, to an era in which culture has acquired value in itself and where there's a need— I'm not saying that it exists—to strive for more professionalism. (1-35)

Therefore unity disappeared in the post-Franco era. This was partly owing to internal tensions within groups, ideologies, parties, and so on that had been previously allied in the anti-Franco movement. It was also due to the fact that the Basque nationalist world had become politically segmented. That is, not only had the general anti-Franco consensus been eclipsed, but Basque nationalist unanimity had fragmented.

Franco's linguistic political repression led, in time, to a growing general awareness of language loss. The process by which the language relinquished much of its communicative function had, obviously, begun prior to the Franco era. However, the regime's repression of Euskara meant that language decline became traumatic; that is, it was no longer experienced as a slow or generic (that is, prompted by impersonal causes) development. Both Basque-speaking and non-Basque-speaking segments of the population experienced a collective feeling of rapid and brutal deprivation.

This growing awareness influenced people to value, even overvalue, the language. Moreover, since it was a response to political repression, this overvaluation came to define the linguistic conflict as a political struggle with the state. The political overvaluing of the language, in turn, revitalized its communicative function in that it motivated people to learn Euskara. It would be hard to explain in any other way the enormous effort invested by a significant proportion of the population in learning Euskara and the pronounced proliferation of ikastolas. These fulfilled the educational strategies for children of parents that positively valued the language. Similarly, one must take into account the fact that professionalization of language instruction generally involved what was generically termed the abertzale Left (radical left-wing Basque nationalist sectors).

During the Franco era, the structure of social plausibility, the maintenance and positive valuation of the language, was formed by what has been referred to here as an intersubjective framework. Within this social space, the language sometimes functioned as a normal means of communication, and always as an expression of belonging to a particular world: a *popular, Basque, anti-Franco,* and symbolically *transgressive* universe. Using Euskara in a purely instrumental way as a communicative tool naturally implied, at least for the actors, belonging to the Basque anti-Franco social faction. The participative and instrumental dimensions of the language came together within this intersubjective framework. Those who did not know Euskara, and therefore did not use it, expressed their positive valuation of the language by defending it in Spanish, as well as by ritually using simple Basque expressions in their greetings and farewells within interpersonal relations.

One of the conditions for the political significance of using Euskara and speaking in favor of it was, without doubt, a consciousness of the official negation and prohibition of the language. However, this consciousness was disrupted, to an extent, by several new factors: the emergence of autonomous institutions on the social scene during the post-Franco era, and especially those laws and institutions that established both a new permissiveness and new possibilities to learn the language; new social spaces that, at least formally, allowed and even facilitated its use; and new institutions dedicated to developing a specific linguistic political policy. During this era it did not seem to make as much sense to demonstrate in favor of Euskara, or even to say that one was learning it. This underscores the complexity of the linguistic world compared with symbols such as flags.

A flag is a simple symbol, in that its evaluative-participatory dimension easily commingles with its communicative dimension; or, at the very least, this communicative instrumental dimension is straightforward. It does not require any technical manipulation and, therefore, there is no need for the individual to learn it (by investing significant time and effort).

I-33, when differentiating between "speaking and doing," highlighted precisely this difference between Euskara and the *ikurriña* (the Basque flag): "What's needed is a personal commitment [to learn the language]. That's the qualitative leap, there's the difficulty. It's not like the ikurriña." This is corroborated by I-34: "The language needs more attention than the ikurriña." What these observers imply is that the participatory-evaluative dimension could not be disassociated, during the new situation, from the utilitarian, functional, and instrumental dimension: "The Basque language is a language of adherence to a national culture" (I-31), "and the big problem is that Euskara is not necessary to be generally understood" (I-31). When total official political prohibitions on the language ended, support came to be demonstrated through use: now it was not a question of a banned language but rather of one language being dominated by another (Spanish). At this moment, it became completely valid to socially, rather than linguistically, distinguish between a "Basque by adherence" (one who feels Basque) and a "Basque speaker" (I-31).

This loss of intensity and importance within the intersubjective framework, which came about gradually during the post-Franco era, also meant that the language was less likely to be positively valued in a political sense (its principal maintenance mechanism under Franco). The importance of learning the language shifted from the politically symbolic to the socially practical realm. Informants confirm that, during the post-Franco era, one dimension of the language redoubled in importance. Given its low existing status, it was critical to enhance Euskara's social valuation. In other words, for them Euskara's lack of social prestige was one of the most serious impediments to enhancing its communicative function. I-33 confirmed that "the greatest obstacle was the problem of the language's prestige." Similarly, I-31 observed that:

> there has been one thing that hasn't changed with democracy: the lack of the language's prestige. . . . The old idea, dating from before the war, that to be a civilized person you had to speak Spanish, still existed. . . . Today the language is official and yet the working classes continue to abandon it. . . . Euskara is not necessary to be generally understood. Any future prestige will essentially come from professionals, from those people who are quite educated and with a greater [Basque] national awareness.

During the Franco years, the language was proscribed within administration, education, and the media; that is, it was institutionally excluded. If the language had not been socially excluded, when it acquired official status at the time of the political reform its linguistic normality might have been established, as was the case in Catalonia. By contrast, in the Basque Country the middle and upper classes did not speak Euskara, though many people of lower social orders did. In addition, there was no campaign by the autonomous institutions to lend prestige to the language. The bad example, as far as Euskara's prestige, was set not only by the oligarchy but fundamentally by upper-class Basque nationalists. Today, the language is official, and yet the lower classes continue to abandon it. The old idea, predating the civil war, that to be civilized you had to speak Spanish, persists. Euskara is frequently spoken for purely symbolic reasons, in a way that would be embarrassing were one to speak similarly in Spanish. Xabier Arzallus,[2] when speaking Spanish, carefully selects the proper word (as should anyone when wanting to present a cultured demeanor). When he speaks Euskara, however, he is rustic and provincial.

I-34 introduced another dimension closely related to Euskara's communicative aspect:

> For the student [at the Teacher Training School] an idea exists that if one wants a job one has to study Euskara. They are quite clear about this. As a result, learning Euskara isn't motivated by any internal desire, but only in so far as it might lead to a job. This doesn't mean that there aren't people who do have self-motivation. The idea that if you don't know Euskara you don't have a job spreads from person to person. There are continual protests because of Euskara. They see Euskara as an obligation and usually say that they would learn it if it weren't obligatory, but it would be normal for them never to learn it. If you

don't need Euskara, you don't learn it. Some are happy to do so, and the majority of them learn it because they have to. Some of them are quite against it, but . . . at the end of the day, it's in the curriculum and they have to pass it. Some give the excuse that they're going to teach outside [the Basque Country]. In class you don't sense this opposition, but you do when you speak with them. It's an underlying thing and surfaces from time to time. There's a de facto acceptance of it. Generally, Euskara is very negatively regarded in the Teacher Training School.

This might be termed the pragmatic dimension, where reactions are ambivalent. Obviously, one should be careful about drawing general conclusions from this particular observation by one informant, however qualified and well situated he might be to observe this dimension. What is interesting, though, is that positive and negative attitudes may coexist. On the one hand, the above-mentioned pragmatic evaluation, based on a belief that Euskara may be required in the job market, creates a positive attitude about learning it. It may also produce both an evaluative and emotional rejection of the language—a rejection poorly understood by the educators themselves and therefore not by social linguists either. On the other hand, it is important to remember that the foregoing perspective concerns a very specific and condensed context—that is, a circumscribed center where studying the language meant acquiring that extra special something. Possibly one's attitude depends on whether one is looking at the pragmatic dimension from an individual or a collective point of view (the latter, moreover, is more learned than felt).

What is important to highlight here is the increasingly complex nature of the evaluative dimension of the language, resulting from the new liberalization and institutionalization. During the Franco era, the evaluative dimension of Euskara clearly superseded the communicative one, and, within this, a political evaluation took precedence over other ways of assessing the language. In the post-Franco era, the evaluative and communicative dimensions were more connected and interrelated. Moreover, social and pragmatic questions came to supersede purely political ones.

In group interviews (G-I to G-VIII), the subject of perceptions in the linguistic world was examined more closely. This helped to confirm the accuracy of the conclusions extracted from the individual interviews, and also to probe more deeply into some of their aspects.

In general, and independently of ideological points of view, the idea that Euskara was in a very difficult situation was present throughout the nationalist world:

Euskara is screwed up. . . . Because the truth is that one can get by without it. For me, this is the biggest problem: Euskara isn't necessary, if you don't want it, throughout your whole life; speaking Spanish is enough. (G-I, PNV)

On the one hand, it [Euskara] is experiencing a general trend of social disappearance, abandonment, and unpopularity in cities. On the other, in the smaller towns it lives a dual existence: in part, Euskara has familial and emotional value as well as regards all things *Basque,* yet also it publicly experienced political repression and the contempt of the upper classes. (G-VI, EE)

From what we understand, Euskara might disappear; the current situation cannot be maintained; there's no reason to speak Euskara. (G-VII, HB)

Excepting the opinion of new generations, whose perspective of the Franco era was generally less dramatized, especially so in regard to the language (G-IV and G-VIII), across Basque nationalism's ideological spectrum the interpretations of Euskara's problematic social standing included, explicitly or implicitly, a dramatization of the Franco years as the system that produced the current crisis. However, a division emerged within the Basque nationalist spectrum over the changes that took place with the creation of autonomous institutions during the post-Franco period.

The dramatization of the Franco era was clearly evident in the responses of G-V (PNV), G-VI (EE), and G-III (HB). For G-V, it was clear that even though one of the group members insisted on remembering "objective history" in which Euskara's social decline (owing to social and political pressure) dated from prior to the Franco era, the others persisted in, and insisted on, focusing blame on the Franco regime:

"The *francada*[3] years, when it was prohibited to say *agur* ["goodbye" in Basque], that was the worst time for the language. You have to have lived it. Parents spoke Euskara and didn't teach it to their children. I know cases of people who only found out that their parents spoke Euskara when they were older. But also prior to Franco, even though we might not have known it, Euskara suffered a lot. Without suffering official repression there was social repression: Euskara was the language of peasants. The classy young men of Bilbao used to go to the San Juan dance in Sondika [a small nearby town] where they went crazy dancing, and the village girls, with four words in Spanish, tried to appear intelligent. Yes, the young girls, already in the [nineteen] forties and fifties, didn't want to speak Euskara because they were accused of being provincial. But before the war there was also the problem of the schools. Anyone speaking Euskara was walloped by the teacher. But the problem is at what time people gain a consciousness. And with Franco . . ."

"That's it, that's it . . ."

"Look, if Franco hadn't existed, Euskara would have disappeared. What Franco did was create a consciousness." (G-V)

This highlights how important crisis was as a mechanism for producing meaning for a feature by framing difference. "Crisis" here refers to the appearance of traumatized consciousness of the disappearance of a feature, when, viewed objectively, its loss has been taking place since proverbial time immemorial.

However, as has already been mentioned, the changes taking place after Franco's death were perceived differently according to ideological viewpoints. The most radical position, logically, was that of HB. For the two groups of members belonging to this organization, the situation had not changed substantially and there continued to be strong repression of the language. They concluded that, because the situation of the language was dramatic and the repression continued, its very survival required a general imposition of Euskara throughout the whole Basque Country (G-III, G-VII).

To conclude this examination of the changes in the symbolic realm during the post-Franco era, three topics will be considered: (1) the social belief in the utopian idea of a monolingual Basque Country; (2) the ideological overradicalization of those who worked for the revitalization of the Basque language; and (3) the growing internal Basque conflict, in contrast to its external one (with the state political center).

THE PLAUSIBILITY OF A MONOLINGUAL EUSKADI

At one time, during the Franco years, when there was a complete ban on using the Basque language, when the *impossible* became *possible*, and when positive and unanimous political valuation of the language constituted Euskara's fundamental dimension, a utopian image of the linguistic situation existed: that of an ill-defined Basque monolingual world. However, a certain liberalization and some institutional measures aimed at linguistic development led to a new need among some social sectors, those Basque nationalist sectors popularly termed *posibilistas*, or pragmatists. To them, it seemed possible to replace the possibility/impossibility syndrome by rationalizing the situation politically and linguistically, both in means and objectives. For the pragmatists, it meant the PNV and EE creating a positive climate for the new linguistic reality of bilingualism: "On the other hand, within linguistic circles the ideal image of Euskadi's future has shifted from Basque monolingualism to one of bilingualism. People generally think that, in the abstract, both languages are encouraged. In practice they are not. They think bilingualism is something for other people, since those who speak Euskara already know Spanish" (I-31).

In purely logical terms, and starting from the actual linguistic situation in the Basque Country at that time, bilingualism would have been a necessary intermediary step in achieving an eventual monolingualism. However, such ideal monolingual definitions were not derived logically but rather politically. That is, they clearly involved political questions:

> The bilingual idea emerges as opposed to the monolingual one, and it seems like there is room for everyone. However, bilingualism is a strong idea and there's a lot of confusion about its exact meaning. In abstract terms people accept it, but then a parent obliges their child to learn Euskara at school. . . . I think, whatever the case, there is no clearly defined policy in this country designed to achieve this situation.

Those in favor of a monolingual situation, at heart, realize that they must first strive for bilingualism, yet what happens is that, because of their stance, they reject this. It's impossible to achieve monolingualism without first attaining bilingualism, starting at the place where we are now. (1-34)

Clearly, among people from the non-nationalist world, every ideal linguistic definition met with a different degree of acceptance. As a result, linguistic discourse was completely situated within the framework of collective identity, within the "we" that was precisely at the fundamental center of the general symbolic conflict in the Basque Country. This was a "we" in both a social and a political sense. And this was why the monolingual versus bilingual discourse has noticeable similarities with the more directly political debate of independence versus autonomy. Those who strongly supported autonomy did so as a necessary step toward a final goal that may have been independence. Those who strongly supported bilingualism did so as a necessary step toward establishing monolingualism at some undefined future point. Both positions, each within its own spectrum, accepted an intermediate objective as a lesser evil. Yet they did so as they simultaneously attempted to develop an efficient strategy capable of achieving the ultimate goal (full independence). Those who accepted neither autonomy nor bilingualism as practical intermediate steps generally believed that the institutionalized means (political autonomy) of achieving monolingualism actually impeded the Basque political will to reach the ideal goal.

These differing ideological positions were articulated in a dual context: an external one defined by the Basque Country–Madrid conflict and an internal Basque one. This was why each position defined the other in an ambivalent way. The *posibilista* position considered the center ("Madrid") the enemy and approximated politically the hard-line *rupturista* (rejector) position when the issue was legitimizing political power or the political objectification of the "we." Yet it considered the *rupturistas* as adversaries when the issue was internal rationalization or the rational management of resources. In such complex social situations, one of these postures predominated over the other. Conversely, the same might be said of the *rupturista* position, which emphasized either the struggle against the ancestral enemy, the center, or against the "mistaken sibling" (1-58) (the Basque Autonomous Government), which could even become an authentic adversary if a common enemy of the "family" didn't appear on the horizon. As for political organizations, there was one group that theoretically served to resolve, in logical discursive terms, the conflicts of both sides: EE, or Euzkadiko Ezkerra (Euskadi Left). Perhaps this is why that political party's greatest political resonance was in intellectual circles, where the separation between thinking and doing is greater and a problem's resolution is conceived in abstract intellectual terms.

In order to illustrate the *posibilista* and *rupturista* concepts, one might look at the definitions by 1-33, a high-ranking institutional official within linguistic policy, and

1-32, a member of one of the most radical groups in the linguistic and, of course, political fields:

> So long as we pose utopian goals we'll get nowhere. It's the same with Euskara. We all want a Basque-speaking Euskadi. But one doesn't achieve this by saying I want. This isn't achieved through holding demonstrations.
>
> Before, we all believed in monolingualism, in a Basque-speaking Euskadi. Now one must think about bilingualism. The heart wants monolingualism. Because here one knows full well that Spanish is going to dominate for years to come. The problem is knowing for how many generations we'll have to wait before achieving monolingualism. I reckon that even I won't see bilingualism.
>
> For me, monolingualism sounds the same as independence. I'm not at all sure I'll ever see it. As an agreed aim or objective. (1-33)

> The only possible [linguistic picture] for an abertzale [nationalist] is that throughout Euskadi, both north and south, Euskara is spoken and that it's the only national language. (1-32)

THE OVERRADICALIZED POLITICAL CONSCIOUSNESS OF LANGUAGE MANAGERS
In regard to the world of what might be called the functional managers of the language, one basic fact should be pointed out. As a consequence of their working professionally with the only element considered essential in differentiating Basque identity, their political positions have been "overradicalized" or "additionally radicalized." Their functional stewardship of the language implied that they possessed *objective* and *empirical* criteria by which to politically evaluate individual and group situations and behavior. In short, this was the realm of linguistic radicalism. However, this did not occur as much within those groups who, because of their linguistic origins, might have felt discriminated against by the actual dominance of Spanish: "The fact is that the number of people who might feel linguistically marginalized through not demanding a practical bilingual policy are a minority that, by their very social makeup [rural groups that are the only ones to speak Euskara with any ease], don't create any problems. They don't exercise their linguistic rights" (1-31).

Within this linguistic radicalism, each manager held a critical view of the language policy of all political organizations, both those that they supported and those they did not.

For example, observe the linguistic opinion of 1-31, whose political posture was at least close to that of EE:

> Nationalist political parties do more in terms of political discourse and slogans than in practice. Of course, the one that demands most on bilingual rights is HB and, to some extent, EE. The PNV, nothing, with one notable exception: a week

ago the PNV announced that it was going to demand that all its public representatives learn Euskara within four years.

Two gaps emerge: One, between political discourse and practical demands by
the parties, as a consequence of the fact that establishing bilingualism in administration, education, and the media has very high social and economic costs,
and, in general, the public doesn't think investing in the language is as important as other areas such as roads, health, employment, and so on. . . . Two,
within the parties themselves. The administration, as an aseptic administration,
demands knowledge of Euskara for certain public positions while the nationalist parties themselves don't demand it for their own public representatives. For
me, the scandal isn't that Madrid[4] opposes this; we've been opposing it for years
by not obeying the bilingualism law.

In Catalonia, every Catalan knows Catalan and, therefore, a bilingualism law
favors Catalans. In Euskadi, it's not like that: there's a difference between a
Basque by adherence and a Basque speaker and, therefore, the bilingualism law
is prejudiced against Basques themselves. Thus it's something that is adopted as
a slogan against Madrid, but then they don't apply it at home, because in daily
life the majority don't speak it [Euskara].

[There is] the incongruity of an HB leader who is always shouting out against
the marginalization of Euskara and he hasn't looked in the mirror. I'm also
criticizing certain radical linguistic groups, such as Euskal Herrian Euskaraz
[close to HB] for being too linked to one party, HB, and as a result not criticizing
the party closest to them. (I-31)

Here one can see how the criticism was directed toward everyone, highlighting
the failure to demand that the language be used in administration, education, the
media, and even within the political parties themselves. I-31 criticized the most radical linguistic group, Euskal Herrian Euskaraz, and its incapacity to criticize its closest political ally, HB. Finally, he clearly established a difference between a "Basque by
adherence" and a "Basque speaker," which has already been discussed. I-33, a member of the PNV and a high-ranking official in the campaign to regenerate Basque,
went as far as criticizing his own party. He accused HB of being hypocritical in its
criticism of the Basque Government:

Speaking of Euskara in the press, many experiments have been carried out and
none has worked; it's very difficult to increase the use of Euskara in order to
inform. Yet, why are those criteria from the editorship of *Egin* [a radical nationalist newspaper published in both Spanish and Basque] valid for *Egin* while
those from the Basque Government aren't valid for the Basque Government,
when the audience is the same? This is justifiable in *Egin* and not here. It's
curious that this might enter the same person's *bolo*.[5] This has a very specific
name, mental paranoia. That one person is capable of taking in two processes

that are so identical with two different perspectives; that the leaders who speak the worst Euskara and that are most allowed to speak in Spanish are from HB is truly very curious" (1-33).

According to 1-34, former member of EE and head of the Basque Language Department in the Teacher Training School:

> The Basque Government doesn't have a linguistic policy at the moment. Nor does the PNV. They themselves have to internally contend with the problem of *Batua*–non-*Batua*.[6]
>
> No party has a clear line on what Euskara should be—a linguistic policy. HB is the clearest, although at the same time it's limited in its capacity for doing things. One of HB's contradictions is that many of its leaders don't speak Euskara. The parties don't have a clear idea. And those that do have a clear idea don't have any social impact. Some also have a clear idea, but so extreme. . . . Only a few people have a clear idea. Because no party obeys its own programmatic model. No party follows, within itself, the model that it is attempting to impose on society. In EE there were two or three people who were moving toward a real bilingualism, as was the case in HB and the PNV. The PNV has this internal problem. Some try and impose an archaic form of Bizkaian[7] that is more artificial than *Batua*. (1-34)

One might speculate on what happens when overradicalization is added to political radicalism. 1-32 demanded the imposition of Euskara on the whole population and criticized the PNV and HB in equal measure because they put class interests before those of the Basque nation, both in general politics and in the specific area of Euskara:

> When the parties should be at the service of the Basque nation, it turns out that they aren't. Both the PNV and HB. HASI is Marxist; this means it puts class oppression before national oppression; it wants to establish a national front, but it's a class front because the PNV isn't there. And this is the same as the PNV. It doesn't want independence, the *estatutillo*[8] is enough, and this is because they have economic interests, with the commercial and savings banks. It's like this in politics and the same with Euskara. They put class interests before those of the Basque nation. And one can't put a nation right like that. Why is there no interest in culture or Euskara? Because class is the most important thing. This is certain. If the leaders of Herri Batasuna were to say, "all our leaders have to be Basque speakers, all our speeches in Euskara." (1-32)

THE IMPLOSION OF THE BASQUE CONFLICT

One might now ask to what extent the apparent cultural and linguistic change, along with the emergence of domestic political institutions in Basque society (which shared among their many commitments linguistic development and the regeneration of Euskara), led to an internalization of the conflict, and to what extent, within the social image of the language, the conflict continued to be defined as a political struggle with the power center in Madrid.

This examination shows that there was not a complete internalization of the conflict; the exterior dimension did not disappear, or almost disappear. At least this was the case for a rising internal Basque dimension in which different stances and positions about the language opposed one another. Rather, it appears that a growing complexity in the conflict reinforced the conflict's internal dimension, though without eliminating its external one. All the informants involved in the field of language (1-31 to 1-34) emphasized the multiple internal aspects of the conflict, but none seems to have ceased to bear in mind (at least in the back of their minds) the external dimension.

The existence of two juxtaposing linguistic images—one advocating monolingualism, the other bilingualism—implied the beginning of an internal dimension to the symbolic conflict. Supporters of one or the other idea were in competition for resources within the Basque Country and, furthermore, within the Basque nationalist world.

The discourse of bilingualism attempted to rationalize the situation. It invoked a temporal dimension. "Before" was an obvious reference to the Franco period, to Basque political unity in the face of complete official negation of the language. The present situation required a rational approach; one could not just argue for "utopian objectives." Monolingualism would be a final goal, but one that "at present" remained utopian. Bilingualism would be an intermediate and achievable objective. The claim to a rational approach showed in the call for a scientific definition of the problem ("one knows scientifically") and a stretching of objective time frames ("do things gradually"). The monolingual idea showed the persistence of the "impossible is possible" mechanism, from an era when there was a complete ban on any form of expression.

The two images, bilingualism and Basque monolingualism, parallel those of another dichotomy: rationalization and politicization. Rationalization refers to functionalizing and improving the technical sophistication of linguistic action. Politicization (and the accretion of other nonlinguistic dimensions, such as national construction) refers to the political significance of the act of learning Euskara.

Another place where the internal dimension of the conflict was noticeable was in the informants' definitions of linguistic conflict. For 1-31, "the most obvious conflicts are those of the educational world (public school/ikastola) and that of adult Basque learning (AEK/HABE)." This was corroborated by 1-33 and 1-34. Although they considered such internal divisions a little fictitious (given that the external dimension continued to be more important for them), they recognized that such conflicts had possibly become "more technical" and therefore more internal. For 1-

32, the bigger conflict was definitely with the center. From this perspective came
derogatory and continual references to the autonomous (Vascongadas) institutions
and their definition of internal linguistic problems.

Of course, in the two conflicts mentioned (public school vs. ikastola and AEK vs.
HABE), the internal dimension was an initial defining feature, but the external dimension served as a backdrop within both.

Within the public school/ikastola conflict, those that favored the ikastola as the
principal context for completing EGB (Enseñanza General Básica; Basic General Education, or the primary educational level) were afraid of the continued control of the
public school system "by Madrid." For I-31, within the "ikastola realm" there was
greater opportunity to preserve "Basque control," whereas the realm of the "public
school" implied joining the "central system" and therefore being subject to "Madrid
policy." Even taking into account that the "ikastola system" might turn into a privileged educational network, given autonomous institutional support, his final verdict
was clear: "dismantling the ikastolas is too risky." I-33 described the external dimension in similar terms.

One also encounters the external dimension in the AEK-HABE conflict, although in
more subtle form. I-32 was clearly in favor of AEK, and, in declaring this support, he
stated his thoughts about the politico-territorial dimension:

> AEK is right in a more important way, because it exists throughout the territory
> of Euskal Herria and territoriality is basic. A Basque can never relinquish
> Navarre or North Euskadi. AEK has achieved this territoriality. Furthermore,
> AEK has gained twenty-thousand-something students and has a worthy experi-
> ence. Some new gentlemen then arrive and sink AEK. For two reasons: because
> they want everything concerning Euskara, as with everything else, to be in their
> hands and they don't let anyone have what they believe to be theirs. This is logi-
> cal for a party, but not for a government. Secondly, AEK has a *proletaritis* problem,
> in other words, *izquierditis* ["leftitis"];[9] that's where LKI [Liga Komunista Irault-
> zailea; the Revolutionary Communist League] is involved in certain high places;
> and they're experiencing what also happened to many in HB, that they give pri-
> macy to class over nation. And the right-wing Vascongado Government can't
> accept it.

From the other (more *posibilista*) viewpoint, more inclined to the functional rationalization of teaching the language, AEK's own positions imbued the organization
with extralinguistic characteristics:

> AEK is a globe. It's what has the most students, but it lacks adequate teaching
> staff. And they don't accept any kind of control. Now the *euskaltegis*[10] can say
> that they are affiliated with AEK. However, this wasn't the case before. In the

beginning, AEK rejected the euskaltegis because it said they prevented grass-roots movements from emerging out of the neighborhoods. A nucleus should emerge in every neighborhood. At that time, it viewed the euskaltegis as professionalism, as a phantom that would do away with the neighborhood movements, the feminists, homosexuals, ecologists, and so on. The character that appears in AEK texts wears a sticker; he comes out of a demonstration. (I-34)

I-31 described the situation in the following way:

> When Labayen was minister of culture, the Basque Government saw the need to do something in this area and suggested to AEK that it institutionally organize the [language] campaign, with a degree of economic and administrative control from the Basque Government. AEK was controlled, generally, by people in HB and positioned itself in favor of marginalized groups: feminists, homosexuals, and so on. This was a mistake because it should have embraced the population as a whole. In its texts, magazines, and so on there was tremendous sectarianism. One must also distinguish Bizkaia, where AEK was most important, from Navarre, Gipuzkoa, and so on. A deluded individual was in charge of Bizkaia. AEK didn't agree to any control of its finances, teachers, or texts and, as a result, the Basque Government started HABE.

As a final observation on this conflict, here are the thoughts of I-33, a high-ranking official in HABE:

> There is one way to look at the HABE-AEK conflict: in terms of people that didn't find it hard to give up the connotative aspect of language learning. What we [HABE] had to do was build centers, a school in the academic sense of the word, whose function was didactic, period. That is, as a public organization we couldn't get involved in other issues. We had to impart Euskara to as many people as possible, which is what we did as a public organization. It was very different from what AEK did, where it was important to stir up people: if they learned Euskara, all fine and well, but that wasn't as important as promoting an *abertzale* [nationalist] consciousness. For AEK, whether a teacher was qualified or not wasn't important, and it principally criticized us for being too linked to the academy. And you [AEK] aren't [linked], because you can't be, I would argue, because 70 percent of your teachers have no academic qualifications and nearly 50 percent don't even have an Euskara qualification, or even an academic qualification. What, then, is the goal?
>
> Is it the revival of the language or political mobilization and consciousness-raising? The objectives were, then, totally different. They tell us that HABE's project is very conditioned, that it has only academic connotations. And, of course, it is. They should go to the most important glotto-didactic centers in the world and see how they teach languages there! What we're most interested in

is the most efficient way to teach a language. That's what we're interested in. Do they even know that pedagogy and glotto-didactics exist, that there are theories and so on?

One should point out that the linguistic area is more complex today. There is a fully developed internal dimension of conflict, although this doesn't mean that the external one has disappeared. Indeed, both external and internal dimensions are made up of subtle and complex factors. The internal dimension sometimes refers to what happens territorially in the Basque Country and at other times to what happens in the "Basque world," the world of language, culture, and nationalism. Consequently, the external dimension refers to the political center of the state, or to what happens inside the Basque Country but outside this "Basque world."

One should also mention the fact that this outburst of a positive political valuation of the language has been perceived in quite general terms: "Euskara belongs to everyone, but, in truth, it's not enough to *say* it, one must *do* something. Here a lot of people speak about saving Euskara but they do very little, almost nothing: everything is just words and, naturally, it's easy to talk, but they have to do something about it." (G-I, PNV)

The comments of G-III (HB) confirmed the attitude that, besides merely advocating the language, everyone's personal involvement was important. They also expressed the opinion that speaking was different from doing, and that the problem stemmed from the fact that "we all know and understand Spanish."

Finally, the basic analogies and differences in regard to the language issue emerging from different ideological perspectives within nationalism will be outlined here. In both PNV and HB discourse, language was an essential element of cultural differentiation and the Basque nation. Both parties saw the need for linguistic recovery. However, for the PNV this implied making the linguistic world in general, along with language instruction and the political implementation of progressive measures in particular, more functional. For HB there had to be a fundamental leap in linguistic policy, with the basic objective being to maintain the link between Euskara speakers and learners, on the one hand, and the radical political project on the other. EE's discourse basically attempted to be rational about goals. But this abstract rationality toward the linguistic problem was difficult to accept for those who began with an emotional sense of belonging prior to the problem being rationally defined:

Because if we're Basque it's because we speak Euskara. . . . Now nobody can say that they can't learn Euskara or they can't speak it; those who don't do so don't want to. Much is said about the subject of Euskara, but nobody remembers what it represents for us. (G-I, PNV)

Those in AEK, and in HB generally, have raised the issue of Euskara as a political flag. . . . They're not working in favor of it as a cultural phenomenon. And I say

AEK though I could mention others. Sometimes, even we ourselves [the PNV] also tend to falsify the importance of the language. Falsify in the sense of using it as a weapon to be launched against a political adversary, more than working in favor of Euskara, because people should learn the language, because it's something inseparable from the Basque people and must be a cultural necessity. (G-V, PNV)

We've reached the point that we don't know who we are, what our language is. There are people who, on losing the language, don't know if they're Spanish or French or what . . . they are. This is the problem: that we think in terms of parameters from a foreign culture that has been imposed on us. (G-III, HB)

What's happening now is that a Basque-speaking approach is considered radical, when all it does is defend its own language in an unfavorable situation. . . . The institutions don't take it seriously—they're afraid of confrontation. They should confront more radically an opposition that always reflects a centralist approach. We should be like the Jews in Israel: oblige everyone to learn Euskara. In this one must be radical; if there's no obligation, if there's no pressure, Euskara will never be recovered. (G-VII, HB)

In G-II one can discern a prototypical attempt to rationalize linguistic discourse in extreme terms, which concluded, "Spanish is a Basque language because 95 percent of Basques share it as a first language. Perhaps the Basque language par excellence" (G-II, EE).

Transformation of Physical Forms of State Violence (Factor B) and ETA Violence (Factor C)

The purpose in the preceding section was not to describe and analyze the actual changes that took place in Factor A (symbolic violence of the state), but rather to simply observe how perceptions changed. We will now consider Factors B and C in the same terms, namely the changing attitudes of Basque nationalist social actors toward physical violence.

Interviews with I-37 to I-44 (inclusive) will be the principal sources of information for this analysis. These informants were chosen for their political makeup: former *etarras*, or ETA activists, from both the "military" and "politico-military" factions; EE adherents; PNV members experiencing current familial problems because of repression; and HB loyalists. An attempt will be made to establish the range of attitudes about both state violence (Factor B) and ETA violence (Factor C), with two objectives in mind. On the one hand, we wanted to understand if there was a single continuum of attitudes, or if they had diverged. On the other, we wanted to determine the extent to which the aspects that did emerge regarding both Factors B and C in official political discourses were consonant with private lives or individual experience and perspectives.

EVALUATIONS OF THE POLITICAL CHANGE

In general, evaluations of the political changes that occurred after Franco's death ranged from relatively positive to completely negative. These were related to the perceptions of autonomous institutions and, in particular, the Basque Government and the Statute of Autonomy.

Not surprisingly, within the nationalist spectrum, the most positive evaluation of the political changes, of the statute and the new institutions, came from the PNV's political sphere. I-11 (PNV) affirmed that

there's a lot that has been accomplished; many conditions have been inserted into this statute; if we had the complete statute, as we should, then even more would be achieved. . . . Little has been achieved, but with this constitution the central government has limited many laws for Euskadi; you can't achieve what you want, they prevent a lot of things. . . . The basic problem is Navarre, they haven't allowed it to be here with Euskadi. Euskadi's biggest enemy is the central government; it's always been that way. We won't manage, nor do we expect, to get independence here. One can't say what might happen, but currently the situation is much better than before, because a lot has been achieved, a lot. . . . It's not like before, when Franco fined you for not flying the national flag on your balcony. Euskara is prospering after the ikastolas have developed a lot.

From this political position the political changes in general, and autonomy in particular, were seen as positive; yet, the goal of independence—which for this informant was an obvious right—had not been realized. Confrontation with the central state would remain. Moreover, contemporary politics were gradated toward the future. Regarding independence, although not viable today, "one can't say what might happen" later.

What was evident in this temperate (moderate and relatively positive) evaluation was that the image of the state, above all in terms of repression, continued to be extremely negative:

There's more repression, much more than before; if before there were forty now there are four hundred [state police]. Although it doesn't bother them, they're going to bother others; they're going in search of others, therefore they also pay the consequences for getting involved. There are a lot more prisoners than in Franco's time. The French government is complaisant regarding GAL [Grupos Antiterroristas de Liberación; Antiterrorist Liberation Groups, protagonists of a Spanish government-sponsored dirty war against ETA that lasted from 1983 to 1987]. The Madrid government is guilty along with the complaisant French. (I-41)

The most negative perception of the political changes was to be found in the world of HB. For the two informants belonging to this political coalition, the changes after Franco's death were thoroughly negative, to be summed up in terms such as "disillusionment" (I-43) or "discouragement" (I-44).

Both of these perspectives confirm a gradual privatization of social life, in the sense of a progressive disinterest in politics, and especially a steady diminishing of popular mobilization. This, along with the parallel steady absorption of political activity by political parties, which, ultimately, meant the construction of a political sphere differentiated from daily life, and, especially after the intensely personalized political experiences of the Franco era, resulted in a growing political indifference, if not downright avoidance of politics, by many social actors:

> The change entailed a shift of political power toward the parties and away from the formerly potent church. Parties have become the main channels for the exercise of power. During the Franco era, the people participated, acted, but they didn't think about power itself. There's been a split between those who exercise power and those who are governed. The result is a certain disillusionment. If, during Franco's time, Basques struggled to participate, now there is no participation—which is frustrating.
>
> But perhaps the worst thing about the change is that utopian ideas have faded and the illusions of many people were extinguished.
>
> The entrance of political parties onto the scene has implied that they are now the only channel through which to participate. It's very difficult for people to participate in parties. Furthermore, participation cannot terminate in the parties. These have become bureaucratized. The consequence is an even greater disillusionment, because one realizes that this channel is insufficient. (I-43)

> Furthermore, the panorama is discouraging. At an economic level we're worse off than ever. Movements that were leading the charge have been made official. The system has been able to absorb all rebellion, and the problem that now arises is the following: who made these changes?
>
> The state appears as something remote, too distant to touch; it doesn't form part of my everyday life. The conflict with the state isn't so important just because I'm a nationalist, although for that reason too, but because there are also other factors. But the conflict is not as vigorous as before; the determination to confront has decreased. (I-44)

However, there was not as clear a decreasing intensity in popular mobilizations (see table 5.1). José Manuel Mata (1993, 80–93) provides the most exhaustive and

TABLE 5.1 *Number of Radical Nationalist Mobilizations, 1978–1988*

Year	Total	%
1978	283	10
1979	241	8
1980	261	9
1981	280	9
1982	177	6
1983	302	10
1984	222	8
1985	108	4
1986	163	6
1987	721	24
1988	190	6
Total	2,948	100

Source: Mata 1993, 83.

detailed account of radical nationalist mobilization for the years 1978–98. The interviews with I-43 and I-44 were conducted in 1984, during a time of relative decline in mobilizations.[11]

Elsewhere, within the HB sphere, three ideas continued to dominate: the real state was that represented by the political center; this state continued to severely repress the Basque Country; and, finally, both the Statute of Autonomy and the autonomous government did not represent real power, although they did serve to reduce political tension:

> The state's image is driven by fear. The insecurity and fear that people have today reinforces the state's image as an all-embracing protector. The state is something given. When one accepts its rules, this implies that one accepts apparatuses that it sets up. The Vitoria government [the Basque Autonomous Government] is very moderate; it seems as if it's afraid to do things. What is most lacking is definition. Although perhaps the most important thing is the nondefinition of a national project. They have shown too much confidence in the state, and the political setting it has come up with is very precarious. It seems like the Vitoria government hasn't done much, although perhaps they haven't been able to do any more. (I-43)

I think that the Basque Country–Madrid contradiction has declined. The statute [of Autonomy] nonsense works for people and moderates the conflict. I don't see what the statute has been any good for. It seems the same whether there's a statute or not. The same, more or less, happens with the constitution. It's a front that is no good for anything. It doesn't affect anyone.

The PNV is associated with the [Spanish] government, and has a governmental image, but not that of a state. The Basque government is associated with the PNV. But Madrid is the state [and] the PNV is something else; it governs but it's not a state. (1-44)

Before moving on to the EE political sphere, let's consider two views of the political change by a couple of former ETA members—one from the military branch (1-37) and another from the politico-military wing (1-38). Both perceived the change in completely negative terms, since the transformation was seen, above all, as one of form, not substance. However, despite this shared opinion, there were profound differences in the two perceptions:

> With the political reform after Franco's death things changed, yes, a lot, but not substantially, that is, in getting underway with building this country, in every aspect in a cultural sense and in every institution in a political sense. That's the thing; everything is still subordinate to Madrid's centralism. Although they've allowed a Basque government that says it supports the culture and, above all, Euskara, the repression is the same and there's still a lot of fear.
>
> These autonomous institutions have modified the outlook of the country, of course. I reckon a good part of the population has been integrated into the reform process, through the PNV and the institutions. It is true that the people are getting more disillusioned with the statute. They're realizing that there's not as much power in the statute as they thought. More or less they control what the diputaciones [provincial governments] controlled before. They don't control a lot more, education and things like that. But really nothing's changed.
>
> The politicians and those of ETA are the ones that take part, but everyday people no. Everyday people don't even demonstrate anymore. Nobody participates now, nobody goes anywhere now. When there's a demonstration now, there is no mobilization, because it's not so important. It's the same during election time. There'll be more and more abstention, I reckon. But, nobody takes part. Who represents more or less what I think? Herri Batasuna? Then I'll vote for Herri Batasuna! But that's it, no more. Because it's not that the people aren't interested, it's just that it's not worth anything. (1-37)

The change that took place after Franco's death has been discouraging. All that energy shown by the people has been shut up in laws and parliaments. The most important thing in Euskadi is Euskadi, and after Franco it has been turned into a feudal kingdom.

Everyone thought the city halls were going to have more control and specific powers, and be closer to the people. However, political life has become very controlled, to such an extent that nobody bothers about the interests of the people; everything is against the people. The autonomous pact itself, arranged at the outset, was an illusion because, above all, the PNV didn't press for everything that it should and could have.

In general, the changes have been more cosmetic than substantial. Things are done, but always at a price for us. There's no imagination and the big parties (the PNV, PSOE, and PP) are against us. In fact, Vitoria hasn't done anything. The big laws that they might have changed have been passed on to the Constitutional Court. The autonomous institutions display little independence. This situation generates a lot of frustration, but inside there's a lot of anger that could explode. (1-38)

As one can see, the informants concurred in a series of appraisals: the change had not been substantial; there had been a growing privatization of life (lack of participation, integration, enclosure of popular energy in laws and parliaments, distancing of municipal government from the citizenry); these autonomous institutions that "integrated" or "shut up" "popular energy" didn't have real power ("what the diputaciones controlled before," they hadn't "done anything" and had "little independence"); the Basque Country still suffered the same repression it did under Franco; and so on.

On the other hand, there was also an important difference in the observations of these two. 1-37 was skeptical from the beginning of the political rationalization process that took place in the post-Franco era. In contrast, 1-38 expressed disenchantment or dismay that what might have been failed to materialize, which suggests a certain confidence in the party system itself and democratic institutions in the abstract. This difference captures perfectly the basic historical distinction between the two most important branches of ETA: that is, the difference between believing (politico-military) or not (military) in the need for political control (by political parties or professional politicians) of the general sociopolitical process, especially violence. The attitude of the military wing toward violence was closer to Weberian models regarding values and affective behavior. The politico-military wing conceived of violence as a political instrument for gradually achieving objectives; in other words, it followed the Weberian rational behavior model more closely in terms of goals, and was therefore subject to an analysis of the political situation that took into account the real center of power: the state.

The Weberian distinction is essential in this instance, where the difference resided in advocating the independence of Euskadi as a value (affectively protected) or as a final goal in a chain of intermediate objectives. The difference was also framed as an ethic of absolute values versus one of pragmatic responsibility. Within an ethic of absolute values, violence was already the outcome. One did not have to wait for it nor predict it, since it tried to sustain a value or restore it if violated, treating any side effects of such action as secondary. Action itself, then, whether value oriented or affective, was the outcome. Also, within this mindset, and given the felt intensity of the underlying fundamental values in which the actors had been socialized, all action was to some degree affective.

A detailed analysis of these theoretical disquisitions is beyond the scope of this book, but it may be worthwhile to point out a difference in the immediacy of the response (action) to a stimulus: rational action in the maintenance of values might be more thought out, preconceived, and planned (though not its results or effects) than affective action, which would be more of an immediate response to a stimulus.

In reality this distinction also captures, in very general terms, the different ideological structures and behavior of the HB and EE spheres. Having examined the HB viewpoint, let's now consider EE:

> The change has been frustrating. There's a lot of disillusionment because we thought it might have been one thing and it's turned out to be another. What we wanted doesn't seem possible now. We thought something new would come about; however, this hasn't been the case. The reasons for this are complex. One would have to say that it [the change] hasn't been led by the forces of the Left. Furthermore, the parties accepted the reform. This had negative consequences, given that we struggled for a break [with the system] and this didn't happen in Euskadi. Another of the causes was that the parties were very weak. Their image is overvalued because they're not deeply rooted. The Statute of Autonomy could have been an instrument of change, but the state hasn't fulfilled its promises. The struggle with Madrid continues to demonstrate the state's lack of understanding. Things can't be fixed while Madrid continues to misunderstand what the struggle for national liberation means. What does seem obvious is that after Franco there were many dreams, but the reality has woken us up; we thought the impossible would become possible in a short time; this has proved to be wrong and, obviously, this is frustrating.
>
> The institutions emerging out of the Statute of Autonomy are unfamiliar to most Basque people. There's a widespread ignorance of them. People think they only exist to settle domestic problems and that the big solutions to the most pressing problems will still be resolved by the state. There's widespread ignorance of what the autonomous institutions are able to do. The biggest mistake that the PNV made was in not knowing how to bring the people closer to the institutions.
>
> As such, people still think that solutions to the most important real problems will come from the state and not the autonomous institutions. (I-39)

However, you look at it, the change has been frustrating. The transition hasn't filled the void as was hoped. The work undertaken during these last few years hasn't come up to expectations. A lot of years playing around for nothing.

There's still a fucking fear of a coup d'état. The most discouraging thing, for those who take part in politics, is that people equate you with the Right and say that politics is shit and all politicians are the same, without making any distinction. It's unfair to say that all of them are the same, that all they think about is getting ahead in life. But what hasn't changed is the scant political formation of people; there's a great lack of political culture. Even in many social spheres, to confess that you're a member of a political party breeds mistrust. This is a frustrating situation: you've struggled all your life and now you find yourself in the situation where, in many places if you say from what position you're coming, people begin to look at you in surprise and some even find you suspicious. . . . What is certain is that there are greater freedoms, less helplessness, greater possibilities to come together; there's a different atmosphere. You have to face things in a different way. Yet, despite the fact that this is true, you end up short, you don't complete everything, there's a great distance between the objectives we struggle for and the reality, a lack of culture and a lot of emptiness, that is difficult to overcome.

As for the state, one might talk in terms of two attitudes. Some have thrown in with the state and others have not, seeing it as the natural enemy, which one must be against. In general, and despite autonomy, people think that Madrid's laws are effective while those of the Basque Country are not. Only the church and the Spanish parliament. The Basque Government is only an administrator. The Basque Government is symbolic. The Statute of Autonomy hasn't managed to institutionalize the parliament. It has no jurisdiction to legislate. They move in narrow confines. They administer what has been ceded, but they don't create new laws; therefore its activity passes unnoticed. There's an identification between the PNV and the Basque Government. People believe the PNV should govern the Basque Country, and there are some, and not especially from the PNV, who identify Euskadi with the PNV. Subjectively, there are people who vote for the PSOE, but think that the only party that can win elections in the Basque Country is the PNV. They oppose them for sport, but not out of conviction. (1-40)

One can see how, within the EE sphere, there was a sense of frustration over the post-Franco institutionalization process. This contrasted with the attitude in HB, where there was complete denial from the outset that the new institutions implied any change. The EE informants approved of the adopted autonomous political system (though obviously as an intermediate step leading to the final goal of independence), but they were frustrated with the nature of this institutionalization. An interesting, ambivalent perspective on political parties emerged out of this. On the one hand, EE adherents saw the need to channel politics through political parties; on the other, they lamented bureaucratization of politics and distance from daily life. In other words, they accepted channeling political activity, but they regretted the separation of it from everyday reality, that is, the differentiation of politics from social life:

> The parties are weak. In general they haven't been able to reach the people. Nor have left-wing parties achieved this. The members themselves don't know how to reach them. What does seem true is that the parties don't respond to everyone's needs. They're bureaucratized. One of their biggest problems is that they are so obsessed with their image that they don't accomplish what they want to do. They're very controlled by the image that society has of them. (1-39)

> One must distinguish among political parties. One can't speak about parties in general, because their social and political concepts are very different. They do less than they could. They don't get involved in the problems of everyday life. People continue to look at power as something external that doesn't touch on everyday life. Despite these limitations, they're essential. If in every organization there's a tendency toward bureaucratization, this is also the case with parties. The reasons for this are that it is very demanding to give an opinion. To be up to date, one must be well informed; if not, the people remain isolated. (1-40)

Fundamental to instrumental rationality is a separate decision-making center. Yet the basic point about EE's other component, Basque nationalism, was that its somewhat populist outlook denied the separation between the activity of the social base and decisions taken by the leadership. In this sense, within EE one found a certain distortion of the relation between both components, since they made contradictory demands. The same happened in the PNV, which, being a Basque nationalist party and therefore populist in that sense, assumed specific governmental responsibilities that demanded of it instrumental rationality. This produced a tension between the need to centralize the party or government and "turning to base support" out of habit, the need to mediate its own internal conflicts and using potential populist power against the central power.

THE IMAGE OF THE POLICE

The HB and EE informants had similar images of both the state police and the Ertzaintza (Basque Autonomous Police). Essentially, they shared a negative view of the state police and a hopefully expectant one of the autonomous counterpart.

There was a very negative generic view of the state police. The terms used included "innocent detentions" and "provocation" (1-41); "a wretched and irretrievable image," "they play out their bad mood," "torture" (1-43); "same as always," "the people don't go near them," "they're frightening," "repression" (1-44); "the same image [as during Franco's time]," "normal people tremble when they [the police] are in the street with their machine guns" (1-37); "people who torture," "the police rule," "they are fucking way above the democratic institutions," "people insult them," "they're against the people" (I-8); "an image equivalent to evil," "they've changed their image, but just because of that they're not going to trick us," "they represent repression," "they're not worried about the Basque problem, they come to conquered territory," "they maintain the order of the colonial government," "the best thing they can do is go away" (I-9).

As one can see, the police continued to have a Francoist image; indeed, the problem was ingrained and irreversible:

> On the other hand, the Ertzaintza doesn't have a precise image. People are expectant. What will happen when they have more powers? Until now they've only taken charge of traffic issues, and they've proved to be helpful and friendly; however, let's see what happens when they have more authority. People still don't take them very seriously. The thing is that they still don't look like the police; let's see what happens when they really have to use their guns. But I will say that, at the moment, their image differs from the other lot. In fact, in the towns people are going to embrace the Ertzaintza; they talk about it and say it publicly; and friends and the cuadrilla admit as much without any problem—it seems natural to them. I wonder what would happen if some of these people started saying that they were going to join the Civil Guard or the National Police. They'd be ostracized; people would run away from them. (I-40)

There was generally a certain degree of sympathy for the autonomous police, and positive qualities were attributed to them: "closer to the people," "more local," and more "aesthetic." However, some doubt remained over the fact that they still had not taken charge of an essential issue: "public order."[12] With this in mind, respondents tended to leave a wholly positive evaluation of the Ertzaintza to the future, indicating doubt about what would happen when the Ertzaintza took charge, which would ultimately occur fully in the 1990s.

Within what might generically be termed the left-wing Basque nationalist spectrum, then, informants (I-43, I-44, I-38, I-39, and I-40) all held a *relatively* positive image of the autonomous police, highlighting their positive qualities while also expressing doubts about the future.

THE IMAGE OF ETA'S VIOLENCE

The political parties' own internal official discourse shows acceptance or condemnation of ETA's violence to be a dividing line between them. PNV and EE clearly did not see violence as having a positive political function. The discourse of these parties favored negotiation and social reinsertion of former activists. On the other hand, within the discourse of HB was a positive valuation of the political efficacy of armed violence, accompanied by constant references to independence, amnesty, and the expulsion of the state security forces.

What is now interesting is whether the social actors also shared such a clear perspective of the violence. In short, they did not. At this level the picture was hazier.

Their social discourse was more ambiguous and punctuated by internal divisions. Of these, perhaps the most important fault line was that between sentiment and reason, likely a consequence of the violence's personal meaning in the Basque Country. Some of the actors had direct personal experience with the physical violence of the state, or knew a relative or friend who did. Further, there was usually someone in their social circle who had been close to ETA's violence or possibly even currently belonged to the organization.

As nearly all the informants observed, the romantic stereotype of prisoners had diminished, as well as the capacity of that stereotype to mobilize the popular will. However, the number of prisoners at the end of the 1980s was still quite large, and there was no indication in any of the three Basque nationalist political variants (probably given the personal and historical recollections of previous eras) that people considered ETA activists to be terrorists. Indeed, even within the most rationally negative discourse about armed violence's political function, there was an explicit refusal to classify them as such.

I-41, a member of the PNV with close family members who were political refugees abroad, was clearly ambivalent. On the one hand, adopting a political and ethical point of view, he negatively evaluated ETA's violence: "ETA's actions do harm. If you want something, we want peace, and to find peace you have to be at peace. . . . What does the most harm is the killing, but it's the same on both sides [the police and ETA]. Nobody should kill anyone." However, a little later, to a certain degree, he justified ETA:

> The subjects of social reinsertion, deportations, and so on don't solve the problem. The only solution would be independence, as they want, and achieving independence, that would do away with the struggle. . . . There's terrorism on both sides because yes, ETA is terrorist because it has kidnapped, killed, planted bombs, but they weren't all done by ETA. There are others that weren't done by ETA. . . . ETA fights for Euskadi. If they steal it's because they need to. They blame ETA for many things. Most people are against ETA, and now more than ever. Before, when they killed someone, they [people] used to say "he must have done something," but now they don't. (I-41)

The interview with I-43 revealed a position that, within HB, could be considered critical of ETA violence and even HB itself. There was no ethical denial of ETA, but there was criticism—as opposed to a condemnation—of its political function. There was also some recognition of a decline in ETA's positive image. At the same time, ETA's actual existence was justified on the basis of the deception created by the political change, above all by the Statute of Autonomy. The political criticism of ETA and HB was, it is argued here, a typical internal discourse within HB regarding political organization itself: the incessant negativity of ETA and HB and their lack of a constructive political agenda.

I-43 framed the violence in ethical terms, but there was no symmetry between his perception of violence "against all things Basque" and "Basque violence" (ETA). Besides a criticism of ETA's violence (some actions are "demented"), one also sees in this informant's thinking an affective bond ("they endorse with their heart"):

The ETA problem is very complex and one must understand it on different levels. There are at least two kinds of violence in the Basque Country: a guilty, unwanted violence and a guilty, necessary violence. Thus, for example, Spanish culture practices nonguilty violence. The violence objectively practiced by an immigrant against the Basque differential reality is not guilty. However, the violence practiced by the state is guilty. The violence of central power is guilty. Next to these one finds ETA violence. It's true that ETA's image has changed over time. At present, ETA doesn't represent the Basque people, given that there are other political expressions, which implies that its monopoly has been broken. Furthermore, ETA has carried out specific demented actions. Its activity has been displaced and its actions remain unconnected to a political perspective. In short, ETA continues because there's a profound disappointment with the Basque project; the statute is a completely political game. This isn't what we wanted; we wanted to open up that channel more. The fact that such falsehood exists might have contributed to not considering the question directly. [That] might also be important. It's also the case that ETA might be the savior that liberates me while I stay at home. ETA might be a projection of the frustrations and the idol with which I identify. The problem is that neither ETA nor HB is constructive. In fact, there's a gap between ETA and those close to ETA. Nobody can figure out a connection. Whatever the case, the members of ETA are not terrorists. They are an amalgam of idealism, frustration, and so on.

ETA has demonstrated its capacity to destroy; what remains to be seen is a similar ability to create. Many actions are endorsed, above all with their hearts, but ETA has made many mistakes. It's carried out demented acts that do it great harm. It's not the same killing a high-ranking official as it is a normal citizen; while one can understand the first concept, the second is incomprehensible. Every day one misses the construction of a Basque national project. (I-43)

I-44 offered another critical perspective of ETA violence from within Herri Batasuna. This individual also saw no equivalence between state and ETA violence ("now we hear nonsense like having to denounce violence from wherever it comes"). This informant doubted that a position moderately favorable of ETA violence would be socially acceptable, although he favored it. This reflects a tension between what ETA must do politically and what it does in reality, but the informant didn't explicitly condemn the violence in ethical or political terms:

I feel very sorry for the ETA guys. Now they don't have anything to do, it's absurd. Now they can't carry on like Robin Hood. They can't do your dirty work; that time has already gone. ETA's role has been very important, but today many things have changed the situation. ETA is still around because people don't want to give up with some things still unresolved; they want radical measures and think that it's the only force capable of making inroads into the existing problem. Sometimes they see in ETA a savior that will solve their problems, while they stay at home. It looks like they're having a tantrum; things can't go on like this. One can't say that ETA has demobilized; but what one can say is that ETA continues to be at the front, when it should have gone to the rear in order to let people organize and express themselves.

Taking responsibility for demobilization hasn't been apparent. It emerges naturally out of general demobilization. (1-44)

1-37 (a former member of the military faction of ETA) openly favored ETA's armed violence and was clearly convinced that, more or less explicitly, a large part of the Basque people believed in the political necessity of this tactic. He clearly echoed the distinct perspectives being compared here: the political discourse of political parties versus social actors' attitudes:

People are a lot less against ETA than the political parties say. People aren't so exasperated with ETA. Yet it depends a lot on what sectors you're talking about. You see sectors close to the PNV that aren't against such actions in general, but yes if it's a poor sergeant or a poor private they've killed. Now other things happen, like the other day when they killed that captain in Navarre; in general people were pleased because it seems like he organized everything regarding the border, which might have been related to the GAL. And, in general, people thought it was fine. I believe the Basque people accept the violence with all its consequences. And many people are conscious of the fact that there needs to be violence, more and more, and the problem is that there's a great impotence; but there is a will. (1-37)

1-38 (a former member of the politico-military faction of ETA) offered a more critical and reflective statement on ETA violence. In its attempt to be rational and rationalizing, the statement revealed a clear tension between a reasoned denial of the political function of violence and an acceptance of it on emotional grounds. Also evident is a tension between absolute values and emotions, on the one hand, and responsibility for political consequences on the other:

ETA is not the most adequate method of fighting; it hasn't produced a mass response. First of all, there's also repression and no social capacity to respond to it. Nor has ETA created a base to respond to this repression. This is a result of the fact that people placed too much confidence in ETA and abandoned organizational structures that might have given the Basque people this response. From this point of view, ETA's weakness is obvious; it has depended too much on the voice that screamed: "ETA, kill them." ETA often didn't realize that who really gained from the struggle was the PNV; ETA has been good for the PNV.

What happens is that there's a split between what one thinks and what one does. It often seems like we're living in the past. This is clear, above all, in attitudes toward violence. Often it is said about ETA: what these people do is what has to be done. There are moments of regression, or even a rupture between theory and practice. People can speak a lot about doing things, but when it comes time to keep one's word they forget. Therefore, when they consider leaving ETA they ask themselves: "Yes, but where do we go?" There are no projects; one has to be radical in looking at ourselves. What happens is that the Basque people are still screwed; if someone has to respond, and I'm not capable, there must be someone to respond for me. But moreover, people need a missionary, a myth. This possibly masks the lack of responsibility, and the answer is always that someone else responds. Furthermore, it's quite clear that ETA offers an efficient image; for example, Lemoniz[13] has been closed down. For normal people, ETA seems efficient. This image is also obvious when they carry out an act; when it doesn't personally touch [people], there's support. It screws things up quite a lot when they get it wrong and kill normal people, or even with the tax [ETA's demand for money from businesses] on small businessmen using family capital. When they ask important businessmen and you know they've paid up, you're happy. This is because you don't trust the institutions to come up with the answer. Moreover, one still has to get rid of Madrid. If there's nothing that does any harm [the threat of ETA's violence], you can't get rid of it. People's mentality still works like in Franco's time: nationalism doesn't work by throwing in the sponge; someone must respond. (1-38)

The language of 1-39 (a member of EE) was similar to that of 1-38, but this informant's lack of personal experience with armed violence meant greater rationalizing. That said, he too noted the difference between the what was felt after the death of an ETA member and what was felt after the death of a policeman:

ETA's image is harmful. During Franco's time it was impossible to criticize them; any mistake was justified. Now they're a destabilizing factor. They get in the way of an alliance of the Left. They tire people. ETA's activity is one of the most pressing reasons to be demoralized. Armed activity demoralizes people. It replaces popular activity because people think that others are capable of doing what you cannot. The reasons for all this go way back. In Franco's time this replacement took place. Although ETA didn't seek it, this replacement took place. There's no reason now for ETA to continue; it carries on through inertia. Its activity doesn't terrorize people, but rather bores them.

This can be seen when the cops kill an ETA member. People are more pissed off when an ETA member is killed than a Civil Guard member. But this has changed a lot; through inertia people think that they're fighters. (I-38)

I-40 (a member of EE) underscored the division between reason and sentiment when talking about ETA. Indeed, for this informant it was explicitly thematicized:

It [ETA] continues to exist through historical inertia; moreover, one must understand that it came out of rural towns with a very defined and clear mentality.
Euskadi is Euskadi and one must free it, and there's no gray area. But also
because it was a very narrow-minded society, made up of a paternalist, domi-
neering core that was incapable of conducting conversations without resorting
to insults and so forth; it was also the result of a very typical personality. It
wasn't surprising that for some sectors, they were defending Euskadi's essence.
For adolescents, they played an epic or heroic role. Young people need this role
and ETA filled the requirements; it was an organization in love with the epic.
There are even kids who arrive at the paradox of being against the armed
struggle, in favor of pacifism and also of ETA. There are also people who still
think they live in Franco's time; they think that the years haven't passed by,
that nothing has changed here and, therefore, that ETA is still necessary. They
don't understand very well what they count for today; I reckon they don't understand what the struggle means, and that this condensed historical inertia
and indebtedness are stronger than [ETA's] need to remain in existence.

I feel more when they kill an ETA kid than some guy from the Civil Guard;
heart and *head* don't think the same. (I-40)

One has to conclude that there was a lack of congruity between political party official discourse and social actors' discourse. Moreover, the latter was strongly am-bivalent in evaluating ETA's violence. The limits of official political positions were marked by acceptance or rejection of that violence; within the actors' discourse was an ambiguity and tension between contradictory evaluations. Ethical, political, and sentimental evaluations commingled within a complex framework. Indeed, they did not even have to be mutually reconcilable within each social actor.

The division between reason and sentiment occurred within all ideologies that were, more or less, Basque nationalist. However, perhaps the most paradigmatic and self-aware expression was from members of EE, precisely because it was the political organization that made the greatest attempt to be politically rational and to exclude nonrational elements from its discourse. Within the PNV milieu there appeared to be less reflection. That is, there was less of a conscious connection between rationaliz-ing denial and sentimental support. The HB environment was characterized by both a sentimental and political acceptance of violence, ranging from pure and simple embracement to some political criticism of the way in which it was carried out. This was quite clearly the least ambivalent perspective. Paraphrasing Weber, it might be argued that this was rational behavior related to some affectively protected values.

On the other hand, all these disquisitions about the discourse on violence revealed a basic fact more or less recognized by everyone: namely, the general and gradual erosion of ETA's positive image throughout the 1980s. What happened was that the process of political change begun after Franco's death enabled and facilitated the emergence of an instrumental political rationality (the possibility of political parties and organizations taking part in the system, autonomous political institutions, and so on). As a result, the affective support for ETA's violence that developed during the Franco era within the heart of Basque nationalism was weakened by a discourse that favored instrumental political rationality.

One should highlight two further points about ETA's image. The first is the influence (regarding Factors B and C) of new phenomena. For those interviewed, the most striking new development was the appearance and activity of the so-called GAL (Antiterrorist Liberation Groups). Most of the informants referred to a more or less direct collusion between the Spanish government and this armed group. According to I-41 (PNV), "the French government is complicit in the GAL issue," and he attributed "blame" to the Spanish government. For I-43 (HB), "there might be collusion with the state apparatus; maybe someone in the apparatus is involved, partly encouraging this." For I-44 (HB), "powerful people are clearly behind it [financiers, military personnel]; maybe the government has nothing to do with it, although its [GAL's] activity is very good for it; what does seem likely is that they have ties to the military class." I-37 (a former ETA military member) referred to "that thing, the GAL thing; the Spanish police and the socialist government can't be doing it alone; the CIA or something like that must be involved." I-38 (a former ETA politico-military member) argued that, "for many people GAL goes beyond the state," and for others the confrontation between ETA and GAL was "a mafia war."

The second point is that, once again, practically all the informants spoke of a loss of mobilizing capacity in regard to the prisoners' issue and a decline in ETA's romantic image. This meant (although not only this) that there was a weakening of identification with ETA or, in more cautious terms, a decline in the social and political importance of affective identification with ETA (I-38, I-40, I-43, and I-44).

If one takes into account that, throughout the discourse analyzed here, there was at the same time a complete negation of those state elements practicing official violence, one must conclude that in the 1980s, within the Basque nationalist world, the social actors oscillated between two positions about socially legitimizing political violence: some of them defended ETA's violence; for the remainder, however, the violence lacked legitimacy, because neither the state's nor ETA's violence could be condoned. Indeed, for these social actors, violence is never legitimate.

Previously, it was demonstrated how, during the Franco era, there was a strong and progressive relationship between the factors producing legitimacy (affective ad-

TABLE 5.2 *Change in Image of* ETA *Members, 1978–1989*

Image	1978	1989
Patriots	13%	5%
Idealists	35%	18%
Manipulators	33%	11%
Crazy people	11%	16%
Criminals	7%	16%
Don't know/no response	1%	34%
Total	100%	100%

Source: Llera 1994, 103.

hesion) of ETA violence and those leading to the delegitimation (renunciation) of state violence. However, during the 1980s a consciousness arose, unrelated to any attitude toward ETA activity, that delegitimized state violence. This meant that within the Basque nationalist world state violence continued to be unanimously rejected. Nevertheless, the negation of state violence did not mean a positive evaluation of ETA's actions. However, there remained an important sector—what might be termed the ideological milieu of HB—where state violence denial and a positive evaluation ETA violence still coexist; and within those sectors that rejected state violence, but did not politically evaluate ETA positively, there remained a division between reason and sentiment. Within these latter sectors, there appears to have been a complex amalgam of a negative politico-rational evaluation of ETA violence and a positive evaluation of it in sentimental or emotional terms. The mixture was owing to the varying personal experience with the two kinds of violence in the recent past—one's *lived history*.

Finally, one should highlight that the general population's attitude toward ETA violence has evolved. Although polls are not the ideal method with which to gather information about such a delicate question, there is little alternative. Llera (1994, 99–119) offers a series of indicators. The conclusion, apart from a significant increase in those who *did not know* or *did not respond*,[14] is that ETA's violence was viewed as progressively less legitimate. This is evident in table 5.2.

This chapter has analyzed perceptions of the new situation that began with the death of Franco, especially of the various types of physical and symbolic violence. Allowing the Basque language to be used and permitting its educational institutionalization signaled a major relaxation of Factor A (symbolic violence practiced by the state) and had a number of consequences. Among these, three stand out: the persistence of a social belief in the utopian idea of a monolingual Basque Country; the overradicalization of the so-called functional managers of the language; and a certain implosion of the Basque conflict (that is, its growth within the Basque Country itself).

As for how the new situation affected the forms of physical violence, the perception (of at least a part of the general population) continued to be that the political change had been insignificant and that, to some extent, ETA's violence still made sense. However, affective support for it declined in most of the Basque nationalist population. Within this majority, a mechanism referred to here as the division between reason and sentiment allowed a certain ambivalent attitude toward ETA's violence. As a consequence, those people who condemned the violence for political reasons could continue to feel a degree of affective identification with it.

The parties' political discourse, which was rationalizing and denied the liberating value of the violence, prevented a *continuum* of nationalist attitudes regarding ETA. Nevertheless, there was a continuum of different attitudes among the (Basque nationalist) population based on the efficiency of compartmentalizing reason and sentiment. Those people who still affirmed the need for violence with political objectives could remain politically close to those who rationally rejected this need but felt a certain affective harmony with it. In the epilogue, a new development will be discussed: how this mechanism, which allowed an internal or individual division between reason and sentiment and, therefore, proximity between more radical and less radical nationalist sectors, has been progressively weakened. This, in turn, led to a certain fission within Basque nationalism.

After analyzing how perceptions of different kinds of violence have changed, there remains one more change to consider, in the other axis of the nationalist reproduction model: namely, the intersubjectivity that formed part of the oppositional subculture during Franco's reign. This is the subject of the following chapter.

Chapter Six

The Privatization of Social Life and the New

Political Institutionalization

In the Basque Country during the Franco era, as we have noted, the intersubjective (cuadrilla) and associative (church and recreational) networks acquired tremendous political influence. This was expressed best in the symbolic space of the street, which had become an established sphere or stage of political activity. The goal of this chapter is to understand to what extent and in what ways these complex intersubjective and associative networks, through their public projection, both hindered the political modernization process that sought to institutionalize democracy and distanced it from the daily lives of social actors.

During the post-Franco years, and even following the introduction of a differentiated political sphere (a Basque government, Basque parliament, Basque high court of justice, and so on), an essential part of political life remained beyond separate Basque control. Spain's central government retained important political power. Furthermore, the complex interactive and associative network still had an important (though declining) political influence. On the one hand, the collective interactive life of the cuadrillas and associations was still politically important, and those new political organizations associated with the post-Franco era (nonclandestine political parties) were themselves characterized by intense social interaction. This was especially true of Basque nationalist parties, which, as ideologically interclass heterogeneous formations, needed frameworks within which different social classes could plausibly interact.

After Franco's death, the Spanish state itself proposed, through certain anticipated mechanisms of succession and with the collaboration of the vast majority of more or less organized political forces, to carry out a political transition that would lead to state formation comparable to Western (and above all European) democracies. The Spanish state that emerged out of the civil war had not managed—had not even tried—to gain legitimacy among important sectors of the population. Personalized authoritarian central power led to considerable "anti-Francoism." This underscored a problem of legitimacy that was two sided. At the moment of the Transition, the problem was framed in the following way: for some people it was the particular government that had occupied central power that had not achieved legitimacy; for others, central power itself had become illegitimate by not representing the social and political meaning of their community. Put more succinctly, the Franco regime reproduced day after day, and in a seemingly widespread way, the old problem of "España roja" (Red Spain) and "España rota" (Broken Spain; that is, a Spain threatened by internal divisions rooted in the conflict between center and periphery). Therefore, a principal task of the political Transition was the nationalization of the state (Moya 1978). A dual reconciliation was necessary: between Right and Left and between center and periphery.

In schematic terms, the vertical dimension of this reconciliation (Right and Left in political terms) called for a democratization of state structures. This meant establishing political representation in dual fashion: ensuring that it emanated from the citizens' popular will and safeguarding the integrity and autonomy of the political sphere as a representational setting for political action and actors. The horizontal dimension of this reconciliation (between the center and certain peripheries) called for the framing of an established center that could no longer be omnipotent. The State of the Autonomies was the political response to these demands, bringing with it a series of both old and new factors and terminology: decentralization and autonomy, the federal state, nation and nationalities, nation and regions, nation of nations, peoples of Spain, and so on. The solution to this doubly complex challenge was put in terms of reverence for a dominant symbol: the constitution. In fact, this was no more than an agreement about wanting to agree, thereby establishing the rules of the game through which specific accords might be reached.

During the Franco years, Spanish civil society had been subjected to extreme pressure as a result of the lack of freedom of expression and association—the key mechanisms through which social discontent is expressed. During the immediate post-Franco era, important social sectors, on seeing the political sphere weakened by rising discontent, engaged in street demonstrations. This took the form of both strikes and festivals, with social drama threatening to eclipse political transition. Out of this emerged a belief that political and social life had to separate for reconciliation to occur. Then came the notion of privatizing social life while depriving it of political projection. With the (complex) nationalization of the state, privatization of social life, and the political rationalization of society, Spain attempted to assimilate the sociopolitical customs of European parliamentary democracies.

Clearly the aforementioned processes met additional difficulties in the Basque Country. One need only look at the results there of the constitutional referendum (table 6.1), the numerical and percentile support for Basque nationalism in general elections (table 6.2), and the significantly greater number of social and political mobilizations that took place in the Basque Provinces.

What follows, first, is an analytical description of the overall meaning of these processes of the privatization of life and political rationalization in modern Western countries. Second will be a brief description of the particular difficulties that such

TABLE 6.1 *Results of 1978 Referendum on Spanish Constitution*

	Percentage of Votes Cast				
Electoral District	Abstention	Yes	No	Void and Blank	Total
Araba	41	42.5	11	5.5	100
Gipuzkoa	56.5	28	13	2.5	100
Bizkaia	56	32	9	3	100
Basque Autonomous Community	55	31	11	3	100
Navarrese Autonomous Community	34	49	11	6	100
BAC + NAC	50	35	11	4	100
Spain	32	60	5	3	100

Source: El País, December 8, 1978.

TABLE 6.2 *Votes in Favor of Basque Nationalist Parties in Spanish General Elections*

General Legislative Elections	Total Votes Cast	Total Nationalist Votes	Nationalist Votes as a % of Total Votes Cast
1977	1,035,207	357,610	35.54
1979	1,020,793	505,075	49.48
1982	1,220,817	647,077	53.00
1986	1,113,447	597,807	53.69
1989	1,116,034	659,667	59.11
1993	1,206,137	580,419	48.12
1996	1,241,747	574,274	46.25
2000*	1,109,319	433,974	39.12

Sources: Aranzadi, Juaristi, and Unzueta 1994, and the official website of the Basque Government: www.euskadi.net/elecciones.
*The Basque nationalist vote is somewhat reduced owing to the nonparticipation of radical Basque nationalist groups in the elections.

processes encountered in the Basque Country during the Franco years. Finally, the changes that began to take place during the post-Franco period will be analyzed.

The Privatization of Life

As Conrad Lodziak observes, "By privatism we mean social and political withdrawal or abstinence, and coupled with this a central focus on family and domestic life, and/or some form of self-absorption. Then the concept of privatism is sufficiently broad to accommodate all the major cultural trends. Indeed, some concept of privatism does figure in a wide range of debates focused on particular aspects of contemporary culture. Thus discussions on privatism are to be found in the debates addressing the emergence and expansion of the 'affluent working class,' on the gendered public-private divide, on collective and self-identity, on the disappearance of traditional communities, and on the ideology of individualism" (1995, 74–75).[1]

According to Habermas, the process whereby life is privatized is a complex shaped by three basic syndromes. First, there is the civic privatism syndrome. This gradually limits the individual's input in relation to the state. In other words, there is progressively less orientation toward the popular or political will and greater emphasis on the state's output—that is, toward the advantages (benefits and services) that the state provides individuals (Habermas 1975; Held 1989, 92).

The remaining two syndromes are familial and professional privatism. They influence the family and the individual, respectively, in matters of conspicuous consumption and leisure activity and professional careerism and status competition. The close relationship between the first syndrome and the two remaining ones in the production of life's social meaning occurs in the following way: social meaning gradually disappears in the public-political sphere and is reestablished in a fundamental way within the privacy of the family. In turn, interaction becomes parisitical, especially through the mass media.

The beginning of the phenomenon described here as the privatization of life— that is, a complex relationship produced in Western societies among the economic, cultural, and political spheres—can be traced back to the nineteenth century (Turner 1993). However, it was during the early twentieth century that such privatism really became widespread. During this time, private and mass consumption, followed by the emergence of the welfare state (a socialized form of consumption), came to constitute the underlying social plausibility of this complex phenomenon (Turner 1993; Brittan 1977). Bell attributes importance to the appearance, at the beginning of the twentieth century, of three innovations: the assembly production line technique associated with the automobile industry, marketing and publicity, and credit sales (Bell 1976). He also discusses the political consequences of these changes, especially their role in the decline of political ideologies in the 1950s (Bell 1988).

Perhaps Brittan (1977, 24) is right when he argues that everyday life is not a modern invention, but that mass production, and especially mass consumption, would profoundly change its character. Giddens agrees: "Consumption under the domination of the mass markets is essentially a novel phenomenon, which participates directly in processes of the continuous reshaping of the conditions of day-to-day life" (1991, 199).

The automobile, as Bell (1976) asserts, is the prototypical consumer product that changed everyday life, along with the values that fed it. Another significant phenomenon in the same vein was increased access to home ownership. This was facilitated by states through their subsidization of both production and demand, depending on the economic climate (Doling 1993, 72, 80). Domestic appliances transformed domestic life. These goods, along with related benefits such as greater mobility and leisure-time vacations, came to shape the behavior, values, and interests of westerners (Inglehart 1977, 1989). Even matters of identity could be added to this list, although their inclusion would require a long explanation (Lodziak 1995, 48 ff.).[2]

The manipulation of identities thesis (Lodziak 1995, 45–72) advances the interesting idea that consumption involves not only the creation of needs but of conflicts; such conflicts can be resolved only by channeling them into consumption (Lasch 1991b, 518). Bauman argues that "consumption guides the tensions and conflicts which emerge out of political and social subsystems to a sphere where they are symbolically transfigured and blurred" (Bauman 1992, 53). In another work, I discuss the 1960s strategy of channeling the ecological conflict into consumption of the environment, an environment created by a new productive sector and consumed collectively (Pérez-Agote 1976).

The other side of this coin would be the political apathy of the citizenry (Van Deth 1989; Bennet 1986). This growing disinterest in politics is reflected, according to Lodziak, "in the declining membership of traditional political parties and trades unions, together with an increasingly widespread tendency for people to place their energies into private solutions to the problems they face," which implies a "loss of faith in collective and political solutions" (1995, 75). Although many arguments seem to imply belief in a mythological golden age in which most citizens were truly interested in politics, there does appear to have been a loss of faith in political parties as channeling agents of citizens' interests in government (Offe 1990).[3]

Moreover, a number of unelected forces have emerged that, in alliance with governments, make decisions about the most important questions outside the framework of parliaments and political parties: governmental unions and employer commissions, for example, as well as the decisions taken by experts (Offe 1988; Arblaster 1987). One commentator points out that "the genetic engineering revolution is extraparliamentary" (Beck 1994, 47).

Here the discussion will follow the more limited aspect of civil privatism—

limited in the sense of a privatization of life process that implies gradual social separation of the sphere of everyday life from the political one. This takes place because citizens are increasingly more interested in what the state has to offer them (mainly physical benefits and social security) and less so in their own participation in the process of shaping the political will.

According to Habermas:

> This problem is resolved through a system of formal democracy. Genuine participation of citizens in the processes of political will-formation . . . that is, substantive democracy, would bring to consciousness the contradiction between administratively socialized production and the continued private appropriation and use of surplus value. In order to keep this contradiction from being thematicized, then, the administrative system must be sufficiently independent of legitimating will-formation. The arrangement of formal democratic institutions and procedures permits administrative decisions to be made largely independently of specific motives of the citizens. This takes place through a legitimation process that elicits generalized motives—that is, diffuse mass loyalty—but avoids participation. (1975, 36)

The public sphere generally expanded and became more autonomous in the formation of legitimate political will, especially through the electoral process. These (electoral) moments were held at ritually constituted times and arose exclusively out of "generalized motives." Genuine popular participation declined as daily life became less politicized.

Eisenstadt, when discussing the basic characteristics of political modernization, argues that "among specific types of organization which serve to articulate political demands, interest groups, social movements, public opinion, and political parties are especially important. To some extent one might consider the first three of these as components of the final one, that is, of the parties, which are the most articulated forms of modern political organization" (1969, 29).

Parties play a crucial role in framing a differentiated political sphere, channeling political concerns and forces toward it and translating them into more rational terms, that is, terms for defining objectives and developing means with which to achieve them. According to Eisenstadt: "Parties (or other organizations of the same variety) achieve this integration through the development of specific partisan organs, leadership, and a program; through the inclusion within the party itself of diverse specific interests close to the governing interests as well as more general objectives that may be attractive to a wider public; and through the translation of inclusive and diffuse objectives of social movements into more realistic appraisals of specific political goals, problems, and dilemmas, articulated through some partisan organizations and activities or similar channels" (1969, 33).

Through this translation of interests into objectives and means, political parties shape political life in terms of their own internal rationalization and bureaucratization. As such, they gradually distance bureaucratic organization (especially its highest level), not only from the electorate at large but also from their own members. Typically, parties implement an internal process that parallels their stance toward the exterior, one that gradually disassociates day-to-day life from politics. In other words, parties tend to foster a gradual decline in political participation and, at the very least, deprive it of any decision-making power. This means that decisions are made only at the highest bureaucratic levels. Furthermore, this leadership interfaces with different circles of voters and members in selectively framed ways, excepting during prearranged ritualized moments: political rallies and electoral campaigns.

Following Weber's (1978) treatment of open and closed social relations, one might argue that political parties remove themselves from general societal interactions, while the upper level of their internal bureaucracy loses touch with its own rank and file and the wider electorate.

The Politicization of Basque Social Life During the Franco Years

Adapting the preceding theoretical considerations to the Basque case, one might say that political life during the Franco years lacked formal democratic legitimacy (in the sense of the existence of representative electoral rituals) and that the political sphere was not just differentiated from daily life but actually exorcized from it. The main relationship between the political sphere and daily life lay in the confrontation between two forms of violence. As a result, political violence itself occupied a central place in society. This symbolic centrality was connected to everyday life through individuals' personal and collective experience of state violence and through the gradual affective embrace of ETA's violence as the only possible public response to an imposed silence.[4]

As previously stated in the historical treatment of the Franco years,[5] from 1970 onward collective life (essentially through voluntary associations and the cuadrilla) spilled out onto the streets at crucial moments.

The Privatization of Life and Political Rationalization During the Post-Franco Period

Those complex processes associated with the Franco period, the mutual reinforcement (interactive life/ETA violence) and confrontation (between the foregoing binomial and state violence), undoubtedly posed the greatest challenge to political reform in the post-Franco era. The street was a politically important space[6] (important both sui generis and in the "social evaluation" of "popular support" for the legitimacy of a political posture measured by the number of demonstrators) where collective inter-active life competed for political importance with elections. Then too, after Franco's death a number of political organizations came into being under ETA's symbolic um-brella—as expressed through one of its two branches ("military" and "politico-military"). Thus EIA (Euskal Iraultzarako Alderdia; the Basque Revolutionary Party) was born under the guidance of the "politico-military" branch, along with a series of parties that would later become the Herri Batasuna political coalition, under the influence of the "military" wing.

The affective identification with violence by (at that time youthful) sectors of the population led (in regard to the foundation of these political formations) to a com-plex phenomenon. This can be analyzed through consideration of a key moment: the so-called Freedom March of August 1977.[7] This affective identification with ETA did not lead to a massive recruitment of young people in those parties whose previ-ous legitimacy stemmed from armed violence. A large part of the radicalized popula-tion remained at the fringes of this political semi-institutionalization. For them there was only one political objective (independence for the Basque Country along with radical social transformation), but there were several political strategies. Their political and social space was the street; and it was there that they expressed their slogans, the most important being "ETA, Herria zurekin" ("ETA, the people are with you"): ETA was the image of a unified Basque movement—without any divisions or political parties—struggling against social and national oppression. In fact, this radicalized collectivity did not accept the internal division of ETA or division among parties. It claimed to be against political parties—antiparty. This led parties founded under the symbolic warranty of ETA to introduce ambivalence into their discourse. They attempted to differentiate themselves while seeking to capitalize on the sym-bolic capital of a violence that commanded the affective support of important seg-ments of the population.

The general panorama of Basque nationalist politics after the death of Franco in-cluded the PNV, which was quickly reconstituted within the Basque Country, along with the new formations of HB and EE.[8] All of these parties were plagued by impor-tant internal tensions, deriving mainly from the cross-class and populist nature of their ranks. These tensions developed out of the contrast between those forces favor-ing bureaucratic consolidation of the party and society's rich interactive life in gen-eral and those forces peculiar to each political organization and derived as well from different attitudes toward the violence among their base support and membership, and from the range of different ideological postures within each of the parties. Herri Batasuna identified most with the violence and experienced the least tension as a result of organizational bureaucracy. It was perhaps more a movement than political party and reflected radical (especially nationalist) discontent in society. It encom-passed a great diversity of popular movements, and the coalition issued frequent calls for popular mobilization. Taken together, these factors indicate that HB was the least closed organization (in the Weberian sense), since it was difficult to draw a boundary between its political formation and general social interaction. That it had the least bureaucratic tension can also be attributed to its having the lowest predilection for regularized and prioritized objectives, as well as the means to achieve them. Still, there was a degree of tension in HB between the central membership core that did not accept any political programming as long as determined "minimal demands" were not met and those who made sporadic calls for participation in the "Vascongadas's institutions"—that is, in institutions that did not fulfill such demands. Several internal organic debates took place over the issue of participation. HB was, therefore, the political formation that most clearly inherited the "impossible is possible" mechanism, the unitary or antiparty tendencies, and the symbolic capitalization of the violence.

Within Euskadiko Ezkerra there was a declining tension between bureaucratization of the party and identification with the violence. This tension was an inheritance of the symbolic warranty itself—that is, it derived from the politico-military wing of ETA, which advocated political control of violence rather than unbridled militant violence. Eventually, it was transformed into a tension between party and armed group. As the organization gradually distanced itself from its violent origins and moved toward forming a party in the traditional sense, this tension disappeared. However, much of the previous strain was transformed into a subjective internal personal tension among the leaders and members who were personally and affectively differentially committed to the violence. This was the tension between political reason and sentiment already alluded to. Another strain within EE was between the national and social agendas, reflecting the political origins of the members. Of all the groups, then, EE was the most closed and, to a certain extent, most closely approximated a traditional political party.

Finally, the tensions within the PNV essentially developed from its interclass nature. These were accentuated when its activity within the Basque Country grew and, especially, after it became governmental. Other internal tensions were quite strong as well: for example, between the push to form a very centralized and bureaucratized party and the tremendously populist and interactive structure of the PNV, as well as its democratic and decentralized tradition. Moreover, its key position within the Basque Autonomous Government's political structures placed it at the vortex of Basque-Madrid tensions, as well as internal Basque Country ones. This, in turn, encouraged a certain arbitrariness on the part of the leadership in seeking to formulate a common PNV front. Nevertheless, as the key political force between two (Spanish and Basque) symbolic political spaces, the PNV was often politically ambiguous. During the 1980s, it was sometimes impossible for the PNV to take a clear stand on either of the two confrontational forms of violence. It usually criticized both ETA and

Spanish state violence simultaneously and advocated only vague solutions to be achieved through the autonomous political process.

The Post-Franco Intersubjective Framework

As during late Francoism, during the post-Franco period the basic elements of the intersubjective framework were the associative network, the cuadrilla (groups of friends), and poteo (barhopping). These three social phenomena—one might say institutions—were firmly interrelated. Indeed, one could argue they were three aspects of the same complex world. The associative network underpinned the formation of many cuadrillas, many of which in turn constituted the foundation of formal associations. Cuadrillas shared a basic ritual of the group's cyclical maintenance: poteo. And poteo served as the point of contact among different cuadrillas that led to establishment of relations between different associations. This all implied, then, a framework, a complex world that, during the Franco era, acquired an important role in maintaining, comprehensively reproducing, and radicalizing Basque nationalist consciousness. As a result, it became a basic element in the rising affective identification with ETA's violence.

Putnam contends that the term *social capital* was invented at least six times during the twentieth century, "each time to call attention to the ways in which our lives are made more productive by social ties" (2000, 19). Social capital has an individual as well as collective dimension, a private and collective face. The former refers not only to private benefit, understood in an economic sense, but to other aspects of human life that make it more acceptable. However, it is true that such aspects are difficult to quantify. Moreover, social capital implies two collective effects: "frequent interaction among a diverse set of peoples tends to produce a norm of general reciprocity. Civil engagement and social capital entail mutual obligation and responsibility for action" (Putnam 2000, 21). Putnam further distinguishes two types of social capital: "bridging" (or inclusive) and "bonding" (or exclusive). "Bonding social capital is . . . good for 'getting by,' but bridging social capital is crucial for 'getting ahead'" (2000, 23). The first of these is vital (as a means of survival) when the group in question is being dominated.

The complex of intersubjective relations maintained during the Franco years—through the family, the cuadrillas, and the cuadrillas' ritual meeting in the poteo—implied a high level of "bonding social capital." Its political capacity was enormous: the political expressions were, first, social maintenance and even extension, along with political radicalization, of the Basque nationalist symbolic universe; and, second, rising affective support for, and even involvement in, the violence of ETA.

The intensity of this bonding social capital decreased during the post-Franco era, as did its political expressions. However, in the epilogue we will consider how this strong social bonding, along with its marked political expressions, continues to exist, operating more and more fully within the restricted spaces of radical nationalism: territories (associations, bars, and even areas made up of streets or neighborhoods, as well as particular towns) where ritualized intergenerational relations still survive.

We will now consider the declining intensity of bonding social capital and the political effects of the transition to a democratic regime.

Almost certainly, in every Basque urban center during the Franco years, there emerged a central area (more widespread in some places than others) for collective encounters through the ritual act of poteo. This ritual became the symbolic pillar of community in the neighborhoods or towns where it thrived. Evidently not everyone participated in the poteo, nor did everyone who frequented the central area or areas. However, such places became the critical public and political points of reference. With the gradual institutionalization of the democratic regime, this exclusive centrality began to disappear.

It is especially interesting to look at this practice in the Santutxu[9] neighborhood of Bilbao (I-39 to I-49). This is because it was a place of rapid demographic growth within a larger metropolitan area. I-69, a general informant on social life in the neighborhood, described it in the following terms:

> Perhaps before anything else it's important to point out that it's a neighborhood that has grown a lot throughout this time [fifteen years], with a lot of immigrants and, therefore, it's become a very internally segmented neighborhood; consequently, during the Franco era El Carmelo became the center of neighborhood life, [but] it has lost importance owing to the emergence of new centers and places to meet.
>
> Young people are changing the poteo rules; they prefer pubs and disco bars that are springing up in the neighborhood, especially in the new area, significantly reducing any political commitments.
>
> Before, there were many cuadrillas in the central area [El Carmelo], and they were always linked to associative centers. They were people who greatly identified with the neighborhood, with Basque objectives and a sociopolitical response to the system. Poteo was the way through which one belonged to the neighborhood, together with dinners, fiestas, mobilizations, and other cultural activities that were always led by these cuadrillas.
>
> Now [intersubjective relations] have lost their vitality and importance, despite the fact that they still exist. They've lost the cohesive centrality of the associative movement. They have less political impact. The habits associated with free time have changed, losing that overvaluation that poteo had and leading to a greater dispersion. The solidity of relationships has been lost.
>
> Before now those involved in associations led a cuadrilla lifestyle, with very

informal relationships, even within one geographical location [El Carmelo] and daily itinerary. On the other hand, the same cuadrillas mixed together in different associative levels. (1-69)

There was a "central" and "cohesive" area of social life with political influence that constituted a point of reference. In other words, political mobilizations from the 1970s onward (and in general throughout the Franco era) and political consciousness had a *sense of unity* based squarely on a thick network of interpersonal relations. This was confirmed by another general informant about the neighborhood (1-70): "Before, the associative life of the neighborhood was characterized by personal and political interaction and by the unitary nature of its organization and activities."

In the 1980s, there seems to have been a gradual loss of this social centrality, political unity, and a spatial reference in the El Carmelo district of Santutxu neighborhood. However, it should be pointed out that in the other population center chosen for this analysis (Tolosa), such centrality was more dispersed, and that its quality (in being a discrete point of reference) was not as relevant since it encompassed a whole historical population center, that is, a town. Thus, there was less of a tendency in Tolosa for the point of reference to erode during the post-Franco era.

THE CUADRILLA

One could argue that the cuadrilla world was essentially masculine, although there were mixed ones and even mergers between male and female cuadrillas. In the interviews with cuadrilla participants (1-64, 1-65, 1-66, 1-74, 1-75, and 1-76) there were no particular references to women, except when indicating that, as a result of an engagement or marriage, one of their members had withdrawn from the group.

Within cuadrillas of young people the dichotomy between study and work was not an impediment to the functioning of the group. It appears that within those cuadrillas composed of members who both worked and studied, studying was a more prestigious social activity than work (that is, the labor of a young person without much formal education). However, the prestige conferred by greater prosperity compensated for this somewhat: "those who worked had more money and that's prestige" (1-66).

We can now consider the ways in which the cuadrilla evolved during the 1980s. First, increasingly one's intimate personal relations were not restricted to cuadrillas. Cuadrilla members could find people in whom to confide their personal problems, both through other (specific and particular) members of the cuadrilla and outside of it:

Personal problems emerged only at an interindividual level. Such problems never came out when everyone was together. (1-64)

With time, everyone began to experience more personal individual problems; it was a topic of conversation among some members, but not among everyone. (1-65)

Personal problems didn't come out; nobody dared speak about them, although they wanted to. When we spoke of such things it was after a fiesta when a few of us remained. (1-66)

Within cuadrillas of young people under twenty-five years of age in the 1980s, a relative lack of interest in transcendental collective and political values was increasingly apparent. Cuadrilla members became more interested in personalized values and less in a common political ideology. As many members sought more intimacy, group numbers dwindled. Furthermore, political ideology as a foundational and maintenance mechanism of the group fell out of use. Perhaps one should ask whether, in fact, cuadrillas were declining as the basic form of peer group formation, possibly being displaced by smaller circles of friends with less public presence. In general, one can say that the frequency of cuadrilla relations fell. As will be seen, poteo declined considerably on working days. Many cuadrillas met only on the weekend (1-64, 1-65, and 1-66).

We might now outline a series of five features of the evolution of cuadrillas in the 1980s.

First, there was a strong decline in the frequency of cuadrilla relations, especially in the basic group maintenance ritual, the poteo. "The cuadrilla has disappeared in many towns" (1-45). Although this statement might seem a bit hyperbolic, it does indicate a decline in the frequency of cuadrilla interaction.

Second, the greatest decline took place in intermediate age groups, that is, within age groups that underwent the greatest political radicalism in the 1980s: "The cuadrilla is now for those up to twenty-four. A [cuadrilla] of over twenty-four-year-olds doesn't exist any more. The ones who get married or, for whatever reason, split it up. . . . You'll see people between forty and sixty, and between seventeen and twenty-two, doing poteo. You don't see anyone in between those ages any more, although there are exceptions" (1-45).

Third, there was a progressive privatization of cuadrillas, in the sense of a decline in relations among them. Partly this was a separation between cuadrillas of the young and old. This was the case in Santutxu for cuadrillas in general. In Tolosa, 1-64 observed that from 1975–76 onward there was a gradual distancing among cuadrillas of those with differing political views, as well as those of different ages (1-64). The decline in relations also occurred because of decreasing communication among young people's cuadrillas—"there's a lack of connection between cuadrillas, like there was before; young people are scattered all over the place" (1-74))—and between cuadrillas in general for political reasons: "People don't have as good a time as before during the poteo. There used to be more interchange. Before, there were more cuadrillas that were more like friends and now there aren't, because one person is HB and another is EE. During the Franco era everyone was together against him" (1-68).

The progressive privatization also occurred in the sense of a general loss of external or political projection by the cuadrilla. In Santutxu, I-74 stated that the *jatorra*[10] cuadrillas that had been organizing events for fifteen or twenty years continued with the daily poteo but didn't do anything now in the neighborhood. In Tolosa, attention was drawn to the fact that the cuadrilla's only visible presence came during the carnival fiestas[11] (I-60, I-64, and I-65).

Another important indication of the declining political function of the cuadrilla has to do with the so-called pro-amnesty (for convicted ETA operatives) committees—one of the most characteristic institutions in the relationship between the intersubjective framework and radical Basque nationalist politics. The committees were basically articulated through family and cuadrilla relationships. However, as one informant pointed out: "[The cuadrilla] still continues to directly control the *pelas*[12] [for the prisoners] in a few places. However, this is less and less typical given that, as the committee has taken over this role, the cuadrilla as a source of aid for the prisoners has disappeared. There have been cases of cuadrillas forming a part of the committees, but these have not been widespread. What's happened is that, although cuadrillas were very important and even at the heart of founding the committees, they later lost their importance (I-51).

Fourth, there are two observations to make about the political direction of cuadrillas: those concerning relations between parties and cuadrillas and those concerning the political homogeneity of the cuadrillas.

In the first instance, the general traditional world of cuadrillas seems to have been related to some specific political ideologies and, especially, with specific political parties. Of course, it was also related to the Basque nationalist world and to the two most clearly nationalist parties: the PNV and HB.

In Tolosa, I-64 observed that each party, and especially PNV and HB, "has at least one typical cuadrilla" and that "those who take part most in cuadrillas are those of PNV," while "HB cuadrillas are incredibly closed." I-67 confirmed the latter observation: "cuadrillas are politically differentiated, most obviously those of HB. These don't mix very much, but keep their distance." As for EE, commenting on his party's incapacity to call meetings in the town, the EE informant in Tolosa himself said that "before, there were cuadrillas of members and they organized a meeting more easily," and that "EE people" move around "as individuals, not as a party."

Things were the same in Santutxu in that the cuadrilla structured plausibility; it was a way of maintaining the symbolic nationalist universe (I-74).

In both Santutxu and Tolosa, adult cuadrillas were generally more politically homogeneous and more politicized than their younger counterparts (I-64, I-67, I-76, I-77, I-78, and I-45).

With the emergence of political parties and the need to politically situate oneself (in terms of sympathy or membership), many new tensions developed that led to divisions among the cuadrillas. This rupture of a relative unanimity—anti-Franco in general and Basque nationalist in particular—led to an ideological splintering among these groups of friends. This phenomenon was clearly observed by the owners of two obligatory bars on the poteo route of Tolosa: "quite a violent split began" among the cuadrillas after Franco's death and with the emergence of political parties; according to this informant, "before" nobody spoke because people were "afraid to speak"; then people started to talk and with this came the splitting up of many cuadrillas. "Now anything political was avoided" (1-67). 1-68 corroborated this political fragmentation of the cuadrilla, illustrating it with a (typical) story of the collapse of friendship when one person joined HB and the other EE. This political division was evidently at the heart of what, in an old militarist sense, was termed the "abertzale [patriot] Left," a term that ideologically described a large part of the most politically radicalized population. In fact, the greatest problems regarding new definitions (in terms of specific political organizations) were faced by those individuals who shared a left-wing nationalist outlook. From 1980 onward, a certain dedramatization took place with the decline in the social virulence associated with politics.

1-77, the owner of a bar in Santutxu, and therefore a privileged observer of cuadrillas during the poteo ritual, delineated the changes in this ritual's communicative content:

> Before, the basic topics, in order, were: politics, soccer, the future and what was going to happen or how it was going to turn out, problems in the neighborhood, etc. Now, also in order: Athletic [the Bilbao soccer team], soccer, the cinema and shows, politics in general [especially among young people and from a left-wing perspective], unemployment and personal problems, [and] a lot less about problems in the neighborhood.
>
> There aren't usually any arguments, but before there was more debate, especially of a political kind.

One can conclude that young people spoke more about personal problems and unemployment than they did about political matters; that they discussed politics less than older people; that when they did broach politics they were more interested in the issue of peace and alternative movements and in politics in general (in a broader and less personal way); and that such personal aspects of politics emerged again through the specific experience of repression.

As for the older cuadrillas: members spoke less about politics than before, but still more than young people; as with young people, when they did speak about politics it was in a wider and less personal sense than before; the recrudescence of such personal aspects and feelings of political unanimity emerged in direct relation to specific experiences of repression; and, again in the same way as with young people, the economic crisis and unemployment came to occupy a central place in their conversations.[13]

A fifth and final feature of the cuadrilla's evolution in the 1980s consists of a series of differences between younger and older cuadrillas, identified through the observations of some informants:

Generally speaking, and by way of introduction, one might argue that both the numbers and size of cuadrillas fell. Similarly, poteo (as a cuadrilla ritual) also declined. However, these declines did not affect cuadrillas of the young and old in the same way, thereby highlighting the differences between them:

> What stands out is the individualism of people. Cuadrillas are disappearing, getting smaller and smaller all the time. The biggest change is that people follow more and more their own tastes and think more and more about themselves.
>
> You see more political, and all kinds of, pluralism; people can give their opinion in a better way; they judge things more and have more criteria.
>
> Before, cuadrillas of up to thirty people used to come here and now they're usually about four or five people; the cuadrillas formed by young people now are of the smaller kind. (I-74)

People now needed greater cultural commonality to speak about various subjects more deeply. As a result, the cuadrillas' numbers fell and the topics of conversation changed (I-77).

Cuadrillas of older people were bigger (I-76); more unified by politics (I-76); more internally homogeneous and divided among themselves by politics (I-76, I-77, and I-78); and had a greater external influence (I-79). Those of younger people were smaller (I-76, I-77, and I-78) and had less external influence (I-79).

It also appears that adult cuadrillas and those made up younger people were structured in different ways: the former were more formalized and hierarchical, the latter more egalitarian and based on friendship relations. The younger cuadrillas were also more intimate and fostered more open debate among their members. As has already been pointed out, they tended to be more like "groups of friends" than cuadrillas in the more traditional sense:

> Within cuadrillas, above all the large and older ones, there was and is an implicit hierarchy of prestige, of weight, that controls the rest; it pressures them into going here and there, into thinking one way, etc. Above all, in those cuadrillas composed of forty-year-olds there's an alienation: a few of them decided the route, the topic of conversation, the schedule, etc.; there was more internal control and censorship, more ritual and permanence; they were more obliged to keep up the show.
>
> Now it doesn't happen like that: young people are more independent; the cuadrillas are more egalitarian and have more intimate and friendly relations. There's less ritual and also less stability and permanence.
>
> The older cuadrillas come nearly every day, although they're more like groups of friends now.

Young people argue more, while the older ones control themselves more and argue much less.

Bars of the same area are usually labeled, in such a way that there are some cuadrillas that select bars [some do and others don't] mainly for political reasons.

You see in this, and in other things, that here a way of being Basque has been created and this has been imposed by the PNV cuadrillas.

However, the young people are more open and give less importance to these things, although they also make choices. (I-77)

For those of the new generation, defined here as those below the age of twenty-four or twenty-five, the cuadrilla met partially, but certainly not entirely, their needs for interpersonal communication. The cuadrilla world was created through a series of values that might be termed transcendental (and especially political), through communicative raw material shaped principally by politics and violence, and through both an individual and collective dimension. As such, members turned into political instigators and actors, and personal or intimate problems did not arise within the cuadrilla as such. The new generation adopted a dual direction in regard to its values, losing interest in politics and religion as "sacred canopies" but reintegrating into these a sense of a social option, as a kind of search for community through involvement in a small group. This dual direction was a kind of hedonism related to free time and mass consumption, but also a heightened evaluation of a life laden with values (such as friendship, intimacy, and communication) that called for this small group to be maintained. The cuadrilla, despite any political or social interest it may have fostered, did not fulfill the need for more personalized interrelations.

THE POTEO

Since the poteo was the principal daily ritual through which the cuadrilla was maintained, one could argue that the previously mentioned changes in the world of the cuadrilla would have profound effects for this custom: the declining importance of political subjects and a general change in the nature of communicative content; a decline in communication among different cuadrillas and especially the separation between younger and older people; and the diminishing size of cuadrillas generally, especially those of the young. Still, the specific changes that took place in the poteo ritual should be outlined.

First, the frequency of actually doing poteo decreased. In Santutxu, the specialist informants (bar owners) observed a general decline: "the frequency of poteo has fallen" (I-77); "the txikiteo [poteo] custom has declined" (I-78). In Tolosa, the poteo custom transformed into a more specifically weekend ritual when the cuadrillas would get together (I-64, I-65, and I-66). This was confirmed by the two informants who were bar owners. They also differentiated (in economic terms) between the beginning and the end of the month (I-67 and I-68).

As for how the poteo was done, 1-68 established a significant difference between older and younger people: the former did more poteo, in that they visited between twenty and twenty-five bars during the route, and they spoke less; the younger people visited fewer bars (between eight and ten) and spoke more (1-68).

Reflecting the then current generational "lack of connection," there was a hesitancy on the part of older people to enter places labeled as "for young people" and vice versa (1-78).

In terms of the kind of drinks ordered, all four specialized informants (bar owners) agreed completely that just as the older people drank wine exclusively, the younger the customers, the more varied their consumption: *zuritos*[14] and even sodas. On weekends, just as the poteo shifted to more "urban" areas, so these young people drank more cocktails (rum and coke, for example) (1-67, 1-68, 1-77, and 1-78). According to 1-77, drinking habits were clearly related to age differences: those in their forties drank only wine; those between twenty and thirty drank both wine and other drinks. I-79, to differentiate cuadrillas of over or under twenty-five years of age, said of the latter: "those of today are less stable, more disintegrated, more sporadic, etc., and they don't even drink wine" (1-79).

Finally, according to our informants in both Tolosa and Santutxu, the cuadrillas followed a set itinerary; that is, they had fixed routes and hours (1-67, 1-68, and 1-70). Since cuadrillas became politically fragmented around the time of the appearance of political parties, both the routes and the bars frequented were increasingly differentiated politically (1-70 and 1-77).

THE DECLINE OF IMPLICIT POLITICAL FUNCTIONS

As is clear from the preceding sections, politics gradually lost influence within the intersubjective framework, with the framework itself losing importance. Remember that politics and violence made up the basic communicative content within the intersubjective world during the Franco years, both before 1970 (a period described here as having a collectively clandestine nature) and after this date. It was precisely after 1970 that this same intersubjective world burst out on to the streets and was maintained through popular mobilizations whose base of support was the intersubjective framework.[15] During the Franco era this framework had a number of implicitly political functions: in brief, socialization functions within the Basque nationalist symbolic universe; functions of maintenance and political radicalization within this same universe; and, subsequently, political mobilization.

As has been observed in this chapter, during the 1980s politics lost this power within the intersubjective framework, a loss reflected in a number of ways:

1. The intersubjective social framework's centrality faded, in the sense that it declined as *the* exponent of social and political life for those individuals of a certain social nucleus (towns or neighborhoods) and as, therefore, a point of reference.

2. The numbers and size of cuadrillas declined, particularly among the youth.

3. Young people searched for more personalized relationships that were less influenced by politics. They tended to form intimate groups of friends more than cuadrillas.

4. Relations within the young cuadrillas became less hierarchical and formalized (combined with a greater possibility to express and debate subjects) and, of course, less politicized.

5. Cuadrilla life tended to become privatized; there was a decline in the relations among cuadrillas; and they lost their external and political projections.

6. At the time of the distancing of the political from the social (1980) and beyond, the appearance of political parties coincided with a decline in the cuadrillas' importance. The older groups were, in all respects, more politically homogeneous, while those of the younger people were more plural or, more accurately, less focused on and interested in politics.

7. Politics declined in importance as communicative content; there was relative growth in major-issue politics, experienced through the mass media, in relation to personal politics; and personal politics grew in importance during moments of state repression.

8. Poteo frequency declined, above all among the most politically radical generation, and routes became politically differentiated.

9. The importance of the associative world declined quantitatively (which will be discussed in the following section).

It is important to underscore that the intersubjective framework lost its social importance, as did politics within it. However, if political radicalism survived and yet was not expressed daily through the intersubjective space owing to the rise of social control, should there not have been a return to clandestine activity by the most radical nationalist sectors? This question would be more valid if one looked at the 1990s in relation to the 1980s.

A politico-rational discourse would be imposed on the attitudinal continuum, and, as will be seen in the epilogue, this provoked a strong ideological split—not only in the Basque Country in general, but within the Basque nationalist world in particular—between those who accepted and those who did not accept the violence of ETA.

There was a general decline in individual political activity and a relative lack of interest in politics (in the personal or day-to-day sense of the Franco era). Furthermore, there was a growing lack of interest in politics, along with declining political and associative activity in general, among people under twenty-five (in the 1980s)—the new generation (I-65, I-66, I-68, I-70, I-74, I-75, I-76, I-77, and I-79).[16]

Political organizations also began to assume increased control of the associative world, possibly channeling some specific interests. However, whatever the case, they removed individuals from unitary participation through the intersubjective world generally and the associative world in particular (1-59, 1-70, 1-71, and in general from 1-59 to 1-79).

The Associative Framework in the Post-Franco Period

Our information about the associative world was principally obtained through eight individual and insightful interviews (1-51 to 1-58) with leaders in a number of different social fields.

The associations of greatest interest to this study were those believed to have formed central mechanisms in the reproduction of the nationalist consciousness during the Franco years—plus the pro-amnesty committees or councils, which, logically, did not exist during the bleakest years of the dictatorship. These latter groups were included because they constituted a very significant kind of associative organization in the great political ferment achieved through the intersubjective framework during the initial post-Franco years.

Thus the focus here is not on the new types of association that emerged during the last years of Franco and that continue to prosper, such as those made up of ecologists, anti-military activists, feminists, and so on. Such groups are not representative. That is, they cannot be viewed as heirs of a logic and a process associated with the particular social mechanisms of reproducing Basque nationalist consciousness during the Franco years. Other associations that during the Franco years spearheaded the citizens' movement, namely those associated with urban social conflict, have not been analyzed either. In 1-52, one can observe the total, or near total, loss of an individual's social activism.

Within this analysis of different kinds of associations, five common features emerged. Indeed, one might consider them the general characteristics or tendencies of the process of change in the associative world during the 1980s. Each will be considered below.

DECLINING STRENGTH AND RELEVANCE

There was a progressive decline in the strength and relevance of the associative world. This is evident in quantitative terms; that is, there was a gradual decline, within each realm, of the number of associations. In a qualitative sense, there was a gradual decline in the participation, that is, commitment, of persons in the associative world.

In the case of religious associations, those more or less connected to the church, 1-53 clearly differentiated between popular and doctrinal communities, with the former (which flourished especially after the Second Vatican Council) being more directed toward a sociopolitical commitment; while the latter (which flourished after the death of Franco) were more spiritual. Popular collectivities stagnated during the 1980s, while the doctrinal ones, which were more numerous and had increased during the 1970s, disappeared altogether during the 1990s. I-54 seemed to have a slightly more optimistic outlook about the more spiritual communities in the 1980s: "They grew without any problem: they started in sixty-five and experienced a big increase, especially from the democratic transition onward, even achieving official recognition and aid" (I-54).

The collectivities that were more associated with political and social commitment grew in the 1960s as platforms favoring both ecclesiastical protest and renovation, as well as political action. From the beginning of the transition onward, however, there was a gradual abandonment of this political activism.

In the case of folkloric associations, and in particular those associated with dancing, one might point to a decline in the number of groups. However, this was possibly slightly offset by the creation, in many municipalities, of dance groups formed by the respective city halls. There was also a decline in the number of members of these groups. With the legalization of political parties, "people began to disappear from groups, and the impression of those of us who continued in this mess was that they left us in the lurch." Between 1975 and 1980 there was symbolic intensity when "folk shows were performed all over the place," but later it became "too much" and the number of fiestas the groups attended fell. More importantly, there was also a sharp decline in the social life of these groups (I-55).

The situation of the "hiking clubs" in the 1980s was captured perfectly by I-57:

> The current situation of the hiking clubs is relatively good. It seems like after a period of decline, people want to go hiking again. If this is true, and it seems as if excursions have grown during the last few years, the same thing hasn't happened with the clubs. New members only trickle in. People go hiking more, but they don't join hiking clubs.
>
> Within the clubs you can see a certain evolution. Before, the clubs organized a lot of hikers' bus excursions and the members took part. Today the excursions are quite spaced out and fewer people come. People prefer to use their cars, because they say that it gives them more independence. This is also because there are certain types of people who do more high-risk hiking and, of course, the clubs can't organize large-scale excursions to those mountains.

The youth movement in the 1980s, in one informant's opinion, was "almost nonexistent" (I-56). The movement more or less favoring Basque political autonomy and that connected with neighborhood associations all but disappeared. That tied to the church was greatly weakened in general, although it did have a certain potential (as was observed earlier in this section): namely, of a doctrinal or spiritual kind belonging to the post-Franco period but not typical of the previous era:

At the moment, youth associational movements are quite weak. Here there are no places to meet that aren't connected to consumption. Autonomous associational movements, which existed during Franco's time, have practically disappeared. Thus the network of youth clubs has disappeared, [as have those] youth associational movements dependent on neighborhood associations. There only remains a certain kind of associational movement tied to the church and whose activity is more for "catechumenical [doctrinal] people" than for young people. Furthermore, this kind of young peoples' world lacks internal consistency and is very ideologically biased. If, during Franco's time, the church sheltered an inclusive kind of associational movement, nowadays it concentrates more and more on its [own] strength, to the point of converting these groups into exclusive forms. Only in those places where there's still a nice young priest are there youth associations, although they're very weak. (1-56)

The scout movement (largely tied to the church) was very difficult to modernize. This was obvious from the observations of 1-56, who contended that it was in clear decline:

Another of the associational forms that still operates is the scout movement. These kinds of associations are directed, mostly, at children rather than adolescents. At the same time, the scout movement maintains very close relations with the church. A goodly number of the places they use belong to the church. However, even these forms are in decline, having lost a great deal of their strength. (1-56)

During the 1980s, political parties did not manage to develop youth associations that might have replaced the previous groups. Only the PNV (with EGI) and HB (with Jarrai) achieved some kind of organization, however rare:

Another form of association that exists, although also with little importance, is the political one. With the exception of the PNV's youth organization [EGI] and the scant importance of Jarrai [KAS], the remaining political organizations lack political associations for young people. Even those two groups mentioned have a scarce presence in the adolescents' world. Even if EGI claims to have 1,500 members, its dynamism is practically zero, except in some *batzokis* [PNV centers], and its general presence is rare. The Jarrai case is similar, although no one knows the number of members they have; their only presence appears to be in the schools of some radicalized areas. (1-56)

While one might harbor reservations about this generalization, there did seem to be a greater decrease of youth associative groups in urban areas than in areas of lower population concentration. 1-56 pointed out that this was more the case in

Bizkaia, with Greater Bilbao's intense urbanization, than in Gipuzkoa, whose population concentration is more multipolar:

> It seems like the geographical factor, an unequal urban organization, has significantly influenced this associative instability. Thus, for example, while in Bizkaia the crisis appears to be very acute, in Gipuzkoa there are centers where associative groups are still being developed in vigorous fashion [the Gohierri, Upper Deba, and so on]. This seems to be due to the urban conditions, which in some cases atomize the young people, while in others allow the establishment of interpersonal relations. Medium- and small-scale populations more easily allow the maintenance of a certain associative network. (1-56)

In regard to the pro-amnesty committees, 1-51 pointed out a pattern of decline at the end of the 1980s. Generally speaking, these committees existed in population centers with prisoners. At that time, one could even say there were more committees than before. However, fewer individuals took part in them and, ultimately, there was an important reduction in both participation and militancy:

> There are pro-amnesty committees in every town in the Basque Country, but especially in those places where there are prisoners. There's a direct relation between those towns and neighborhoods where there are prisoners or refugees and the existence of these committees.
>
> The provinces that have the most committees are Bizkaia and Gipuzkoa. Both have fifty committees. Navarre has fifteen committees and Araba only six. Logically, this is closely related to the place of origin of the prisoners and exiles.
>
> Nowadays, there are more amnesty committees than before, but there are fewer people. While the number of people forming the committee used to oscillate between eleven and twenty odd, today it is between seven and eleven people. There is unquestionably less involvement nowadays, and the importance of the committees has declined. If, during the initial years of the transition, the committee was a cohesive body that integrated people from all backgrounds and, moreover, posited an alternative to the incarceration of prisoners and flight of refugees, nowadays this has substantially changed. The reasons for this change are varied and related to the change in objective conditions in the Basque Country. Among those that stand out, one might mention the division within the opposition. This division has come about between those who accepted the reform, the *reformistas*, and those who opted for a break [with the system]. (1-51)

In examining the internal structure of both these committees and the intersubjective framework in general, it is interesting that cuadrillas composed of friends of prisoners disappeared as central elements in these committees:

As regards the cuadrilla, it still continues to directly control the pelas [money for the prisoners] in a few places. However, this is less and less typical given that, as the committee has taken over this role, the cuadrilla as a focus of prisoners' aid has disappeared. There have been cases of cuadrillas forming a part of the committees, but this has not been widespread. What has happened is that, although cuadrillas were very important and even at the heart of founding the committees, they later lost their importance. (1-51)

DECLINE IN POLITICAL PROJECTION

One dedicated political activist lamented and summed up the depoliticization of the associative and intersubjective world as follows: "I was almost one of the founders of ETA, and, at the time, one of our functions was to create hiking associations and things like that. Groups had a political function; it was thought out, consciously organized" (1-37).

The implicit, even hidden and concealed, functions of the intersubjective framework in general and the associative world in particular during the Franco years have already been discussed: namely, the socialization and maintenance of a form of political consciousness and, later, a political mobilization of the populace. During the Franco years, one witnessed the progressive growth of the associative world's political influence. However, with the legalization of political parties in the post-Franco era, there was a gradual depoliticization of this associative world. This depoliticization could be viewed as a simple channeling of citizens' political concerns through the political parties, and as a reflection, on the one hand, of citizens' declining interest in personal politics and, on the other, of their relatively renewed fascination (as spectators) with a differentiated political scenario, along with its creation.

Let us consider what happened in each of the previously examined associative sectors in order to establish the meaning of this depoliticization in terms of the so-called political rationalization.

In the case of religious associations that were more or less tied to the church, the decline in political influence can be seen from a number of viewpoints. First, the situation changed from domination by popular collectivities to domination by catechumenical ones. The latter were more spiritual and based less on social or political commitment (1-53). Second, interest in social and political issues gradually declined among the popular collectivities, reflected in a progressive drift toward more specific problems (1-53). Third, within the popular collectivities there was even a gradual shift from political commitment to a more individualized one (1-53 and 1-54). 1-54, asked about the function of religious communities, replied in terms of "before and now": "Before: (1) From an internal or ecclesiastical point of view, [there was] religious ideological renovation and a protest against the official church. (2) From an external or social point of view, [there was] sociopolitical change and in response to the needs of

Basque society. Now: the place, meaning and identification of the individual [is focused] in contemporary society" (1-54).

Within dance groups there was a clear diminishment of their hidden political function and a widespread lack of interest among political parties in these associations.

> Dance groups have passed through an evolution. Most of them were created in the sixties. You danced out of patriotism; you didn't understand that it was just another facet. Before, everyone was a nationalist. We danced because it was our way of being patriotic. Everything was a question of nationalist politics. Everyone who had some degree of restlessness spent some time in the groups. These [groups] brought together many young people. In many groups people started to get involved politically. I remember in 1971, when the police arrested twenty-four people on the left bank [of Bilbao], accusing them of belonging to ETA's cultural front. Well, the twenty-four of them were members of dance groups. In fact, there was a [dance] group that almost disappeared and almost all its members were arrested in the raid. With this I want to explain to you that before the groups were political; people came to be patriotic and that was the most important thing; dance was a cover.
>
> I often say that the groups were a clandestine batzoki [PNV center]. Then when the era of legalizing parties came along, people began to disappear from groups and the impression that those of us who continued in this mess had was that they left us in the lurch. They became less interested in folklore and dance and went to the batzokis or just got involved in party activities.
>
> With this attitude, they revealed that they weren't too interested in dance groups.
>
> Of course, before, they used to come to have a snack or a few drinks and it was a way of being patriotic. Now they've moved to the batzokis and they don't show up, at least much, in the groups.
>
> Nor do the parties show any special interest in capitalizing on the experience of these groups. There might be people who, at an individual level, are members of parties. Of the groups that I know, they are perhaps mostly PNV people. But, just because of this, we can't say that this group has one or another kind of orientation. I suppose that this is also the case because neither is the PNV interested. In fact, many batzokis have created their own dance groups. (1-55)

The capacity to mobilize people, through both the dance groups and their coordinating institutions, also decreased, as did groups' strictly political dimension. This political dimension had, of course, emerged because of the political prohibition on performing Basque dances in public during the initial years of the Franco regime: "Possibly, in comparison with previous years, the patriotic element has been lost, but now everything is more authentic. They get involved because they're interested in dance; they don't use it as a screen in order to do other things" (1-55).

Hiking groups, too, lost their previously hidden political function and gradually became depoliticized:

> Before democracy came, many people used to go hiking, and, not only did they enjoy this activity, they used to speak about politics and many other things that they could not discuss in other circumstances. It always seemed to me that, occasionally, going to these mountains became a kind of nationalist school. One often went in a group and sang songs in Euskara, even circulating propaganda. Hikes used to be patriotic. This happened a lot. You must realize that it was very difficult to control such activities in the mountains.
>
> After Franco died, there was a certain decline among the clubs. The appearance of democracy also influenced this, but not too much. In the beginning, it provoked a degree of apathy among some sectors, but afterward they began to function again. Today you must also appreciate that the clubs aren't politicized, and that you don't need to go hiking to find a safe place to speak about politics. Today people go hiking and nothing else. This has also brought with it more freedom. (I-57)

In youth associational groups in general, there was a move toward clearer and fewer political objectives. As a result, the groups lost their socializing capacity in the political arena and, of course, a mobilizing capacity.

> The most evident consequence [of democracy] has been the demobilization of young people. They've disappeared from the streets and shut themselves up at home. There's also exclusion. Before, the associations didn't make distinctions; everyone participated in them; they were inclusive. Now, however, the associations are more privatized; they only take in certain kinds of people and their objectives are clearer.
>
> The generational change has mainly had repercussions in the previously mentioned aspects. There's been a change from collective options to individual solutions. Young people's lives are more privatized, more oriented toward consumption, [and] with fewer possibilities to do something. (I-56)

With the pro-amnesty committees, it was not a matter (as in the previous cases) of associative depoliticization. These associations had an obvious political dimension. However, the committees lost a great deal of their cohesive and mobilizing strength. Furthermore, they gradually lost touch with political parties, excepting HB and (to a lesser extent) the extrainstitutional extreme Left (I-51).

RELATIVE REFUNCTIONALIZATION

As a logical companion to its loss of political meaning, the associative world also underwent refunctionalization. Given the tremendous diversity of associations, this refunctionalization assumed different forms. Some associations simply adopted the explicit functions and objectives that had veiled their former clandestine activities. Others adopted new functions. However, generally speaking, a transformation took place from a politicized associative world of diffuse, hidden functions to a less politicized one in which functions were more explicit and objectives more specific. Moreover, there was a transformation from an associative world of multiple appearances that masked quite similar diffuse functions (in the sense of a complexity of seemingly different, yet completely interrelated, groups) to one with a plurality of groups with fewer connections.

Still, this diversified associative panorama did retain remnants of characteristics linked to maintenance of the Basque symbolic universe, although often divested of any political content. That is, there were still groups that defined themselves as Basque and whose members manifested a more cultural or ethnic sense of belonging than a political one. In many cases, there was a complete assumption of Basque collective identity and a relinquishing of any direct political dimension. In these instances, the social definition of all things Basque ceased being political and became more cultural (language, culture, folklore, and even a love of hiking). This reflected the organizational complexity of differential features that structured this collective identity consciousness, while articulating at different essentialist levels elements that had originated in different historical eras.

In the case of religious associations and the church, there is the already mentioned tendency toward less social and political commitment and greater spirituality—within a general stagnation of this associative sector. This was part of a general process of refunctionalization of religion in the West, characterized by the withdrawal of religion from the public sphere and its increasing refuge in various levels of private sociality and also by the gradual loss of importance, also within the private sphere, of church-oriented religion, along with the appearance of a phenomenon categorized by Luckmann as "invisible religion" (1967).

Regarding this second characteristic, the growth in importance of spiritual associations has been described here in connection with the other popular collectivities and their gradual relinquishing of all political involvement. To this might be added the very ingrained primary group nature of all of these kinds of associative groupings.

In the folkloric associations there was a refunctionalization in the strictest sense of the word. The dance groups gradually recovered their singular and explicit functional dimension:

> Now people only come to dance: they're more authentic. They come because they're interested in dancing. It is true that most of the people who are in groups either have nationalist sympathies or their families are nationalist. But now you don't need dance groups to be political. That form of being patriotic has been lost; yet, exactly because of this, Basquism has triumphed. Because now you realize that dance and folklore in general form part of the essential qualities

of the Basque Country, and you can serve it in many ways. One realizes that folklore is one branch of being Basque. It's profoundly Basque. (I-55)

Therefore, a refunctionalization paralleled the loss of an overtly political function. This allowed for the possibility of defining *all things Basque* (the social image of differentiating) outside the *political* realm and through different cultural elements seen to be *objective* and *essential* by the actors. I-55 counterpoised *patriotism*, as a political definition of all things Basque, with *Basquism* as a cultural definition, in terms of *essence*. Politics detracted from all things Basque, in the sense that (and here collective memory is operative) in those moments when Basque culture was politically persecuted any affective adherence toward all things Basque (folklore, language, and so on) was politically positive. The positive evaluation of all things Basque was politically sufficient during times when such things were officially prohibited. When it was once again possible to express publicly all things Basque, however, for those people that functionally manipulated the symbols of difference (in this case, dance) affective discursive adhesion was no longer enough; it became necessary to participate in the construction and reconstruction of objectively differentiating ethnic elements in order to guarantee their survival and thereby guarantee the survival of the identity.

For these reasons, those people described above as the functional manipulators of symbols of differentiating elements (those actors who worked daily on their reproduction) developed an alternative critical reality to that of political actors and institutions. As guarantors of these differential elements, they possessed very clear criteria for evaluating the behavior of political actors, political parties, and institutions. This has already been discussed in regard to the linguistic world, where those actors that professionally worked in it on a day-to-day basis came to evaluate politics through linguistic criteria. In reference to dance groups, one informant continually made complaints and criticized. He denounced the lack of interest from the political parties, the complete absence of relations with the Spanish central government, and a dearth of support from the Basque government (which he approached unsuccessfully for a subsidy on multiple occasions). To the litany, he added a general complaint about the Basque Country's administration, as well as a narrower one about its poor municipal governments (I-55).

Corresponding to all this was a generally positive attitude toward the functional change, toward refunctionalization. Those who remained in groups accepted the change and evaluated it in positive terms. In fact, they were so optimistic that they regarded it as a strategy for future greater advances, in the sense of developing additional pedagogical functions and publicizing their *social worth*. In other words, they proposed reaching out to society as a whole for support to sustain differentiating essential *Basque cultural elements* (I-55).

It is worth adding that these groups continued to maintain the symbolic Basque nationalist universe, and with the same communal or collective orientation they had always had: "People, in the beginning, join groups through their parents. These tell them that they must go and they go. Later, from the age of fourteen onward, they come because they like to dance; dancing appeals to them. Also because they like the atmosphere; they meet people [and] even form cuadrillas" (1-55).

The emerging tendencies in hiking groups seemed quite similar to those of the dance groups. Here, also, there was refunctionalization in the strictest sense of the term:

> This [hiking] also happened before, but people were more politicized and often the club was too; now people are looking more for recreation, to engage in an activity that they like. Politically speaking, they lived in a more relaxed environment and this is noticeable in the club. Today they come, mostly, to go hiking.
>
> Even though the people who run the club might be members [of a party] or have political sympathies, normally this isn't reflected in the club; I already told you that today the club only goes hiking and the other thing is left to other occasions. (1-57)

There was also in hiking groups, although logically to a lesser extent than in dance groups, a certain essentializing of the activity that made up its explicit and, at the time, complete function. An image of the *mountain* emerged, of *climbing the mountain* as something connected (although in a weaker or less essentialist sense than that of dancing) to a way of being Basque, to all things Basque: "One must realize that in the Basque Country there's always been a great interest in hiking. It seems to be something inseparable from the Basque people, who live surrounded by mountains" (1-57).

Nor was the communal dimension lost:

> People go to the club because they like to have an activity and here they find people with the same interests. The club gives you an opportunity to know other people, organize activities, etc. Perhaps this is the most important thing; people find an atmosphere that they share with others; they have a good time, meet friends.
>
> You normally start hiking either with your family or with your cuadrilla. The relationship between hiking and the cuadrilla is very deep. Hiking created the cuadrilla. (1-57)

Finally, as was the case with dance groups, there was a relatively optimistic outlook and positive evaluation of the associative refunctionalization of the hiking groups. Further, and complementary to this phenomenon, there emerged what we have termed, in regard to dance groups, overfunctionalization. This refers to the claim by these groups that they contributed something *essential* (in this case to the currently fashionable environmentalism) to the broad process of socializing Basque society in general:

Future perspectives are good. The clubs must move toward an integrating form of hiking; in other words, you have to teach people not only to hike in the mountains but to know them; you must do more ecological work. For this you must go to the schools and teach the kids about the mountains, what they mean, and so forth.

You've also got to make it possible, through courses, for people to learn hiking techniques and broaden their ecological knowledge about the matter. Of course, this is along with excursions and so on, which have been typical in the clubs. (1-57)

In the case of youth associations, there were those, in the 1980s, whose function, just as during the Franco years, was essentially a general socializing of young people with an important political dimension. Consequently, in that decade (and apart from the religious associations already discussed), within the world of young people, there were mainly recreational associations, that is, single-function ones.

As for the autonomous youth associational movements, their decline was so rapid that the challenge for all of their leaders and the existing associations became whether or not to approach the formal (governmental) institutions for assistance. One informant was so pessimistic and his evaluation of the change—more quantitative than functional—so negative, that for him the only possible future solution to the problem was for the associations to be sponsored by public institutions. This, at the very least, was paradoxical:

Future prospects don't seem too promising. In the medium term, it seems that young people might be bombarded by gifts of services and special offers by the institutions. These offers will be in accordance with a certain quality of life.

It's also possible that the prospects depend on the capacity of institutional bodies to create confidence and a future for young people. Thus, problems like unemployment might be weighing down the future of young people and conditioning their capacity to carry out their projects.

But, of course, the future doesn't seem to be linked to a common development, to autonomous production on the part of young people, in organizational and associative projects. It appears that we're heading more and more toward the privatization of life. If a young person looks for services, they can only be found through consumption. It doesn't seem possible, at least in the medium term, for youth associational movements to reappear; rather it seems as if the institutions generating services might replace them, and [then] autonomous creative associational movements will give way to associational groups as a form of consumption. (1-56)

In the case of the pro-amnesty committees, an internal functional division seems to have occurred:

Within the committees there are more women than men. There are approximately two women for every man. In the committees, there are no old people and very few relatives. The reason perhaps is that these people get together in the family committees and they have their own dynamic.

The relatives have lost specific influence with the passing of time. Their political importance within the committees is today very small. Nowadays, direct support for the prisoner or refugee is more propagandistic; they serve as a loudspeaker before society, but they've lost the influence of their vanguard role. This varies in the different provinces, given that in Bizkaia there are specific family committees, while in the other provinces there aren't. But, of course, the role of the relatives is today more one of support and propaganda than political influence.

The family is still behind the prisoner, although not in a political sense; this isn't the most important aspect because, in spite of everything, affective support still exists. (1-51)

In other words, as a general trend, political functions were taken over by members of the committees who were not related to the prisoners. The families refunctionalized the committee, or, for their own part, they constituted it as an association of practical support for the prisoners. The separation was not emphatic, since these same relatives also undertook propagandistic, and therefore political, activities at specific times. Yet, having lost the capacity to mobilize, a fundamental element of the committee—the relative—spent more time on financial aid questions. As has already been stated, cuadrillas of friends disappeared from the committees, having once been (in most cases) at the heart of their founding (1-51).

Faced with the change, the general attitude of relatives was a negative evaluation of the committees and a wish to recover the political capacity they once had. Nevertheless, there is little optimism in this regard: "the weariness that makes objectives, considered important, recedes into time" (1-51).

YOUTH OVERPRIVATIZATION

The three identified characteristics all relate to a general process of privatization of life: a decline in the number of associations, in the number of members, and in participation in these associations; a decline in the external, and above all political, influence of the surviving associative life; and a tendency toward functionalization in more specific, concrete, and, thus, more private terms. However, it should be pointed out that generational change accelerated the general privatization process. In short, it was within youth sectors of the population that privatization was more pronounced.

In the case of religious and ecclesiastical associational movements, given the general movement from the nodal point of popular collectivities to the spiritual ones, young people seemed to have been less sensitive to political problems than to inter-personal and intrapersonal ones. As a result, they did not join existing popular groups but tended more toward forming spiritual collectivities (1-53). Youth enlist-ment seems to have taken place through "Confirmation catechumen":

> The parishes themselves are those that are most capable of organizing young people, and in fact they've invented that very thing that serves them well. Be-fore, it was catechism for the First Communion, and now they've prolonged it until Confirmation. They keep the thing going in more stable fashion. (1-52)

> Communities composed exclusively of young people are emerging, especially in post-Confirmation environments. (1-53)

> Among youth sectors [between fifteen and twenty years of age], they organize what are termed Confirmation catechumen with an important human poten-tial for attracting groups of young people. (1-54)

The general panorama of religious associational movements was captured per-fectly by 1-54:

1. There is recruitment of youth through platforms created by the official church itself, through Confirmation catechumen.
2. There's an aging in the CPS [Cristianos para el Socialismo; Christians for Socialism] and within the popular collectivities, whose minimum age is around thirty.
3. Despite everything, within those communities with "a missionary spirit," and where the individual and the community play a central role [Pentecostals and Faith and Justice], there's a certain rejuvenation.

In every aspect, the dance groups experienced a youthful overprivatization: "The generational change is quite obvious. Today there are fewer kids coming to dance than before, and their motivations are different. They're not so politicized. But they are more authentic; they come to dance because it's an art, and that's the best thing of all" (1-55).

In the case of the hiking associations, one should remember that "after the death of Franco there was a certain decline in clubs," "but little by little hiking became popular again"; "people go hiking more, but associate with one another less"; and "before, the clubs used to organize more hikers' bus excursions and the members used to participate," while "today the excursions are more spaced out and fewer people attend"; they use "the car, because it gives them more independence and there's a kind of person who does more dangerous hiking" (1-57). "Young people nowadays feel like having strong emotions. Before, we went in for hiking, walking, and little else. Only a few people knew the techniques of [rock] climbing. Today a lot of young people get into mountaineering through climbing techniques. Before, when you learned things like that, you did so by necessity, to round out your preparation as a mountaineer" (I-57).

In the youth associations in general, there was disaffection with collective problems, together with a bifurcation of the interests and values of the young that was reflected in the privatization of consumption and in a focus on the individual's personal problems and quest for inner satisfaction (resulting, as noted, in a reduction in the size of the cuadrilla and its transformation into a friendship group):

> The member joins an association because he or she wants to meet other people, live with people, do things together. Possibly they hope to find friendship among the others. Although young people do things together [going hiking, going on excursions, etc.], the important thing at the end of the day is searching for friends, meeting people who understand one another.
>
> Before, young people spent more time in the streets; going out together was more common; they spent less time at home, etc. Nowadays, many young people listen to music and watch television. They spend a lot of time at home. They shut themselves away in their room and spend their lives there. Young people search for their intimacy like that. Possibly they're more individualistic; they're less concerned with collective solutions and, when they do think about these, they do so for their own security.
>
> This situation has repercussions, especially in the lack of youth affiliation. They couldn't care less. They're interested in associations to the extent that they offer them services consumption.
>
> Generally speaking, their situation is fairly contradictory. On the one hand, they want people to respect their personal space, they're individualistic; but at the same time they want to meet other young people. (I-56)

The overprivatization of young people also affected the pro-amnesty committees. There were not many older people in these groups, and "most young people aren't on the committees, although their makeup is youthful, with an average of between twenty and thirty years of age" (I-51). Taking into account the tardy appearance of these groups, one might speculate that their composition in the 1980s was fundamentally based on the youngest sectors of the previous generation (25–40 years of age), along with some young people of the new generation. However, in general, one could say that the tendency of the youth was to not take part in this associative sector.[17]

ASSOCIATIVE SECULARIZATION

There was a similar privatization of religion that paralleled the general privatization of life. Consequently, religious practice withdrew from the public sphere of political legitimacy or illegitimacy, taking refuge in the private realm. Indeed, the revamping of the church's involvement in daily life involved greater attention by the hierarchy to private spirituality. The focus was primarily on the youth, with extending and reinforcing their period of religious tutelage through renovation of the social meaning of the sacrament of Confirmation. However, while the church hierarchy worked increasingly with social actors in the private sphere, it did not resign itself to withdrawal from the public one. We need only recall the work of the church in the field of education and, more specifically, in educational policy, along with its frequent discourse about the problem of violence in the Basque Country. Within this public sphere, the church addressed an "undifferentiated public" as well as the political institutions. Within the private sphere it approached specific groups, encouraging and promoting them: "The church has been quite important. In many towns the priests encouraged people to go hiking through parish clubs. But this was important once; now it isn't" (1-57).

From the beginning there was an intimate relationship among "hiking," "dancing," and the church, which gradually dissolved, paralleling the depoliticization of these sectors.

As for church work in the private sphere, the importance of post-Confirmation groups has already been highlighted. One should also remember that, in the 1980s, "there was no other politico-social organization that had more influence with Basque youth than the church" (1-54). In the private sphere, the official ecclesiastical hierarchy—conscious of the general privatization of life, the predominance of spirituality over politico-social commitment, and, thus, the abandonment on the part of some religious groups of criticism of church leadership—attempted to regain the initiative regarding privatized religion.

This chapter has addressed the decline following Franco's death of those social mechanisms that formed the architecture of what Johnston (1991b) terms the oppositional subculture of Basque nationalism. During the Franco era, this subculture consisted of a refunctionalization of certain social mechanisms that operated in the private realm of social life, as a way of reproducing the nationalist consciousness. Given the control exercised by the state in the public sphere (above all during the initial years of the authoritarian regime), this reproduction had to be secured through private mechanisms and with the aid of the church's most hidden side. At the same time, there was generational radicalization within Basque nationalism itself. This led to the foundation of a violent nationalist organization that, slowly, gained the affective adherence of new social sectors. The physical violence of ETA, confronted by the symbolic and physical violence of the state, shaped a violent complex that in turn made up the material and the principal content of the intersubjective communication that defined the oppositional subculture.

The previous chapter explored the transformation of these different types of violence brought about by the transition to democracy, especially as they impacted the Basque nationalist world. The new democratic regime presented the possibility of reproducing nationalist consciousness in the public sphere (freedom of political association, public ikastola system, teaching of the Basque language in private and public institutions, mass media in Euskara, especially through Basque public television, and so on). It also weakened not only those private mechanisms that guaranteed the aforementioned reproduction during the Franco era but their political projection and their capacity for political socializing. New generations had not experienced a familial environment subjected to clandestine ideological, cultural, and linguistic circumstances. Eventually, intersubjective relations in the private sphere stopped being politically predetermined as a breeding ground of nationalism and became definitively depoliticized. And, finally, the associative world refunctionalized, thereby losing its previous hidden function of political socialization.

These were the undoubted consequences of a politico-administrative objectification of autonomous Basque identity, or the recognition of Basque autonomous authority through the establishment of the so-called State of the Autonomies. This objectification, however, which corresponded to a politico-administrative variety that was examined at the end of the first section of chapter 1, has not totally satisfied Basque nationalist aspirations, both because it implies subordination to the Spanish state and because it does not include Navarre (nor, of course, the French part of the Basque Country). It has, however, satisfied some people (even if it did not fulfill all their aspirations) because it did imply that the problems with the Spanish state would continue to be dealt with exclusively through political means. For others (those more radical sectors of radical nationalism), it confirmed what one can achieve through violent means—the assertion being that without the threat of ETA the Basque Autonomous Community would have remained a pipe dream. For them the preferred agenda is to employ violence until *territorial integrity* and independence are achieved.

Nevertheless, within moderate and even some radical Basque nationalist sectors, creation of the Basque Autonomous Community meant a profound weakening of the nationalist reproduction paradigm created during the Franco dictatorship and the emergence of new mechanisms for political reproduction and struggle. Many in the radical sectors, however, strained to affirm that the changes were unimportant and continued to emphasize the need to carry on with the violent resistance begun during the Franco era. Within this context, the differentiation between means and ends acquired the highest political relevance within Basque nationalism. Its segments wavered between moments of reunification (agreement on common objectives) and division (resulting from a growing disagreement over the use of violent methods).

Taken together, these implied a new situation and, consequently, the current need to look for a new analytic paradigm with which to understand Basque nationalist reproduction. First, one must examine more closely the public reproduction system and the depoliticization of collective life, and even the resocialization or re-ethnicization of all things Basque. Second, one must look at attempts to perpetuate the old model within a radical social world that became more and more self-contained. Finally, one must shed some light on the dynamic relations between these phenomena. In the epilogue, then, an attempt will be made to offer a new direction for research by highlighting some of the elements of this pending model.

Epilogue

This epilogue is not meant to end but rather to begin the book. The goal is to establish a brief picture of what is happening with those elements that facilitate the reproduction of Basque nationalism at the end of the century and millennium. This does not entail presenting a complete picture of what a new theoretical model of Basque nationalist reproduction might look like but rather a series of reflections, supported by some assiduously collected empirical data, that might assist in the elaboration of such a model. Both a dual and a more complex approach are called for.

A dual approach is necessary because there is a part of Basque society that operates through those channels established by the new political institutions, through the progressive privatization of life, and through the incorporation into social life of the generally more heterogeneous new generations; but also because a minority sector (that is nevertheless numerically relevant) continues to believe that democratization has not substantially changed the recognition of Euskadi as a nation and thus acts as if ETA's violence still makes political sense. For an analysis of this latter social world, the model employed earlier for the Franco period is still valuable as a frame of reference—given that some people say the situation has not changed and continue to behave as if this were true, thus fulfilling their own prophecy. However, this world is increasingly isolated and self-referential, insofar as the discourse of most political parties has led to a gradual social delegitimizing of ETA's violence. Nevertheless, this new model should also be more complex because it must take into account the complicated relations between these two social dimensions and perspectives.

Having proposed to look at the problem in a new way, I now offer a series of elements (schematically developed) with which to approach it.

The Current Coexistence of Political Generations Within Basque Nationalism

At present, several generations (in sociopolitical terms) coexist within Basque nationalism. Their identity matrix has differed over time in response to rapid and intense periods of social and political change. The milestones that marked their formation were the Spanish Civil War (1936–39), the Franco era (1939–75), and the period of political autonomy (1975 on). Consequently, one might demarcate (in an approximate way) the following political cohorts within the nationalist world:

1. The prewar generation: For those born and socialized (in political terms) prior to and during the Spanish Civil War, the prototypical model of identity would be religious or, more accurately, politico-religious—that is, a Basque nationalist political identity defended and legitimized in religious terms.

2. The postwar generation of the difficult Franco years: Those born after the civil war were politically socialized during the most rigid (initial) era of Franco's rule. With this generation came a certain radicalization of Basque nationalism. This coalesced into youthful generational support that in the family (intra-familial, intergenerational relations) acquired an ambivalent character: that is, affective identification with parents humiliated and frustrated by the civil war, as well as confrontation with them over their political inactivity. The visible part of this iceberg emerged in the creation of ETA. This generation inverted its identity: that is, it became totally politicized, judging and evaluating everything from a political perspective, including religion. Furthermore, as religion was secularized, politics became sacred.

3. The generation of the decadent Franco years and the political autonomy: Those born in the 1960s and thereafter were socialized politically during a declining period of Franco's rule or during the era of the political transition. From 1970 onward, nationalism came to dominate the public political sphere. This generation was socialized during an era when the political space par excellence was the street. It was influenced by the privatizing forces of social life and the institutionalizing forces of an increasingly differentiated political world. Within the consciousness of this generation, the Franco era was dedramatized. The harsh rule of a dictator went from being experienced directly to being history recounted by the previous generation. However, this generation also experienced strong politicization in its collective life: it did not embrace privatization.

4. The new generation of those born in the 1980s: The Franco years were totally dedramatized for these protagonists. They were socialized in a richly differentiated and consolidated political world. At the same time, this generation became disinterested in institutional politics. It was a more plural and tolerant generation in the sense that the formation of its inter pares groups had not been determined solely by political options. It experienced strong privatization, but new forms of social and political participation also emerged. As a result of this dedramatization and political secularization, a certain depoliticization of all things Basque took place, along with a re-ethnicization. By this I mean that differential symbols of all things Basque became important in themselves and not according to their political value and influence. This re-ethnicization of all things Basque became socially plausible only within a social context in which all things Basque were socially secure and their validity was taken for granted.

The public system of social integration in schools and the workplace, along with the essential opportunities for Basque cultural expression, as well as intrafamilial, intergenerational relations (the private integrative system), all led to the emergence of differing types of youth adaptation or nonadaptation. The most extreme form of the latter was day-to-day urban street violence (to be examined below).

The Process of Political Institutionalization

The process of political institutionalization was principally determined by the following elements:
1. A change in the form of political legitimacy
2. The introduction of an autonomous differentiated institutional sphere that (to a certain extent) objectified collective identity
3. Freedom of political association (through political parties) and expression in the public sphere
4. The existence of political, juridico-administrative, and economic resources of the new institutions dedicated to the development of cultural and linguistic elements in which the consciousness of Basque national identity was anchored

These elements shaped the transition from a reproduction and sociopolitical model developed in the context of an authoritarian regime (with total political control of the public sphere) to a democratic-autonomous alternative.

Initially, the model would be defined by:
1. Political control of the public sphere
2. Political and social reproduction of Basque nationalism confined to the private intersubjective realm
3. The progressive affective identification with ETA's violence
4. A unanimous positive political evaluation of the language (Euskara)
5. Violence as a central political referent and as dominant in the political discourse of the intersubjective realm

However, the dominant model following the institutionalization process would be defined by:
1. A public space for democratic legitimacy and expression
2. The reproduction and socialization of Basque nationalist consciousness in both public and private realms
3. Political institutions as a privileged place for "doing" politics
4. A public model of cultural and linguistic development: the plurality of political, cultural, and pragmatic evaluations of the Basque language

These two models carry different logics and dynamics and within Basque nationalism today inform different and coexistent perceptions of political reality. Within the heart of Basque nationalism, then, there are two definitions of the situation, along with two political logics, although they differ considerably in their relative strength. Each logical form is maintained by segments of different generations.

More minoritarian radical Basque nationalism employs the logic that the political Transition has not produced any substantial change in the domination of Spain over the Basque Country. This view is promulgated in every town and neighborhood by the most radical nationalists of the generation of the immediate postwar period and the harsh years of the Franco regime. Its definition of the political situation has gained the adherence and influenced the political behavior of a minority of the younger generations. It is difficult to identify the social origins of the young people swelling the ranks of the actively radical Basque nationalists who employ violence in both a populist urban struggle and through ETA. The number of detainees (considered political prisoners within the radical Basque nationalist world) is similar to that of the Franco era. For radical Basque nationalism, their detention is confirmation that little has changed through the democratic transition.[1] The family with a member that it considers to be a political prisoner is living proof of such an interpretation, as well as a breeding ground for more activists. And young people who, because of family, school, or work, experience frustration or lack of self-esteem might find in this role of victim an appealing avenue for overcoming their personal shortcomings. Whatever the case, the incarceration of youthful activists has created in every town and neighborhood an intergenerational social world in which there abides (collectively and individually) a highly dramatized definition of the political situation in the Basque Country.

A majority of the latest generation has adapted to the conditions of political stability and economic instability.[2] However, a minority has failed to adapt to these conditions (political stability and economic precariousness) and vented its frustrations through day-to-day public urban violence. The former path implied greater individualism, pluralism, and tolerance, manifested through a renunciation of the two aforementioned political models. The latter trajectory embraced definitions from the first model; it assumed that the political transformations of the Transition were irrelevant.[3]

Centripetal and Centrifugal Tendencies in the Basque Nationalist World

The establishment of a regime of associational freedoms and the creation of Basque autonomous political power substantially modified the evolution of the politico-symbolic conflict that engaged Basque nationalism with the central Spanish state. Without resolving the conflict per se, a new situation emerged within the Basque Country in which there was internal competition among Basque actors themselves over new economic, judicial, and politico-symbolic opportunities. The previous anti-Franco front was shattered definitively, which placed intra-Basque-nationalist unity at risk within the Basque Country. Added to the usual tensions between parties, of the political Left and Right within the Spanish centralist state parties, there was also a tension between them and the Basque nationalist world, as well as sociopolitical tension within the latter itself. Basque politics post-Franco therefore developed a plethora of institutional actors. Moderate Basque nationalism remained at the center: at times confronting Spanish state parties and thereby forging a general nationalist front; at others, taking on the radical Basque nationalist world, which implied a certain rapprochement with the centralist state parties. To this, one might add the contemporary division within moderate nationalism. In 1986, Eusko Alkartasuna, or EA, emerged as a new political party formed by dissident former PNV members.

We will now consider the current state of Basque nationalism, and particularly its tendencies toward either fission or fusion. For fission there is the following scenario: the element that symbolically most divides the nationalist universe is the current ethical and political evaluation of ETA's violence.

As has been demonstrated, during the Franco era the violence received strong affective support among widespread sectors of the Basque population. This resulted from an absolute prohibition (in the public sphere) against any ideological or cultural expression that differed from the official line, or even of any dissidence or demonstration of general discontent. For many, the symbolic as well as physical violence practiced by the state legitimized ETA's political violence. And this legitimacy was felt within a quite small and highly compact society. With the Transition, the political discourse of moderate nationalist parties gradually delegitimized ETA's violence. However, there remained a certain division between "reason" and "sentiment." That is, within Basque nationalism, even among those people for whom violence was politically incorrect, there still existed a certain sentimental acceptance of it rooted in personal memory. The political discourse of moderate nationalism, however, increasingly rejected this posture and began denouncing the violence in absolutely negative terms, both in its official discourse and the private discussion of individual members.

Within the political sphere, this tension grew rapidly, especially in the municipalities.[4] A split between HB and the rest of the parties (not only the Basque nationalist ones) became more and more typical: "Isolation; they are doing it to us day in day out, especially out there where they can, in the city halls; it's disgraceful. I mean, the example of Tolosa: we don't even have a board, and when I say we don't even have a board or whatever, they don't let us have any possibility of organizing, planning, of presenting our policies on a board" (G-X, HB).

This institutional isolation worsened, as G-X (HB) recognized, based on ETA's violence against individuals, but also in response to attacks against the headquarters of several political parties and to street violence (*kale borroka*) in general.

This internal confrontation among the different forms of Basque nationalism within the world of political institutions (although not only there) fostered a certain possibility of civil confrontation within the population as a whole.

At certain times and in specific places collective confrontations could take place:

In general, relations [in the neighborhood] are good, positive, calm; the only point of friction and tension at the moment in the neighborhood involves what might happen after these acts of violence we've had during the last few years and this year as well, and which has caused severe and serious friction in the streets. (1-80, Santutxu)

It's not only the young people; it's that there are a lot of older adults and the like that, well, are in favor of this and that and . . . I've had to go outside several times into the street because there's been a confrontation, you know? And I'm not talking about a confrontation with two kids getting into a fistfight. No, no, no; it's such a big crowd that gets into it. It's incredible; you're afraid. (1-80, Santutxu)

On other occasions it was more fear than confrontation: "The great fear I have there is always of that [confrontation]. . . . Like what happened in some demonstrations and things like that" (1-81, Tolosa). This informant recounts how tension arose at certain moments, such as when demonstrations employing one slogan were contested by the shouts of opponents: "[The confrontation] is something that's there, that seems like a bomb that only needs to be lit."

Tension in both neighborhoods and towns where people know each other intimately also affects daily personal life. One member of the PNV in Tolosa told of how, in his neighborhood, political posters were put up in the church: "and my wife hated this and she grabbed them and took them down. . . . Then there were two kids waiting to see if anyone took them down or anything like that . . . and we then exchanged a few choice words with them, but no, nothing happened." [Others speak of the fact that yes, you notice] "hatred in a stare" (G-IX).

Adding to both the personal and collective confrontation was an intense ritualizing of civil confrontation from the moment when certain pacifist rituals, especially those of the organization Gesto por la Paz (A Gesture for Peace; a social movement in the Basque Country dedicated to protesting against ETA violence), began to appear. Its silent demonstrations from time to time, or after an assassination, in every neighborhood and town led to a counterdemonstration of people from the radical Basque nationalist world, often at the same time and place, as an attempt to counteract the social impact of the pacifist rituals. These ritualized confrontations did not often result in physical confrontation, although they produced moments of incredibly emotional and dramatic tension between those who remained silent and those who shouted radical Basque nationalist slogans.

Today, out of fear, only a small group of people go to Gesto por la Paz demonstrations, but there are many who support it through personal commitment or strong conviction:

> Maybe there have been twenty-five people from Gesto por la Paz in the Campa del Muerto; well, every day and systematically opposite them there have been two hundred young people. It's tough. And when they changed streets, to take their message to somewhere else . . . , Santutxu or elsewhere, and to feel a little more protected, well, there are the others there too. (I-80, Santutxu)

> Some stand here, others there . . . I don't know if there's ever been any kind of confrontation. (I-81, Tolosa)

> Nothing's ever happened here . . . the same thing always happens; some shout, yes some, and some others applaud. (I-81, Tolosa)

> The last one I remember, they came to us—we were holding a demonstration . . . Gesto por la Paz, and they came, wanting to hand out the "democratic alternative" and so on. And we didn't want any of it. For example, one of the Jarrai [Continuity; a radical Basque nationalist youth group] lot said to me "are you happy now with these *cipayos* [a derogatory term used by radical Basque nationalists to refer to police officers and the like] in front of you?" But, coincidentally, this individual was from here; then, when the two of us were alone together and all that, this other guy looked away. When he was with the rest of them, well, he had to come across as the brave one. (G-IX, Tolosa)

Also contributing to a certain division within the Basque nationalist world was the appearance of a new form of day-to-day urban youth violence that did not emerge out of mass mobilization.

Kale borroka (street violence), understood in the new way just mentioned, has emerged as a social issue in the last few years. Within the radical youth world there have always been forms of street violence. However, they were the outcome of a mass mobilization, usually a violent ritualizing of the finality of a mass concentration and, in this sense, a predictable though unplanned activity. However, nowadays there is another kind of incident: the arrival in a town or neighborhood of a group of hooded young people who carry out violent acts, such as the torching of buses, establishments, ATM machines, and so on. These are not spontaneous acts, but planned, organized, and led:

> [Before] they broke a window or something like that; moreover it was when there was a demonstration and when, you know, four hooded guys and boom, boom, boom . . . they shot. But now it's not like that. Now they come when you least expect them. . . . There doesn't need to be a demonstration or any fuss like that; they get together and have changed the strategy. Then, when you're least expecting it, all hell breaks loose. (G-IX)

It's not very predictable. Before, if [there was] a demonstration, once the demonstration ended . . . they destroyed trash containers, they set fire to them, they got hold of a bus, they emptied it. (G-IX)

This is not the place for a complete analysis of the origins, causes, behavior, and composition of this youth movement, but it is possible to examine society's perceptions of it. It is generally believed that people begin to take part from a very early age. G-XI spoke of people as young as fourteen or fifteen. I-80 observed that the people he knew "have been very involved. All that Gazte Asanblada [Youth Assembly] stuff was a strategy prior to a . . . strategy of mobilizing people in the streets. At that time a lot of people used to meet—restless, worried kids. And then, on the other hand, there are kids that have a degree of consciousness—some are in prison" (I-80).

G-IX spoke of somewhat older participants, roughly eighteen or nineteen years of age. He mentioned both radical nationalist families and non-nationalist, even immigrant, ones:

A lot of them are . . . from immigrant families, or their grandparents came from somewhere else; and as is well known: of the people who want to achieve social integration, many aren't even Basque-speakers, nor . . . do they think of Euskadi as a nation. . . . And then, people who have a father or uncle in prison, or their father is an HB councillor or of the LAB [Langile Abertzaleen Batzordeak; Nationalist Workers' Commission, the radical nationalist labor union] representative for the area . . . well, a little bit of those from two extremes. (G-IX)

The school environment is where one can start to make contact . . . four in the same classroom when they were in grade school, you know? They formed a little ETA group with another one in another classroom. (I-80)

They've already been contaminated somehow by the time they get to high school because, before going to high school, they come out of religious schools or because they've taken part in the Gazte Asanblada; in fights for example . . . a *gaztetxe* [an underground youth center]. Well they've got into all this there and they've been contaminated there, haven't they? They've been contaminated there. Music too; empathy with musical groups where they meet at concerts, etc. (I-80)

I-80 also highlighted the diverse ideological backgrounds of the families of these young people. Further, he noted that those people who partook in such activities were not necessarily failures at school:

[There's a] complete strategy to attract them, and this has its results. It's had its results. During these last few years, I think that the whole Gazte Asanblada thing has been significant . . . in the high schools Ikasle Abertzaleak [Patriotic Students; a radical nationalist youth organization] has also been a space [in which] . . . such groups have been very effective, radical rock groups. . . . Here they organize the fiestas, the groups they bring in are theirs, and then a lot of people get involved, and as such they make contact with one another. . . . I think that fiestas are also a means . . . of attracting people. . . . I think it's the atmosphere, going camping wherever, an outing whenever. . . . In other words, all of this little world of . . . recreation, of occupying time, of the adrenaline that they pump into their bodies . . . well. (I-80)

Perfectly organized, perfectly organized. During the carnival . . . there were about forty of them or something like that. Some had flares, others had Molotov cocktails, others even had axes; they came one by one and reached the Triangle Square; and they didn't just all run up to the Kutxa [a local bank], or others up to the Banco Guipuzcoano [another bank], [or] others setting fire to the ınem [Instituto Nacional de Empleo; the employment office] . . . that is, it wasn't a case of them arriving and . . ."What should we do?" or "Let's burn the Kutxa." No, no. They arrived, and each one had, let's say, a specific objective . . . a twenty-minute thing, a tense half hour. (G-ıx)

In this interview, G-ıx described other commando-type actions and even spoke of leadership by a visible figure: "Another time, in the Triangle [Square], and in other places, there was someone who would have been a little older than the rest; he was a strong guy, with a white tracksuit; furthermore, [it was] strange because you could see him; you could see him easily, the tracksuit he wore, the white hood and tracksuit and he was the one that was . . . the one that was talking. And he was like the boss . . . he gave them a sign and they went off" (G-ıx).

In Tolosa, people believed that the commandos that functioned in each town were made up of young people from other towns (G-ıx and I-81).

Elsewhere, the Santutxu informant said that the young people involved in kale borroka whom he knew denied being under the control of HB. In fact, according to them, all such activity was controlled by the Gazte Asanblada or something like that (I-80). Therefore, according to this informant, there was self-organization.

From the ranks of HB, this kale borroka was perceived as an aggressive spontaneous response—lacking in any specific purpose—by young people against those who oppressed them: "In Euskal Herria their . . . their aggressiveness is directed against those who are oppressing them, as a result of their frustration or whatever, isn't it? In other words, it's the Civil Guard, the Ertzaintza, capitalism. . . . I think it's an outbreak of authentic rebelliousness . . . family suffering, personal suffering, suffering" (G-x). This group (G-x, HB)spoke of an organized movement, but one planned by young people themselves.

Elsewhere in HB, people thought kale borroka was the result of the organization of certain spectacular violent incidents:

I was there because there were fiestas in Ibarra [Gipuzkoa], and what appeared the day after on television, in the press and the rest, I mean, I said: "I don't know where I was because I didn't see all that, of course"; I saw them burn an automatic teller and I saw a confrontation between young people and *ertzainak* [autonomous government police officers], and later I heard that there had been shots and that a kid had been injured and I don't know what else. I didn't see anything else, but on television it looked like there had been a pitched battle; I didn't see it and I was there having some drinks, so . . . (G-X)

In HB, any doubt about the negative effects of this youth street violence was thematicized: "At the end of the day, ultimately, from our point of view and politically speaking, we see these incidents as an indication that there's a political, ideological problem here and that this is one more reflection of what, at times, well, unfortunately . . . are negative effects . . . here young people, a sector of the young people are using a more and more radical form of struggle and it's having a series of effects . . . very worrying, very worrying" (G-X).

Finally there are the fusions brought about by the intranationalist fission. Wherever there is social tension, its development usually implies greater fusion or strengthening in each of the two extremes. The Basque case is no exception. On the one hand, moderate Basque nationalists have demonstrated a capacity to coexist harmoniously and enter into coalitions with non-Basque nationalist forces. This shows in the pluralism and the series of pacts from the party leadership down to the rank-and-file membership.

On the other hand, the radical nationalist world has also become denser. The radical fusion might be said to consist of the following:

1. The reason versus sentiment distinction that allowed, at least in part, prior large-scale mass mobilizations based on radical sloganeering has declined in relevance. Radical political organizations must undergo a functional change in order to adapt to the new situation. This ranges from attempts to mobilize mass support to forming dedicated, unquestioning membership cores organized around the central doctrine.

2. The central discourse, more and more self-centered and lacking in fault lines, corresponds to a feeling of isolation (G-X).

3. The relative ideological coherence (of a monolithic nature) in inter pares relationships has increased.

4. The radical nationalist cause has become more attractive to young people, compared with other political organizations, as a direct result of the relatively greater politico-religious pluralism of the majority of young inter pares groups.

5. Their attraction to and support of general social conflict is greater.

6. The radical world is an authentic social world in the sense of being a network of attraction and indoctrination,[5] and as a logistical possibility for the activities of the youth movement (radical nationalism's social centers and politically identifiable bars). Generally speaking, both the poteo routes in neighborhoods and towns and the bars themselves have divided along age lines. The only bars in which there continues to be an intergenerational relationship are those that double as radical Basque nationalist centers, that is, bars with political connotations in this sense.

Many of the constituents of radical Basque nationalism, as was evident from the second section of chapter 5, had a stark definition of Basque political reality during the Transition, arguing that nothing had changed since Franco's death. This became a self-fulfilling prophecy (Merton 1949). Since they did not believe in a new state of affairs, they continued to behave as before, some practicing violence and others legitimizing it. So their activities provoked state suppression and imprisonment of the perpetrators of violence, as well as its supporters. For those who had accepted the democratic transition, the incarcerated were common criminals. However, those that had not accepted the transition continued (and continue) to consider them political prisoners. This intergenerational closed world of radical Basque nationalism constituted a structure of social plausibility that maintained favorable definitions and attitudes about the violence. Such attitudes were reproduced at the heart of families who had members in prison—identified as either political prisoners or common criminals, depending on who was speaking about them. The intergenerational world, concentrated in specific areas of each neighborhood or town, probably provided the intersubjective confirmation of these same definitions. This vision may also have been reinforced in the educational realm, although this realm did not take the lead in shaping such attitudes and opinions.

Outlined below, from the perspective of G-X, is the view of the situation still held within the social world of radical nationalism:

1. There is still an oppressive colonial situation of central power over Euskal Herria.
2. Today Euskal Herria still requires a political solution: in general, political independence and strategic political negotiation with ETA.
3. The current political institutionalization has only hindered popular political participation. The political parties are especially responsible for this. The political Transition has not resolved the problems of Euskadi.
4. Youth street violence is the consequence of the political and economic situation in Euskal Herria.

Finally, there are elements that have maintained a sense of general Basque nationalist fusion:[6] The movement in favor of repatriating the prisoners constitutes a principal element of agreement among nationalists:

Right now the demand for the repatriation of the prisoners is coming together here, and there are people . . . who don't see eye to eye at all politically and are coming together. People of different ideologies, people who think in different ways. (G-X, HB)

The fact of having differences with HB doesn't stop them, in regard to the prisoners, from asking to meet us. . . . We should be meeting the councillors, the prisoners' families . . . due to their money problems . . . well, let's see, to at least maintain this relationship and to show that there is common ground between HB and us. (G-IX, PNV)

People that until now haven't been involved in anything and say, "We're going to do something somewhere," get involved, and one way of getting involved is also helping the prisoners; and for me there should be, officially, many should be free. It's as clear as that, at the very least . . . I'm talking about the law. (G-XI, EA)

However such rapprochement was sometimes not so publicly evident.[7]

Another element that led to a certain nationalist fusion was the labor union agreement between LAB and ELA:

As we see in ELA and LAB . . . these labor unions are capable of . . . uniting, bringing people together and leading; I think they're in good shape, better than all the political parties. . . . I think they're fulfilling, taking on, roles that theoretically the political parties should . . .

Then I think that they're on the right track and they must try it there; they must go for it, moreover at all levels, not just at the work level—of course, for that purpose it's a labor union, it has to work at the work level—but also in different matters such as that of Presoak Euskalherrira [Prisoners to the Basque Country]. . . . I think that there, there'll be important progress.

There are people from Herri Batasuna here, people from EA, from other labor unions, that is, in the neighborhoods, the streets, sound people, good people that aren't . . . politically, they're not corrupt, they're not corrupt. (G-X, HB)

Other kinds of plausibility for nationalist rapprochement can be found in the world of Euskara (G-IX).

In sum, once again the future of the Basque Country rests on a razor's edge. The spectrum of attitudes is not a *continuum* any longer. Anti-Franco unity is gone; Basque nationalist solidarity is also breaking down. From a rich array of political positions, the situation has polarized into two extremes. Opposing the violence of ETA is a consensus that accepts the current objective limits of Spanish democracy. This is endorsed as the means of achieving any political objective. By embracing the current system, a majority accept, at least to a degree, its objective limits on political possibilities. But there is still confrontation with those who do not accept such limits and consequently reject the democracy as currently constituted. And the consensus against ETA's violence is at stake every time its proponents use democratic, nonviolent means to test the objective limits of the system.

Given this situation, one might speculate about the possibility of a political negotiation with ETA. This is a strategic area in which the moderate Basque nationalist world and the world of Spanish nationalism fail to come together. From the moderate Basque nationalist perspective, this is a practical problem. While from the perspective of the Spanish nationalist world, it is a politico-ideological problem. The search for a political solution in Ulster during the Blair era intrigued the pragmatic Basque nationalists because it was premised on negotiations. However, those who privilege politico-ideological criteria believe that Ireland and Euskadi are two very different cases. From a scientific viewpoint, and examined closely, every society, group, or social unit is completely unique. However, if one is committed to resolving a problem over which it is impossible to reach agreement on content, then it is possible to negotiate and come to some form of accord only if each party reduces its demands. At the end of the day, achieving accord is more a technical and pragmatic, rather than ideological, challenge.[8]

Notes

1. Bell (1982) thought that the old division within social science between functionalism and Marxism (Gouldner 1970) had been progressively replaced by a split between those who made the paradigm of rational action the sole, or nearly exclusive, principle for explaining social behavior and the remaining approaches. At least today, one cannot draw such a strict division. On the one hand, some champions of the paradigm of rational choice theory, such as Hirschman (1970, 1986), defend the existence of a behavioral pluralism, and others, such as Elster (1983, 1989), reach the point of speaking about a behavioral self-determination that can be both rational and emotional along with hetero-determination through social norms, elements that Gil Calvo (1993) considers very similar to those of the Weberian distinction between rationality, charisma, and tradition. On the other hand, in the field of politics, debates about culture in general (Wuthnow and Witten 1988; Archer 1988) and political culture in particular (Swidler 1986; Klandermans 1988; Sommers 1995a,b), which were so pertinent in the 1980s, have called into question an emphatic distinction between rational and nonrational action (Morán 1996–97).

2. In Max Weber's sense when he states that his work *The Protestant Ethic and the Spirit of Capitalism* (1958) is an example of how ideas achieve historical efficiency. Here the social efficacy of an idea or a definition depends on the level to which it is taken for granted and its social diffusion. Maximum social effectiveness implies being taken totally for granted by the whole population, with everyone behaving in accordance with that definition of reality. Being taken for granted and the level of diffusion are related, in the sense that with religious pluralism religion becomes subjective (Berger 1970, 473 ff.).

3. This is reminiscent of Thomas's (1923) theorem and the distinction made by Merton in "the self-fulfilling prophecy" (1949, 179 ff.).

4. The relationship established by Durkheim between the sacred and the social bond, which he treats strategically as religion and society, is fundamental in this regard (Durkheim 1915).

5. I won't fall into the trap of believing in the universality of what Merton calls "Sumner's syndrome." In fact, not every group is an in-group opposed to an out-group, since it is possible for there to be positive, as well as negative, references to groups that do not belong. For the purpose of this study, I emphasize groups of belonging.

6. Here I invoke the fact that this process of progressively negating or downplaying the symbolic importance of these territories continues today through the process of supranational entity formation, such as that which resulted in the European Union, and, in general, through the process of globalization, which, in a way, can be defined as the deterritorialization of decisions, political as well as others (Pérez-Agote 1999).

7. It is beyond the limits of this study to consider whether "we" conflicts can be found

without a political agenda. Possibly there are some whose political projection is not specifically nationalist—that is, ones that do not contest sovereignty by demanding their own central authority independent of any other.

8. Probably the most characteristic discourse of this type within the nationalist world has been that maintained for a good while by Joseba Arregi, a PNV (Partido Nacionalista Vasco, or Basque Nationalist Party) member of parliament who was minister of culture for the Basque government and Basque nationalism's most notable publicist. The following is an example of his discourse: "What Euskadi needs is for the majority of its citizens to be able to refer to it as a nation to be built by everyone, as a nation capable of sheltering within it, as a society, the majority of its citizens. And for those who think and feel that referring to Euskadi as a nation excludes them by definition, learn to use the term nation to refer to Euskadi, [and] we nationalists will have to learn to relinquish a closed, defined, and definitive concept of the Basque nation, of which we are the only and authentic representatives; we will have to learn to refer to Euskadi as a nation to be built by all, with less essential features and more voluntary and societal ones" (*El Correo*, December 28, 1997).

9. These issues are developed in the section titled "The Radicalization of Basque Nationalism During the Franco Regime" in chap. 3. Compare especially tables 3.6 and 3.7.

10. Individual interviews will be referred to in the following way: "I-17" corresponds to the interview with individual 17. A correlative order is followed through all the stages of the research.

11. The process of industrialization in Araba began after the civil war, and, moreover, it is a territory where, except in some small and insignificant areas, the percentage of Basque speakers is almost indiscernible. The important industry of Navarre was also developed after the civil war, and the growth there of an important radical nationalism (in relation to the moderate one) during the Franco years displays different characteristics from the processes in Gipuzkoa and Bizkaia. This has been analyzed in another work (Pérez-Agote 1989a).

12. At the outset of the research, an outline of the social structure of the Basque Country was prepared. It is clear now that the figures that supported the selection of Tolosa have evolved. Our criteria have been published and can be consulted. See Gurrutxaga, Pérez-Agote, and Unceta (1991).

13. To refer to the group interviews, we used the same system as for identifying interviewed individuals. "G-VI," for example, corresponds to Group VI of interviewees.

14. Although this interview violates the symmetry between Tolosa and Santutxu, we included it for the interest and relevance of its perceptions.

15. It was very difficult to gain access to interview people from the radical milieu.

CHAPTER ONE. COLLECTIVE IDENTITIES AND THEIR POLITICAL DIMENSION

1. Clearly, different positions of symbolic power exist, but one should not succumb to the temptation of seeing in socialization a process in which the socialized person is solely a passive *consumer* of meanings. As Michel de Certeau (1990) has observed, even within consumers, such as cosmopolitan viewers of television commercials, there is a creation

and production of meaning, expressed through forms in which they use that which is presented.

2. Nationalism is understood here as a social movement that tends to socially diffuse a definition of reality constructed in terms of national identity, which implies a performative process of symbolic reality. In this sense, this work follows Liah Greenfeld's idea that nationalism is a phenomenon whose nature is determined not by the character of its elements, the so-called objective factors, but "by a certain organizing principle which makes these elements into a unity and imparts to them a special significance" (Greenfeld 1992, 7). Thus, from a theoretical, and therefore generic, point of view, the nation as an organizing principle that nationalism seeks to extend is a form—one form of giving meaning, of defining a collective reality. The elements that this form claims can differ in each case. Therefore, no one element is especially necessary in itself, but there should be some reference to something. However, two observations should be made. In the first place, the element that nationalist definition attempts to make significant for a people might be in danger of disappearing; that is, nationalism can emerge as the consequence of a trauma produced by the disappearance of a valued cultural feature. In the second place, all social aggregates (groups, collectivities) possess logical prerequisites for their existence. One of these is language as a means of expressing the necessary communication basic to the extension and triumph of the definition. Combining these two observations, one might come up with a nationalist movement that wants to define its reality in terms of a differential language that is in danger of disappearing. This produces the paradox that the claim to nationhood and differential language, to be fully understood, must be made in the replacement language that becomes the logical prerequisite of the social aggregate. In other words, the differential language and the effective means of communication might not coincide: Gaelic can be recovered only through English, Basque recovered only through Spanish. On the other hand, when a form of consciousness is described as traumatic, it means that it occurs as a sudden consequence of considering a current event sufficient cause for the rupture or loss of something that is emotionally protected. This definition of the situation (Thomas 1923) can be true or false, as always; in this work the repression of Euskara (the Basque language) by Franco's regime will be examined. This repression was traumatically experienced and is therefore considered here as the affective cause of Euskara's disappearance, despite the fact that the language had been losing its communicative function since time immemorial.

3. G. Balandier has criticized these positions adequately, especially in his *Anthropologie politique* (1967).

4. The Durkheimian journal *L'Année Sociologique* (1896–97).

5. I use the word "simply" because it is best to simplify the problem, not because the problem is simple. On the one hand, any observation that might be made is representation and so subject to an endless analytical spiral because the goal would be the object-reality. On the other hand, in a general scientific way a problem is usually simplified so that it becomes a practical question where the worth of a concept, model or theory is evaluated. Furthermore, the problem becomes more complicated if representations are imbued with a material character.

6. In his *Tractatus de intellectus emendatione,* Spinoza observes that the idea of Peter is "totally different from Peter himself" (1999, 54).

7. It is also true, however, that in other, non-Western cultures this process of progressive personalization of relations might not be the same. In Bali, for example, "Each of the symbolic orders of person-definition . . . acts to stress and strengthen the standardization, idealization, and generalization implicit in the relation between individuals. . . . The illuminating paradox of Balinese formulations of personhood is that they are—in our terms anyway—depersonalizing" (Geertz 1973, 389–90).

8. Merton distinguishes between collectivity, characterized by a sense of belonging, and group, which to the previous characteristic he adds interaction among members. Furthermore, he proposes the idea of a social category, falling somewhere in between, and approximating Nisbet's statistical aggregate, as a unit of individuals with a common characteristic but with no sense per se of belonging to a whole. According to Nisbet, a social aggregate is a unit of individuals with the shared consciousness of belonging, deriving from the possession, or the supposed possession, of a common feature. For Merton, a social category would be a statistical aggregate ready to form a social aggregate (collectivity or group). Epistemologically, the idea of a social category raises the question of who determines the existence of the inclination to form this social aggregate. In my opinion, it is the social scientist (Nisbet 1970; Merton 1949). An example of a social category can be seen in the uneven nature of gender. The attribute of being male in our society has not come to form a social aggregate. The attribute of being female, however, has not only become a statistical aggregate, it constitutes a social category in that any possessor of this attribute can, if she so wishes, form a collectivity (*feminism*) or even, within this, a specific group (*a feminist cell*).

9. These questions are highly relevant for discussing the current issue of collective rights for cultural minorities. A collective right is an individual right that, in order to be furthered, must be applied to a category of people.

10. Rational instrumental behavior needs prerequisites termed *logical functional prerequisites.* The first and most important of these is establishing a goal. There are those who think that only economic or materially useful goals are rational, but, in reality, all cultures can establish different types of goals, as cultural anthropology has effectively demonstrated. Thus, establishing a goal to be attained does not have to imply rational behavior in itself, since it often involves a traditional kind of behavior. Once this goal is established, rational behavior consists of using adequate means to achieve it. Here, however, another kind of prerequisite emerges, as not all means are always considered by a particular culture (for example, the potential to emigrate in order to earn a decent living before this possibility has been socially institutionalized) and not all the means contemplated are considered legitimate. In social interaction, and for rational action to be available to all those wishing to act, one prerequisite is mutual recognition of the other. If this does not take place, those who feel they have not been recognized will struggle for such recognition, potentially making the very struggle the behavioral goal. As a result, a conflict can emerge that makes cooperation among all parties impossible. One must bear in mind that in social interaction these different parties might be in an unequal power arrangement and, above all, in unequal possession of symbolic power. For this reason, the most powerful party can success-

fully define another behavior that has not fulfilled certain prerequisites as irrational or against reason. From a sociological perspective, a given behavior may be rational in relation to certain stated goals, even if those goals are not the dominant ones of the society in question. Martin Albrow has persuasively argued that what he terms the "Modern Project" is a form of cultural ethnocentrism, because all behaviors that do not propose as their principal goal the creation of wealth are considered not nonrational but directly irrational. Albrow states that in modernity "the expansion of rationality is more properly seen as the categorization of life in terms of the rational/irrational dichotomy rather than as the exclusion of irrationality: There is always a 'pre-rational,' though not necessarily 'antirational' substantive basis to which that dichotomy is applied" (Albrow 1997, 53). Clearly, what is here termed irrational Albrow calls antirational.

11. This imbalance will potentially constitute a form of anomie. On the other hand, surfing the Internet opens up new possibilities of building the relationship between knowledge and effect without the constraint of spatial boundaries.

12. Tiryakian observes that history "became a privileged discipline in the nineteenth century to give a sense of an underlying unity in ages past pointing to national unification and identity as the telos of collective action: Michelet for France, Prescott for the United States, Macaulay for Great Britain, Treitschke for Germany are representative figures of nationalist historians in this context. And, along with 'history,' other aspects of culture were involved in the consolidating of the nation-state, for example, poetry and music (the latter in the form of patriotic hymns, national anthems, and, of course, operas, such as those written by Verdi and Wagner)" (Tiryakian 1989, 120). Douglass argues that the rise of ethnonationalist movements is "intimately intertwined with the emergence of the science of ethnology, social anthropology, genetics and linguistics" (Douglass 1989, 70). With regard to Basque nationalism, Azcona (1984) has explained the role Basque anthropology played in the construction of Basque nationalism's symbolic universe.

CHAPTER TWO. NATIONALISM AS THE POLITICIZATION OF COLLECTIVE IDENTITY

1. The inclusive nature of peripheral nationalism raises complicated questions: Should everyone who inhabits this partial territory be included or not? Should one include only those that belong to the ethnic group in question (potentially moving toward a desire to ethnically cleanse minorities) or all inhabitants? Should one include ethnically related persons inhabiting other territories, even outside the state for example? One must remember, however, that the peripheral nationalist definition of identity is more a function of desire and aspiration than of normative definition easily imposed through the use of political process and power.

2. This is a static diagram. It might be the case that one of the definitions is imposed by (state) force. This was the Basque situation during the Franco dictatorship, as will be seen later. It might also be the case that new definitions, acceptable to everyone, are created. This was what the Spanish state tried to achieve through the formula of the State of the Autonomies in the post-Franco era, which will also be discussed later.

3. Of course, the same could also be said if the conclusion were the reverse or if the reality of Spain was in question.

4. Kohn suggests speaking of nationality rather than the nation, thereby placing more emphasis on the nature of a consciousness that the masses gradually acquire through nationalism (1967, 580–81 n. 9).

5. All these definitions came out of Basque nationalism itself, from different sectors and at different historical moments. There were, moreover, definitions of Basque identity from Spanish centralist nationalist perspectives.

6. Space prevents undertaking a theoretical debate about the concepts of ethnicity and ethnic groups, but it is worth asking one question: When a nation is created through the unequal (as will be seen) merger of various ethnic groups and the elevation of one dialect to the status of national language spoken by all, is not another ethnic group being formed? When a nation is historically successful, does it not constitute, for all that it has been shaped through civic ties among several ethnic groups, a new primordial bond?

7. As will be seen later, nation and state cannot be confused, but neither can one understand the meaning of the nation, in its modern political sense, without reference to a past, present, or future state.

8. This lack of agreement became apparent in the Spanish case with the death of Franco. For some, the Franco regime had been an illegitimate seizure of a legitimate center of power. For others, however, the very center of power was illegitimate, as it did not correspond to their affective national community (Pérez-Agote 1984b, 1987).

9. The nation is a way of secularizing the legitimacy of power.

10. See also chap. 3 of Habermas (1981) and Kühnl (1971).

11. In this sense, the case of Spain is paradigmatic in that there was a secular incapacity on the part of bourgeois sectors to control and rationalize the state, together with a secular weakness in the national educational system.

12. To be explicit, in a society of personal political connections, feelings of territorial belonging exist, but without direct political relevance in the legitimizing system of power. Moreover, there may be a feeling of belonging to a whole, a collective identity, stemming from subjugation to this same personal power. However, this sentiment is not what legitimizes power, even though it may have important political consequences.

13. But this does not mean that with personalistic forms of political power there is no sense of belonging to a community, specifically the sense of belonging of those under the personal power in question. In conclusion, even in this case the legitimacy of personal power does not symbolically stem, in a central and direct way, from this feeling.

14. Nietzsche understood very well the role of history in the construction of myths. His aim was to destroy those myths that humans lived by. For that reason, as Foucault explains, for Nietzsche history would be effective—that is, a destroyer of myths—to the extent that it introduces discontinuity into our selves: what is found at the historical beginning of things is not a still surviving original identity, but the discord of other things or folly (Foucault 1992). However, national history is usually taught as sacred history or canonized to impede any mental manipulation of our origins, which, as has been stated, are arbitrary or, as Nietzsche would say, are the discord of the other things, such as folly or conflict. The legitimating function of history consists in affirming the

existence, from remote origins, of what is only a product or a historical result. According to this idea, the nation has existed since remote times, and during the modern democratic era it managed to endow itself with a representative political structure. For our purposes, however, the nation is a modern historical product.

15. Of course, there are cases in Europe where the nation precedes the state. However, the *idea* of nation, in the strict sense, never precedes the *idea* of the state.

16. He refers to the examples of Italy and, especially, Germany.

17. It is interesting to compare ethnic rebirth with the governmental line on the ethnic question promoted by Soviet social science. Yu V. Bromley (1989) contends that pre-Soviet cultures (gastronomy, craftsmanship, folklore) lived on in the Soviet Union but that a Soviet culture, and therefore Soviet political identity, gradually suffused the entire population.

18. Johnston argues that "parallel to the growth of new (social) movements in the 1970s and 1980s, there was also a proliferation of other ethnic and nationalist kinds" (1994, 369).

19. For a critical survey of the literature concerning relations between social and identity movements, see Hunt, Benford, and Shaw (1994).

20. That is, both are attractive to those who engage in the quest in the same sense as previously established regarding the relationships between the new social movements and peripheral ethnic nationalist movements. See Melucci (1989, 90–92) and Johnston (1994, 369–70).

CHAPTER THREE. THE PROBLEMATIC LEGITIMIZATION OF THE SPANISH STATE
IN THE BASQUE COUNTRY

1. Several novels by Pérez-Galdos allude to this daily social tension in the Basque Country of the nineteenth century, even in times when there was no open warfare.

2. The Bank of Bilbao was created in 1857, at the very beginning of the industrialization process, while that of Bizkaia was established at the start of the twentieth century. Of the two primarily industrial regions of Spain, Catalonia and Euskadi, the triumphant model in the later general industrial development of the state would be the Basque one, namely financial capitalism (Moya 1975).

3. The banks cited in the previous note were, naturally, fundamental to the financial market. In regard to the matrimonial market, the University of Deusto—as a meeting (and matchmaking) place for members of both the aristocracy and the industrial bourgeoisie—was, at the end of the nineteenth century, similarly important.

4. The essential work for understanding Sabino Arana's ideology and his political role is that of Javier Corcuera (1979). For the history of Basque nationalism prior to the rise of Franco, see Payne (1974).

5. Specifically, the industrialist Ramón de la Sota y Llano.

6. In *Los medios de comunicación en el País Vasco*, Coca and Martínez (1993) provide information about the principal daily newspapers and radio stations in the Basque Country, from their foundation and historical phases to their ownership. However, this work

does not contain a systematic analysis of the political and ideological evolution of these media, especially during the Franco years. It does examine the effect of Franco's new state on *El Correo Español–El Pueblo Vasco,* the most important of the daily newspapers published in the Basque Country. *El Pueblo Vasco* was founded in 1910 to defend Basque interests from a Spanish, Catholic, and monarchical position. After the entrance of Franco's troops into Bilbao, in 1937, its old subheading, *Diario Independiente* (Independent Newspaper), had to be replaced by that of *Diario Nacional* (National Newspaper), referring, of course, to the Spanish nation. Shortly afterward, it was forced to merge with *El Correo Español,* a Falangist (fascist) newspaper founded in Bilbao on July 6, 1937. As for what happened later, and specifically from a political point of view, this work discusses only subsequent minor changes related to the paper's slow liberalization, highlighting the modifications that took place after Franco's death in 1975 (Coca and Martínez 1993, 39–48). Saiz Valdivielso (1977) addresses the period 1930–39, offering some interesting information but little analysis. There are also several historical monographs on the principal daily newspapers that are more descriptive than critical or analytical (Lerchundi 1985; El Correo Español–El Pueblo Vasco 1985; Ybarra 1985; Peña 1984). In Lerchundi (1986) there is a brief historical description of the *Gaceta del Norte.* In the 1930s, this newspaper was closely connected to the church. Subsequently, during practically the whole Franco era, it was the hegemonic daily: "As long as the Franco regime remained there would be no sanctions, strikes, or kidnappings. Both the government and the *Gaceta* coincided in defending the unity of Spain, the family and Catholicism in general, so relations were as close as possible" (Lerchundi 1986, 608). As an example of its thoroughly anti-Basque nationalist stance, there is the fact that, even after Franco's death, this newspaper refused to call the *ikurriña* (the Basque flag) the statutory Basque flag, instead referring to it as the *separatist Basque flag* (Lerchundi 1986, 609). From an analysis of the previously cited works, one can make some observations about control and ideology within the Basque press during the Franco years (see table 3.3). Regarding the clandestine press during these years, Pedro Ibarra (1986) systematically evaluates eight publications corresponding to "the six most influential clandestine political groups among anti-Franco public opinion" (namely, the Partido Comunista de España [Spanish Communist Party], the Partido Socialista Obrero Español [Spanish Socialist Party], ETA [before the 1970 split], ETA-V, ETA-VI, and the Movimiento Comunista de Euskadi [Basque Communist Movement]), "another by the so-called unitary groups" (published by independent groups with some influence in the working-class movement), and "the institutional publication of the Basque government-in-exile: the OPE" (Ibarra 1986, 688). The Ibarra work includes as an appendix systematic data about the aforementioned publications and a general catalog of publications that were clandestinely distributed in Euskadi during the Franco years.

7. After Franco's death, this panorama changed significantly, especially with the appearance of two new newspapers: *Deia* (Bilbao, June 1977), connected with the Basque Nationalist Party, and *Egin* (Hernani, October 1977), connected with the more radical elements of the izquierda abertzale (nationalist left). At the same time, new nationalist and leftist (or of both tendencies) journals emerged, such as *Berriak* (communist), *Garaia* (from the ESB group, or socialists of a nationalist persuasion), and *Punto y Hora de Euskal Herria* (radical nationalist), together with others in Basque of a smaller circu-

lation. Altabella (1986) presents a general bibliography of works associated with the history of the press in Araba, Bizkaia, and Gipuzkoa. Similarly, a general overview of these issues is presented by Tuñón de Lara (1986).

8. Radio Nacional (National Radio) and SER (Sociedad Española de Radio Difusión; Spanish Association for Radio Broadcasting).

9. The involvement of a good number of ministers made this faculty even more interesting from these points of view. Cf. Equipo Mundo (1970).

10. The grants came from Fundación Vizcaína Aguirre.

11. Principally, family-run and smaller businesses.

12. The PNV did maintain a clandestine organization within the Basque Country that participated in rare strikes and pubic demonstrations against the dictatorship. It also organized an anti-Franco lobby in several Basque diasporas of Latin America. As far as I am aware, there are no studies available on the business sector's political activity during the Franco dictatorship. Nor are there works on the specifically political meaning of the important Basque cooperative movements, especially that of Arrasate. Regarding the Arrasate cooperative, there are a lot of more general works: one overview with a good bibliography is that of Kasmir (1996); on its historical origins, see Arrieta et al. (1998); on its meaning at the end of the twentieth century, see Bakaikoa et al. (1995); for a point of view from within the movement itself, particularly useful in understanding its symbolic and even mystical dimension, see Larrañaga (n.d.) and Ormaetxea (1997). Finally, one can also consult various publications by the Consejo Superior de Cooperativas de Euskadi (the High Council of Cooperatives in Euskadi).

13. One should remember, although it is difficult to tell from table 3.8 (as it only details the balance between the middle of the nineteenth century and World War I), that an important emigration also took place out of the Basque Country to the Americas. See Douglass and Bilbao (1975).

14. One refers to a general industrialization process because, of course, there was industry in these two provinces prior to these decades. However, it did not manage to counter their negative migration balances.

15. The best indication of this was the vote for HB (the radical Basque nationalist party), although it is not the ideal way of measuring support for ETA. As for public opinion polls, in my opinion they are not the most reliable means of gauging general levels of support.

CHAPTER FOUR. BASQUE NATIONALISM DURING THE FRANCO DICTATORSHIP

1. From this moment onward, nationalism's ideological scope became more and more heterogeneous.

2. Lodziak uses the idea of a culture of opposition in another context, specifically to warn of the need to diffuse a "culture of opposition" within the general process that foments capitalist consumerism. See Lodziak (1995), chaps. 5 and 6.

3. Johnston cites the second edition (1986) of Pérez-Agote (1984b), a work that provides the empirical foundation for this chapter.

4. Similarly, in communist Poland there was a clear tension between church and state. After the October 1956 crisis that provoked a number of changes in Polish society, there

was a period of unfulfilled promises lasting until the end of the 1950s in which "religious instruction was banned from public schools and the relation between the state and the Church deteriorated." Despite this situation, "in the long run only the Polish Church seems to have been an undeniable beneficiary of the Polish October" (Ekiert and Kubik 1999, 30), given that one of the remnants of this crisis was an independent Catholic Church, that is, a church in permanent conflict with the state. Later a diverse series of working-class and student movements emerged, culminating in the creation of Solidarity, its legal repression, and its later clandestine activity. Finally, the totalitarian regime fell. Without doubt, the activity of the church was central to this whole process.

5. One is reminded here of the third level of identity objectification mentioned at the end of the first section of chap. 1, namely the politico-administrative variety.

6. According to Durkheim, there is no difference. In *The Elementary Forms of the Religious Life* (1915), he argues that national political solidarity fulfills the same role of symbolic integration as that of religion in totemic Australian societies that he had studied. On this idea, see Pérez-Agote (1984a).

7. One should remember here that, in Europe at least, the idea of the nation implied a certain secularization of political ties. See chap. 2.

8. Joseba Zulaika (1988) emphasizes the importance in the Basque Country of religion and priests in socialization of the young by means of collective representations of history. Initially, this indoctrination entailed ancient history as a foundational ethnic myth; then through the history of the Spanish Civil War; and, finally, as recent history, experienced as heroism and tragedy, during the difficult years of the Franco dictatorship.

9. The reference here is to the old Spanish debate over whether to define Franco's political system simply as an authoritarian regime (Linz 1976) or more strongly as a dictatorship.

10. At least no recurring references were made to personified leadership by those interviewed, even when they mentioned authors, such as Federico Krutwig, who were quite influential. Frantz Fanon was also, unquestionably, important for some members, mainly because of his ideas about violence purifying and liberating.

11. It should be noted that, over time, some activists did publish their memoirs and thoughts, but usually only after withdrawing from the fray, going into exile, or, commonly, ending up in prison.

12. The reference is to those activists that organized ETA's sixth general assembly and consequently came to be known as ETA-VI. This faction represented an ideological turn toward privileging class concerns over national ones.

13. In the post-Franco period, when clandestine activity was no longer necessary and the first public political figures began to emerge, it was common to see them taking part in the poteo ritual in their natal towns with their cuadrillas. Indeed, this kept them subject to direct social control. However, things began to change drastically with the creation of both an autonomous administrative structure and, as will be explored, with the violent dimension of the conflict, which heightened the need to continually protect one's identity.

14. Cf. tables 3.4 and 3.5.

15. Cf. Núñez (1977a), chap. 6.

16. Cf. Payne (1974), 277–80; Clark (1979); and Moreno Lara (1977). As for publication of books, the deleterious censorship carried out by the Franco regime in regard to political subjects in general, and Basque ones in particular, is explored by Torrealdai (1999). It lists all works censored during this time.

17. Schools that both taught the Basque language and taught subjects in that language.

18. The later section headed "The Role of the Church in the Reproduction of the Basque Language, Culture, and Nationalism" underscores the importance of the church in the production and reproduction of nationalism. For the moment, religion is understood as a belief that permeated the Basque nationalist familial universe during the Franco era. The more institutional role of the church is reflected in the foregoing section. First, though, some mention will be made of the associative world (see section headed "The Associative World and the Cuadrilla"), in which the church also played an important role; and the distinct periods associated with the reproduction of nationalism during the Franco era will also be clearly established (see section headed "The Franco Regime"), since the church was a key element in the legitimization of this political system.

19. Between 1955 and 1956, the Ekin group merged with the youth section of the Basque Nationalist Party (Eusko Gaztedi, or Basque Youth), which strained relations between the PNV and its youth wing. In 1957, a definitive split occurred, and in 1958 ETA was founded as an "abertzale, nondenominational, and democratic movement" (*Documentos Y* 1979, 1:30), in the same way that *Ekin*, in 1952, had defined itself as a "patriotic nondenominational movement" (from *Cuadernos Vascos*, no. 1, "De Santoña a Burgos" [San Juan de Luz: Euskal Elkargoa 1972, 28], cited in Ortzi [1975, 279]).

20. Cuadrillas are groups of friends, normally extensive and lasting. They function during their members' free time. More intimate relations do not take place in the group as a whole but within smaller and more personal subgroups inside the cuadrilla. For an examination of cuadrillas and their important political function, see the author's previously cited works, along with those of Ramírez Goicoechea (1984 and 1991).

21. In 1988, DeMartini distinguished between "lineage and cohort politics" when he pointed out the influence, during the 1960s, that the socialist and pacifist positions of parents had exerted on the ideas of the New Left (DeMartini, in Johnston 1991b, 51–52).

22. Ochotes are popular, and generally male, choirs composed of eight members

23. An established daily drinking round, undertaken by a group of friends (within a cuadrilla), of several bars in their hometown or city neighborhood.

24. The phrase "all things Basque" is used here not in an essentialist way, but rather to refer to that which was perceived by the collectivity as Basque.

25. Bren discusses similar politicization of private activity in Czechoslavakia after the invasion of Warsaw Pact forces put an end to the Prague Spring. Czech president Husak sought normalization in which life would again be "quiet." As a result, two traditional leisure-time activities in the countryside acquired new significance. First, individuals and families were encouraged by the communist regime to acquire small cottages (*chatas*), which was not without irony. Yet this uncharacteristic socialist promotion sought "the benefit gained from the [corresponding] political passivity" (Bren 2002, 134). The other activity, which was traditional among the youth, was "the tramping movement—an alter-

native and less politically agreeable use of the Czech countryside—[which] remained
shrouded in secrecy and silence. Unlike the chata culture, the tramping movement had
been founded on preserving the notion of countryside as 'elsewhere,' as beyond the
reach of state control" (127–28).

26. The later public embrace of the prisoners' issue by political parties would cause
resentment among the cuadrillas.

27. This is not an attempt to divide Franco's rule into specific time periods, but rather
to identify periods of Basque nationalism's reproduction under the regime. That said, it
should be noted that the periods used here conform to the typically identified eras of
Franco's rule. The first corresponds to that period between assumption of power in 1939
and the late 1960s. This was the period of the most severe repression and a certain incapacity of the populace to respond socially or politically. Between the end of the 1960s and
1975, the workers' movement strengthened and political repression also increased.
However, during this time the regime was also forced into political concessions (Maravall 1978, 1981, 23). This allowed for the rapid growth of a certain type of associational
activity: for example, urban social movements in some of the bigger cities, such as Madrid, Barcelona, and Bilbao. As Fusi and Palafox (1998) argue, between 1969 and 1970,
Franco's state began to suffer a crisis that, until his rule ended, was characterized by an
internal debate between an ultraconservative inertia and a degree of liberalization.

28. The financial aristocracy was a social amalgam formed through the progressive
incorporation of financial and industrial elites into the aristocracy that controlled the
state. This took place mainly through the "matrimonial" and financial markets.

29. As an example of this, one need look no further than the Collective Letter of the
Spanish Episcopate, dated July 1, 1937, which legitimized the military uprising and the
war in religious terms.

30. Both the Spanish Right and Basque nationalism claimed to possess an authentic
Catholicism. For the Basque nationalist argument, see Altabella (1939). For that of the
Right, see Iturralde (n.d.). It is interesting that both authors argue that the Basque
clergy was Basque nationalist, although Altabella's assessment of this is obviously more
positive.

31. In chap. 6 of Núñez (1977a), there is a list of the eleven states of exception declared
between 1956 and 1975, with their corresponding duration, territorial range, and judicial
scope. One was applied only to Asturias; one to Asturias, Gipuzkoa, and Bizkaia; five to
Bizkaia and/or Gipuzkoa; and four to the whole of Spain. Clearly, then, the Basque provinces of Gipuzkoa and Bizkaia were the most affected, even more so if one takes into
account that several "states of exception" applied to Spain as a whole came as the result
of events in the Basque Country. Naturally, the corresponding repression was stronger
in the Basque Country than anywhere else.

32. To everyday indiscriminate state violence were added ritual celebrations of indiscriminate violence.

33. On the emergence and development of ETA, see Garmendia (1980), Clark (1984)
and Sullivan (1988).

34. Cf. the present section to chap. 4, "The Burgos Trial," in Sullivan (1988).

35. One exception was the surreptitious nocturnal placing of an ikurriña, or Basque
flag, in a highly visible location.

36. On these ritual occasions the state sent important contingents of security forces to the Basque Country. Because these supplementary forces came from other areas, they were unfamiliar with Basque social realities. This triggered an increase in the level of violence.

37. Moreover, it was within such associations that ETA sought (cf. the previously cited 1960 manual) and found its members. In other words, these associations objectively became the basic mechanism for recruiting members.

38. In 1970 the so-called Burgos Trial, or Tribunal, took place. The severe sentences given to several ETA members by the military tribunal resulted in important popular demonstrations and violent acts.

39. Chapter 5 attempts to describe the complex social and political phenomena that made it difficult to reconstruct politics in the Basque Country into a separate sphere: difficulties of depoliticizing collective life, of reducing politics to political parties, and of converting it to an institutional form.

40. Nevertheless, Sarasola (1976) maintains in his *Historia social de la literatura vasca* (A Social History of the Basque Literature) that in the nineteenth century there occurred an important rise in secular literature in Basque and an important expansion of nonreligious institutions out of which a new intellectual elite emerged. "For the first time in history, the Basque clergy felt seriously threatened. Observing that the ruling classes were establishing themselves outside their control, and with a view to strengthening their ties to people of the lower orders, namely the uncivilized people who spoke Euskara and that were uncivilized because they spoke it, they found themselves needing a tactical change. From this time onward, the clergy came to regard Euskara not as a language like any other, but rather as a rampart they could raise against new ideas. Euskara thus became for the Basque clergy a language that they had to protect in order to maintain their outdated ideas" (Sarasola 1976, 70). This would explain the general acceptance of Carlism among clergymen and, later, similar acceptance of nationalism in Gipuzkoa and Bizkaia prior to the civil war.

41. Johnston uses similar terms to refer to the situation in Catalonia: "The central role played by the Catholic Church in Catalonia derives from two sources. Culturally, there is a historical linkage with a traditional form of nationalism. Structurally, special privileges accorded the church by the Franco regime made it one of the few places one could escape state scrutiny" (Johnston 1991b, 50–51). However, in the Basque case, the relationship between the Basque language and the church was structurally even stronger. This was owing to the markedly rural nature of Euskara during the Franco years, together with the social power and influence that the church enjoyed in rural sectors. On this theme, see Itcaina (2000), who analyzes the historical role of the clergy in relation to the Basque language and culture. He further examines the role of seminaries and novitiates in constructing a competence of identity in Giddens's (1984) terms—that is, in the sense of a competence of subject matter directly related to Basque identity, its construction, and its maintenance. This would imply, to a certain extent, that the clergy assumed the role of the intelligentsia faced with the absence of a professional intellectual, academic, or other relevant sector. As such, the creation and development of a public Basque university has had important secularizing consequences in the post-Franco intellectual world of the Basque Country.

42. A high percentage of initial religious vocations is characteristic of the membership of the radical nationalist political world.

43. There is no systematic bibliography on this topic. See Arpal, Asua, and Dávila (1982) and Gaur (1969), although the latter report refers only to Gipuzkoa.

44. Interviews with I-51 to I-58, corresponding to the series used in chap. 5.

45. A selection of the most important documents can be found in Herria-Eliza (1978). This work provides a simple description of the radicalization of the Basque lower clergy.

46. I will mention here, although space precludes detailed analysis, the change that took place toward the end of the Franco era in certain sectors of the religious establishment due to the reforms of the Second Vatican Council, leading to the progressive introduction of a less conservative discourse in social and political matters. Further, the change gradually had important consequences for the discourse of the Basque religious hierarchy regarding the Basque national problem.

47. Itçaina (2000) examines the emergence of religion and, above all, the clergy in nonreligious social arenas like language, culture, the economy (the cooperative movement), and political identity.

48. These sources have been examined in an area that today comprises the Basque Autonomous Community and Navarre. This has been done for convenience and to make direct use of the sources, as well as because the most religious part of Navarre is found in the northern zone, where Basque culture is very important.

49. The church was attentive, as always, to this generational transformation. Without abandoning its public activity, the church attempted to promote new groups that would correspond to the more private understanding of religion shared by these young people. The key tool in this response was the new stimulus that the old sacrament of Confirmation acquired. Through this tactic, the church hoped to prolong a general tutelage that began in infancy and endured in the communion sacrament (First Communion). What happened, then, was that a number of *post-Confirmation groups* emerged at a moment when the associative world began to decline and those associations that remained were depoliticized. This meant that these same associations began to regain their original functions. At this time the church was best situated (although there is no specific way to gauge its absolute power) to bring young people together in these small groups or communities. However, one cannot conclude from the above observations that the church enjoyed a great capacity to attract large numbers of people.

CHAPTER FIVE. TRANSFORMATIONS WITHIN FORMS OF VIOLENCE
DURING THE POST-FRANCO ERA

1. There were other important changes in political symbolism: the institutionalization of the ikurriña, or Basque flag; permission to use the political denomination *Euskadi;* permission to hold nationalist rituals; the beginnings of symbolically significant political elements such as the Spanish constitution and the Basque Statute of Autonomy, as well as the new autonomous institutions in general. Undoubtedly, there were also changes

in the symbolic evaluation of preexisting political institutions: for example, the Spanish flag and the state itself. The 1980s became the setting for what was termed the War of the Flags. It got that name because some Basques objected to the appearance of Spanish political symbols during festivals and other public acts.

2. Xabier Arzallus was, until recently (2004), president of the Basque Nationalist Party (PNV).

3. A derogatory expression with which the interviewee referred to the Franco regime.

4. A reference to a complaint made by the College of Engineers in Madrid.

5. *Bolo* is a colloquial expression meaning "head."

6. *Batua* means "unified" and refers here to unified or standardized Basque.

7. A reference to Bizkaian, the Basque dialect of the province of Bizkaia.

8. Literally, "the little statute," a derogatory reference to the Statute of Autonomy.

9. A pun on the words *proletarianism* and *leftism*, in terms that imply pathology.

10. Euskaltegis are institutionalized centers for learning Euskara.

11. As an observer, I believe that there was a decline in the number of mobilizations, the number of people involved, and also the level of intensity. However, as will be argued in the epilogue, the most dramatic decline in the mobilizing capacity of radical nationalism took place during the second half of the 1990s. The decline would lead this political faction into new kinds of action, such as street violence (*kale borroka*) and a greater effort in indoctrination.

12. It should be remembered that this information derives from interviews conducted in 1984, or when the Ertzaintza had fewer duties and less latitude than at present.

13. A reference to the Lemoniz nuclear power station in Bizkaia. There were important popular demonstrations against the power plant, and ETA killed one of its engineers, bringing the project to a halt.

14. It is difficult to interpret this large increase, but it seems clear that social control was at least one of the reasons.

CHAPTER SIX. THE PRIVATIZATION OF SOCIAL LIFE
AND THE NEW POLITICAL INSTITUTIONALIZATION

1. Another way of interpreting privatism is as a form of cultural tradition or, rather, as ideological tradition in relation to politics in general and urban politics in particular: "Privatism is the dominant cultural tradition affecting urban policy in the United States and Britain. It is a tradition that encourages a reliance on the private sector as the principal agent of urban change. Privatism stresses the social as well as economic importance of private initiative and competition, and it legitimizes the public consequences of private action" (Barnekov, Boyle, and Rich 1989, 1). In the same vein, see McGovern (1998). Privatism is used here in a different way, as the present approach seeks to define those features that characterize contemporary mass culture. Nor does the current approach involve more psychoanalytic interpretations of privatization, as developed in Sennett (1977) and Lasch (1991a).

2. This explanation even involves the potential chronic deficit of meaning itself in modernity and its continued reproduction through disproportionate consumption, which seems superficial. Those who dispute this thesis would say that postmodernity might be the moment in which meaning becomes less relevant in the day-to-day life of citizens. Some observers, such as Bocock, are somewhere in the middle, arguing that some forms of consumption have become the means of producing individual and collective identity (1993, 67). Conversely, there is "a strong suggestion in much work that people were moving away from social class position as the basis of their self-identification to a more individual approach, where privatized consumption patterns, kinship networks, home, hearth and family become more significant" (Taylor-Gooby 1991, 18).

3. One should remember that, for Offe, mass political participation through political parties and the Keynesian welfare state are the two factors that make capitalism and democracy compatible. However, this suggests that the privatization of life would call such compatibility into question. Moreover, this reversal of the relationship between masses and parties (that is, instead of channeling the demands of the masses, parties shape mass attitudes through the media) means that contemporary life is predisposed to populism. This is because populist movements are only proposals, devoid of any ideology, to reestablish communication between the rulers and the ruled (Wieviorka 1993, chap. 2).

4. Cf. "Public Silence and Violence as an Expressive Language" and "Forms of Violence and Their Role in the Reproduction of Basque Nationalism" in chap. 4.

5. See "Forms of Violence and Their Role in the Reproduction of Basque Nationalism" in chap. 4.

6. See "The Street as a Political Space" in chap. 4.

7. Rather than participating directly, I analyzed this event by recording observations of it in a field diary.

8. EIA later changed into EE (Euskadiko Ezkerra, or Euskadi Left), a political organization that tried to reconcile ideological elements of the Left with those of nationalism. This tension would destroy the organization some years later. Some members defected to other Basque nationalist parties, and EE itself, controlled by those who prioritized left-wing concerns, joined the PSOE. As a result, the Basque section of the PSOE became the PSE-EE (Partido Socialista de Euskadi-Euskadiko Ezkerra; Socialist Party of Euskadi-Basque Left).

9. As mentioned in the introduction, Santutxu was chosen as a principal urban center where some of the fieldwork for this book was undertaken.

10. The Basque word *jatorra* means "genuine."

11. The Shrovetide or carnival fiestas are very popular in Tolosa.

12. A slang reference to pesetas, or money. In other words, money sent to prisoners for their prison expenses.

13. One must remember that in the 1980s unemployment levels rose dramatically in the Basque Autonomous Community and that these interviews took place in 1984. In 1976, the Spanish unemployment rate was 4.8 percent, but only 3.9 percent among the Basque working populace. However, by 1984 the relatively better situation in the Basque Country had reversed. Spanish unemployment levels had risen to around 21.3 percent, but Basque averages had increased even more, reaching 22.85 percent (Pérez-Agote et al. 2001, 47).

14. Small glasses of beer.

15. See "The Franco Regime" in chap. 4.

16. However, it should also be pointed out that when one speaks about depoliticization of the youth, "politics" is being used in the more restricted sense of an attitude toward political parties and the state. "Politics" in a more general, and probably postmodern, sense—namely, as an attitude toward the transformation of culture and mentalities through a living-for-the-moment way of life and through actions focused on the spectacular (activities designed to occupy space/time in the mass media in the 1980s and still more in the 1990s)—was very important. Above all, these activities were carried out by people involved in various movements: feminists, ecologists, antimilitary activists, conscientious objectors and those young people who refused to do military service, people in favor of donating 0.7 percent of the national income to countries of the Southern Hemisphere, and a number of nongovernmental organizations. Special mention should be made of the pacifist movement that attempted to secure social peace in Euskadi (Funes 1998).

17. In general, all the leaders of associations interviewed in this section highlighted the privatizing effects of cars and television. One should remember that these products became widespread only in the 1960s; consequently young people in the 1970s were the first generation to experience them from their infancy. To my knowledge, a systematic analysis has not been undertaken of the transformation of leisure-time habits brought about by the introduction of these amenities. Furthermore, democracy led to a general liberalization in television programming enhancing its appeal. Nor has there been proper study of the impact of the personal computer and the Internet upon the privatization of the individual.

EPILOGUE

1. C. Núñez (1977b, 121) cites the number of Basque political prisoners during the Franco era, beginning with 1969 when there were 862. In 1970, this fell to 396, and it continued to drop until reaching 315 in 1974. In 1975, however, it rose to 632. J. M. Mata (1993, 32) cites statistics for the period between 1978 and 1988. In 1978 there were 102 prisoners, with the number progressively rising until 1982, when there were 485. Following some oscillation, the highest number of prisoners was recorded in 1987: 504.

2. Youth unemployment in the Basque Country reached high levels because of the so-called oil crisis of the 1970s. In 1976, the unemployment level in the Basque Autonomous Community for those between ages sixteen and nineteen was 18.55 percent; and for those between twenty and twenty-four, 16.63 percent. Later, these figures rose. For the younger group the highest level was 74.05 percent in 1982, while for the next oldest group the highest was 55.57 percent in 1985. More recently, and after an important economic recovery, the levels improved. In 1998, the figure was 37.3 percent for the younger group and 31.93 percent for the older one. At present the levels more approximate those before the crisis. According to Eustat (the Institute of Basque Statistics), in the third trimester of 2003 the unemployment of youths between sixteen and twenty-four years of age was 21.1 percent and for those between twenty-five and thirty-four years was 11.5 percent. These

statistics were taken from different editions of the *Encuesta de Población Activa* (EPA; the Survey of the Active Population) by the Instituto Nacional de Estadística (INE; the National Institute of Statistics) in Madrid. See Pérez-Agote et al. (2001).

3. Without fully understanding to what extent situations like unemployment or educational failure affect people's decisions to join organizations that use violent means (either high-intensity ones like ETA or low-intensity forms like that of the kale borroka [street violence]), it seems logical to assume that these organizations constitute a parallel means of recovering one's positive self-esteem.

4. One should remember that, after municipal elections, radical nationalists found themselves in positions of power in a significant number of towns. Sometimes they were in the majority, but an agreement between Spanish centralist and moderate Basque nationalist parties might prevent there being a radical Basque nationalist mayor, thus underscoring the importance of moderate Basque nationalism. Situations could be very different. Whatever the case, the intensity and intimacy of municipal politics give it a certain heightened dramatic quality.

5. On the recent activity of Jarrai (Continuity; a radical nationalist youth group) in the educational realm and indoctrination of recruits into it, see *El Correo,* April 1, 1998.

6. The fusionist tendency was especially apparent during the period of an ETA ceasefire declared on September 16, 1998 (and taking effect ten days later). This led to a period of Basque nationalist fusion that was based on the so-called Lizarra Pact. However, this ended when ETA declared the cease-fire to be over.

7. See *El País,* April 6, 1998. The fact that the PNV did not attend a demonstration in Bilbao in favor of the repatriation of prisoners sponsored by HB, EA, IU, LAB, and ELA demonstrates the unstable nature of those mechanisms or elements from which the above-mentioned tendencies have been deduced.

8. On the historical difficulties in bringing about negotiations between ETA and the Spanish government, see Clark (1990).

Bibliography

Abercrombie, N., S. Hill, and B. S. Turner. 1984. *Dictionary of Sociology*. Harmondsworth: Penguin.

Albrow, M. 1997. *The Global Age: State and Society Beyond Modernity*. Stanford, Calif.: Stanford University Press.

Altabella, J. 1986. "Bibliografía de la historia de la prensa en el País Vasco, con dedicación a Álava, Guipúzcoa y Vizcaya." In *La prensa de los siglos XIX y XX: Metodología, ideología e información: Aspectos económicos y tecnológicos*, edited by M. Tuñón de Lara, 469–83. Bilbao: Servicio Editorial Universidad del País Vasco.

Altabella, P. P. 1939. *El catolicismo de los nacionalistas vascos*. Madrid: Editora Nacional.

Anderson, B. 1983. *Imagined Communities*. London: Verso.

Anuario de la Iglesia en España 1990. 1990. Madrid: Arias Montano.

Aranzadi, J., J. Juaristi, and P. Unzueta. 1994. *Auto de terminación*. Madrid: El País-Aguilar.

Arblaster, A. 1987. *Democracy*. Buckingham: Open University Press.

Archer, M. S. 1988. *Culture and Agency: The Place of Culture in Social Theory*. Cambridge: Cambridge University Press.

Arpal, J., B. Asua, and P. Dávila. 1982. *Educación y sociedad en el País Vasco: Historia y sociología de un proceso*. San Sebastián: Txertoa.

Arrieta, L., et al. 1998. *El movimiento cooperativo en Euskadi, 1884–1936*. Bilbao: Fundación Sabino Arana.

Austin, J. L. 1982. *Cómo hacer cosas con palabras*. Barcelona: Paidós.

Azcona, J. 1984. *Étnia y nacionalismo vasco*. Barcelona: Antropos.

Bakaikoa, B., et al. 1995. *El cooperativismo vasco y el año 2000*. Madrid: Marcial Pons-Gezki.

Balandier, G. 1967. *Anthropologie politique*. Paris: Presses Universitaires de France.

Barnekov, T. K., R. Boyle, and D. Rich. 1989. *Privatism as Urban Policy in Britain and the United States*. Oxford: Oxford University Press.

Bauman, Z. 1992. *Intimations of Postmodernity*. London: Routledge.

Beck, U. 1994. "The Reinvention of Politics: Towards a Theory of Reflexive Modernization." In *Reflexive Modernization: Politics, Tradition, and Aesthetics in the Modern Social Order*, edited by U. Beck, A. Giddens, and S. Lash, 1–55. Stanford, Calif.: Stanford University Press.

Beck, U., A. Giddens, and S. Lash. 1994. *Reflexive Modernization: Politics, Tradition, and Aesthetics in the Modern Social Order*. Stanford, Calif.: Stanford University Press.

Bell, D. 1976. *The Cultural Contradictions of Capitalism*. New York: Basic Books.

———. 1982. *The Social Sciences Since the Second World War.* New Brunswick, N.J.: Transaction Books.

———. 1988. *The End of Ideology: On the Exhaustion of Political Ideas in the Fifties.* Cambridge, Mass.: Cambridge University Press.

Beltza. 1974. *El nacionalismo vasco (1876–1936).* Hendaye: Mugalde.

Benedicto, J., and M. L. Morán, eds. 1995. *Sociedad y política: Temas de sociología política.* Madrid: Alianza.

Bennett, S. E. 1986. *Apathy in America, 1960–1984: Causes and Consequences of Citizen Political Indifference.* Dobbs Ferry, N.Y.: Transnational Publishers.

Beramendi, J. G., R. Máiz, and X. M. Núñez, eds. 1994. *Nationalism in Europe: Past and Present.* Vol. 2. Santiago de Compostela: Universidad de Santiago de Compostela.

Berger, P. 1966. "Identity as a Problem in the Sociology of Knowledge." *Archives Européennes de Sociologie* 7: 105–15.

———. 1967. *The Sacred Canopy: Elements of a Sociological Theory of Religion.* Garden City, N.Y.: Doubleday.

———. 1970. "Instituciones religiosas." In *Sociología,* edited by N. J. Smelser, 419–77. Madrid: Foessa-Euramérica.

Berger, P., and T. Luckmann. 1966. *The Social Construction of Reality: A Treatise on the Sociology of Knowledge.* Garden City, N.Y.: Doubleday.

Berlin, I. 1976. *Vico and Herder: Two Studies in the History of Ideas.* London: Hogarth Press.

———. 1993. "El retorno del bastón: Sobre la ascensión del nacionalismo." In *Teorías del nacionalismo,* edited by G. Delannoi and P-A. Taguieff, 425–49. Barcelona: Paidós.

Birnbaum, P. 1993. "Nacionalismo a la francesa." In *Teorías del nacionalismo,* edited by G. Delannoi and P-A. Taguieff. Barcelona: Paidós.

Bocock, R. 1993. *Consumption.* London: Routledge.

Bourdieu, P. 1977. *Outline of a Theory of Practice.* Translated by Richard Nice. Cambridge: Cambridge University Press.

———. 1988. *Cosas dichas.* Barcelona-Buenos Aires: Gedisa.

Brittan, A. 1977. *The Privatised World.* London: Routledge & Kegan Paul.

Bren, P. 2002. "Weekend Getaways: The 'Chata' the 'Tramp' and the Politics of Private Life in post-1968 Czechoslovakia." In *Socialist Spaces: Site of Everyday Life in the Eastern Bloc,* edited by D. Crowley and S. E. Reid, 123–140. Oxford: Oxford University Press.

Bromley, Y. V. 1989. "Procesos étnicos contemporáneos en la URSS." In *Sociología del nacionalismo,* edited by A. Pérez-Agote, 163–76. Bilbao: Servicio Editorial Universidad del País Vasco.

Cámara de Comercio, Industria, y Navegación de Bilbao. 1978. *Dinámica de la población y del empleo en el País Vasco.* Bilbao.

Caro Baroja, J. 1980. *Estudios vascos VI.* San Sebastián: Txertoa.

Carveth, D. L. 1977. "The Disembodied Dialectic: A Psychoanalytic Critique of Sociological Relativism." *Theory and Society* 4, no. 1 (spring): 73–102.

Certeau, M. de. 1990. *L'invention du quotidien.* Vol. 1, *Arts de faire.* Paris: Gallimard.

Clark, R. P. 1979. *The Basques: The Franco Years and Beyond.* Reno: University of Nevada Press.

———. 1984. *The Basque Insurgents: ETA, 1952–1980.* Madison: University of Wisconsin Press.

———. 1990. *Negotiating With ETA: Obstacles to Peace in the Basque Country.* Reno: University of Nevada Press.

Coca, C., and F. Martinez, coordinators. 1993. *Los medios de comunicación en el País Vasco.* Bilbao: Servicio Editorial de la Universidad del País Vasco.

Connor, W. 1994. "Elites and Ethnonationalism: The Case of Western Europe." In *Nationalism in Europe: Past and Present,* edited by J. G. Beramendi, R. Máiz and X. M. Núñez, 2:349–61. Santiago de Compostela: Universidad de Santiago de Compostela.

Corcuera, J. 1979. *Orígenes, ideología y organización del nacionalismo vasco, 1876–1904.* Madrid: Siglo XXI.

El Correo Español-El Pueblo Vasco. 1985. *El Correo Español-El Pueblo Vasco: 75 años informando.* Bilbao: n.p.

Dalton, R. J. 1988. *Citizen Politics in Western Democracies: Public Opinion and Political Parties in the United States, Great Britain, West Germany, and France.* Chatham, N.J.: Chatham House.

Díez Medrano, J. 1995. *Divided Nations.* Ithaca, N.Y.: Cornell University Press.

Delannoi, G., and P-A. Taguieff, eds. 1993. *Teorías del nacionalismo.* Barcelona: Paidós.

Dinámica de la población y el empleo en el País Vasco. Bilbao: Cámara de Comercio, 1978.

Documentos Y. 1979. San Sebastián: Lur.

Doling, J. 1993. "Encouraging Home Ownership: Trends and Prospects." In *New Perspectives on the Welfare State in Europe,* edited by C. Jones, 64–83. London: Routledge.

Douglass, W. A. 1989. "Crítica de las últimas tendencias en el análisis del nacionalismo." In *Sociología del Nacionalismo,* edited by A. Pérez-Agote, 95–110. Bilbao: Servicio Editorial Universidad del País Vasco.

Douglass, W. A., and J. Bilbao. 1975. *Amerikanuak: Basques in the New World.* Reno: University of Nevada Press.

Dumont, L. 1991. *L'idéologie allemande: France-Allemagne et retour.* Paris: Gallimard.

Duocastella, R., et al. 1967. *Análisis sociológico del catolicismo español.* Barcelona: Nova Terra.

Durkheim, E. 1915. *The Elementary Forms of the Religious Life.* Translated by Joseph Ward Swain. London: G. Allen and Unwin.

Edelman, M. 1988. *Constructing the Public Spectacle.* Chicago: University of Chicago Press.

Eisenstadt, S. N. 1969. "El estado, la sociedad y la formación de centros: Algunos problemas en la evolución de la sociología política." *Revista Española de la Opinión Pública* 18 (October–December): 9–40.

Eisenstadt, S. N., and H. J. Helle, eds. 1985. *Macro Sociological Theory: Perspectives on Sociological Theory.* Beverly Hills: Sage.

Eisenstadt, S. N., and S. Rokkan, eds. 1973. *Building States and Nations.* Beverly Hills: Sage.

Ekiert, G., and J. Kubik. 1999. *Rebellious Civil Society: Popular Protest and Democratic Consolidation in Poland, 1989–1993.* Ann Arbor: University of Michigan Press.

Eliade, M. 1992. *Mystic Stories: The Sacred and the Profane.* Translated by Ana Cartianu. Boulder, Colo.: East European Monographs.

Elias, N. 1983. *The Court Society.* Translated by Edmund Jephcott. New York: Pantheon Books.

Elorza, A. 1978. "Sobre los orígenes literarios del nacionalismo." *Saioak* 2: 69–98.

Elster, J. 1983. *Sour Grapes: Studies in the Subversion of Rationality.* Cambridge: Cambridge University Press.

———. 1989. *The Cement of Society: A Study of Social Order.* Cambridge: Cambridge University Press.

Equipo Mundo. 1970. *Los 90 ministros de Franco.* Madrid: Dopesa.

Foucault, M. 1992. *Microfísica del poder.* Madrid: La Piqueta.

Freud, S. 1972. *Obras completas.* Madrid: Biblioteca Nueva.

Funes, M. J. 1998. *La salida del silencio: Movilizaciones por la paz en Euskadi, 1986–1998.* Madrid: Akal.

Furet, F. 1981. *Interpreting the French Revolution.* Cambridge: Cambridge University Press.

Fusi, J. P. 1984. *El País Vasco: Pluralismo y nacionalidad.* Madrid: Alianza.

———. 1988. *Política, nacionalidad e Iglesia en el País Vasco.* San Sebastián: Txertoa.

Fusi, J. P., and J. Palafox. 1998. *España, 1808–1996: El desafío de la modernidad.* Madrid: Espasa.

Garmendia, J. M. 1980. *Historia de ETA.* San Sebastián: L. Haramburu.

Gaur. 1969. *Así está la enseñanza primaria: Hablan los maestros.* San Sebastián: n.p.

Geertz, C. 1973. *The Interpretation of Cultures.* New York: Basic Books.

Gellner, E. 1983. *Nations and Nationalism.* Ithaca, N.Y.: Cornell University Press.

Giddens, A. 1984. *The Constitution of Society: Outline of the Theory of Structuration.* Cambridge: Polity Press.

———. 1991. *Modernity and Self-Identity.* Stanford: Stanford University Press.

Gil Calvo, E. 1993. "La hipótesis del rol egoísta: Los límites de la teoría de la acción racional." In *Problemas de teoría social contemporánea*, edited by E. Lamo de Espinosa and J. E. Rodríguez Ibáñez, 225–66. Madrid: Centro de Investigaciones Sociológicas.

Gouldner, A. 1970. *The Coming Crisis of Western Sociology.* New York: Basic Books.

Greenfeld, L. 1992. *Nationalism: Five Roads to Modernity.* Cambridge: Harvard University Press.

Gurrutxaga, A., A. Pérez-Agote, and A. Unceta. 1991. *Estructura y procesos sociales en el País Vasco.* 2 vols. Bilbao: Universidad del País Vasco.

Gusfield, J. 1994. "La reflexividad de los movimientos sociales: Revisión de las teorías sobre la sociedad de masas y el comportamiento colectivo." In *Los nuevos movimientos sociales: De la ideología a la identidad,* edited by E. Laraña and J. Gusfield, 93–117. Madrid: Centro de Investigaciones Sociológicas.

Habermas, J. 1975. *Legitimation Crisis.* Boston: Beacon Press.

———. 1981. *L'Espace public: Archéologie de la publicité comme dimension constitutive de la société bourgeoisie.* Paris: Payot.

Haferkamp, H., and N. J. Smelser, eds. 1992. *Social Change and Modernity.* Berkeley and Los Angeles: University of California Press.

Hechter, M. 1989. "El nacionalismo como solidaridad de grupo." In *Sociología del Nacionalismo,* edited by A. Pérez-Agote, 23–36. Bilbao: Servicio Editorial Universidad del País Vasco.

Heelas, P., ed. 1998. *Religion, Modernity, and Postmodernity.* Oxford: Blackwell.

———. 1998. "Introduction: On Differentiation and Dedifferentiation." In *Religion, Modernity, and Postmodernity,* edited by P. Heelas, 1–18. Oxford: Blackwell.

Held, D. 1989. *Political Theory and the Modern State.* Cambridge: Polity Press.

Herria-Eliza. 1978. *Euskadi: Iglesia-Pueblo.* San Sebastián: Auñamendi.

Hirschman, A. 1970. *Exit, Voice, and Loyalty: Responses to Decline in Firms, Organizations, and States.* Cambridge, Mass.: Harvard University Press.

———. 1986. *Interés privado y acción pública.* Mexico City: Fondo de Cultura Económica.

Hogg, M., and D. Abrams. 1988. *Social Identification: A Social Psychology of Intergroup Relations and Group Processes.* London: Routledge.

Hunt, S., R. Benford, and D. Snow. 1994. "Marcos de acción colectiva y campos de identidad en la construcción social de los movimientos." In *Los nuevos movimientos sociales: De la ideología a la identidad,* edited by E. Laraña and J. Gusfield, 221–49. Madrid: Centro de Investigaciones Sociológicas.

Ibarra, P. "La prensa clandestina en Euskadi bajo el franquismo." In *La prensa de los siglos XIX y XX: Metodología, ideología e información: Aspectos económicos y tecnológicos,* edited by M. Tuñón de Lara, 687–711. Bilbao: Servicio Editorial Universidad del País Vasco.

Inglehart, R. 1977. *The Silent Revolution.* Princeton, N.J.: Princeton University Press.

———. 1989. "Political Value Orientations." In *Continuities in Political Action: A Longitudinal Study of Political Orientations in Western Democracies,* by M. Kent Jennings, J. W. van Deth, et al. Berlin: W. de Gruyter.

Itçaina, X. 2000. "Catholicisme et identités basques en France et en Espagne: La construction religieuse de la référence et de la compétence identitaires." Ph.D. diss., Institut d'Etudes Politiques, Université de Bordeaux IV.

Iturralde, J. n.d. *El catolicismo y la cruzada de Franco.* N.p.: Egi-Indarra.

Iztueta, P. 1978. "La Iglesia vasca en la coyuntura política actual." In Herria-Eliza, 135–54.

Jacob, J. E. 1994. *Hills of Conflict: Basque Nationalism in France.* Reno: University of Nevada Press.

Jaureguiberry, F. 1983. "Question nationale et mouvements sociaux en Pays Basque Sud." Ph.D. diss., Ecole des Hautes Etudes en Sciences Sociales, Paris.

Jennings, M. Kent, J. W. Deth, et al. 1989. *Continuities in Political Action: A Longitudinal Study of Political Orientations in Western Democracies.* Berlin: W. de Gruyter.

Johnston, H. 1989. "Toward an Explanation of Church Opposition to Authoritarian Regimes: Religio-Oppositional Subcultures in Poland and Catalonia." *Journal for the Scientific Study of Religion* 28: 493–508.

—. 1991a. "Religio-Nationalist Subcultures and Soviet Nationalisms: Comparisons and Conceptual Refinements." Photocopy.

———. 1991b. *Tales of Nationalism: Catalonia, 1939–1979.* New Brunswick, N.J.: Rutgers University Press.

———. 1994. "Nuevos movimientos sociales y viejos nacionalismos regionales en España y la Unión Soviética." In *Los nuevos movimientos sociales: De la ideología a la identidad,* edited by E. Laraña and J. Gusfield, 369–91. Madrid: Centro de Investigaciones Sociológicas.

Jones, C., ed. 1993. *New Perspectives on the Welfare State in Europe.* London: Routledge.

Jutglar, A. 1968. *Ideologías y clases en la España contemporánea.* Vol. 1, *1808–1874.* Madrid: Editorial Cuadernos para el Diálogo.

———. 1973. *Ideologías y clases en la España contemporánea.* Vol. 2, *1874–1931.* Madrid: Editorial Cuadernos para el Diálogo.

Kasterztein, J. 1981. "Aspects psychosociaux de l'identité." *Social Science Information* 20, no. 1: 95–109.

Kasmir, S. 1996. *The Myth of Mondragón: Cooperatives and Working Class Life in a Basque Town.* Albany: State University of New York Press.

Kedourie, E. 1966. *Nationalism.* London: Hutchinson.

Kierkegaard, S. 1963. *El concepto de angustia.* Madrid: Espasa Calpe.

Klandermans, B., H. Kriesi, and S. Tarrow, eds. 1988. *From Structure to Action: Comparing Social Movements Research Across Cultures.* Greenwich, Conn.: JAI Press.

Kohn, H. 1967. *The Idea of Nationalism.* 1944. New York: Collier Books.

Künhl, R. K. 1971. "El liberalismo." In *Introducción a la ciencia política,* edited by W. Abemdroth and K. Lenk, 49–90. Barcelona: Anagrama.

Lamo de Espinosa, E., and J. E. Rodríguez Ibañez. 1993. *Problemas de teoría social contemporánea.* Madrid: Centro de Investigaciones Sociológicas.

Laraña, E., and J. Gusfield, eds. 1994. *Los nuevos movimientos sociales: De la ideología a la identidad.* Madrid: Centro de Investigaciones Sociológicas.

Larrañaga, J. n.d. *El cooperativismo de Mondragón: Interioridades de una utopía.* N.p.: n.p.

Larronde, J-C. 1977. *El nacionalismo vasco.* San Sebastián: Txertoa.

Lasch, C. 1991a. *The Culture of Narcissism: American Life in an Age of Diminishing Expectations.* New York: Norton.

———. 1991b. *The True and Only Heaven: Progress and Its Critics.* New York: Norton.

Ledrut, R., ed. 1979. *Le pouvoir local.* Paris: Anthropos.

Lefebvre, H. 1972. *La vida cotidiana en el mundo moderno.* Madrid: Alianza.

Lerchundi, A. 1985. *"La Gaceta del Norte": Sus ochenta y tres años de vida.* Bilbao: Servicio Editorial Universidad del País Vasco.

———. 1986. *"La Gaceta del Norte* (1901–1984): Muerte ideológica de un diario." In *La prensa de los siglos XIX y XX: Metodología, ideología e información: Aspectos económicos y tecnológicos,* edited by M. Tuñón de Lara, 603–13. Bilbao: Servicio Editorial Universidad del País Vasco.

Linz, J. L. 1973. "Early State Building and Later Peripheral Nationalisms Against the State: The Case of Spain." In *Building States and Nations,* edited by S. N. Eisenstadt and S. Rokkan, 2:32–116. Beverly Hills: Sage.

———. 1976. "An Authoritarian Regime: Spain." In *Politics and Society in Twentieth Century Spain,* edited by S. G. Payne. New York: New Viewpoints.

Linz, J. L., et al. 1981. *Atlas Electoral del País Vasco.* Madrid: Centro de Investigaciones Sociológicas.

Llera, F. J. 1984. "El sistema de partidos vascos. Distancia ideológica y legitimación política." Paper presented at the IV Spanish Conference on Political Science, Alicante.

———. 1993. "The Construction of the Basque Polarized Pluralism." *Working Papers.* Barcelona: Institut de Ciènces Politiques i Socials.

———. 1994. *Los vascos y la política: El proceso político vasco: Elecciones, partidos, opinión pública y legitimación en el País Vasco.* Bilbao: Servicio Editorial Universidad del País Vasco.

Lodziak, C. 1995. *Manipulating Needs: Capitalism and Culture.* London: Pluto Press.

López Adán, E. 1977. "Sobre las bases sociales de carlismo y del nacionalismo en Alava." *Saioak* 1: 128–35.

Luckmann, T. 1967. *The Invisible Religion.* London: MacMillan.

Lyman, S., and W. A. Douglass. 1973. "Ethnicity: Strategies of Individual and Collective Impression Management." *Social Research* 40, no. 2: 344–65.

Lyman, S., W. A. Douglass, and J. Zulaika. 1994. *Migración, etnicidad y etnonacionalismo.* Bilbao: Servicio Editorial Universidad del País Vasco.

Mannheim, K. 1952. "The Problem of Generations." In *Essays on the Sociology of Knowledge,* by K. Mannheim. London: Routledge & Kegan Paul.

Maravall, J. M. 1978. *Dictadura y disentimiento político.* Madrid: Alfaguara.

———. 1981. *La política de la transición, 1975–1980.* Madrid: Taurus.

Marx, K. 1972. *La ideología alemana.* Barcelona: Grijalbo.

———. 1977. *Capital: A Critique of Political Economy.* Vol. 1. Translated by Ben Fowkes. New York: Vintage Books.

Mata, J. M. 1993. *El nacionalismo vasco radical: Discurso, organización y expresiones.* Bilbao: Servicio Editorial Universidad del País Vasco.

Mauss, M. 1967. *Essais de sociologie.* Paris: Minuit.

McGovern, S. J. 1998. *The Politics of Downtown Development: Dynamic Political Cultures in San Francisco and Washington, D.C.* Lexington, Ky.: University Press of Kentucky.

McNeill, W. 1982. *The Pursuit of Power: Technology, Armed Force, and Society since A.D. 1000.* Chicago: University of Chicago Press.

Melucci, A. 1989. *Nomads of the Present.* London: Hutchinson Radius.

———. 1994. "¿Qué hay de nuevo en los 'nuevos movimientos sociales'?" In *Los nuevos movimientos sociales: De la ideología a la identidad,* edited by E. Laraña and J. Gusfield, 119–49. Madrid: Centro de Investigaciones Sociológicas.

Merton, R. K. 1949. *Social Theory and Social Structure: Towards the Codification of Theory and Research.* Glencoe, Ill.: Free Press.

———. 1976. *Sociological Ambivalence and Other Essays.* New York: Free Press.

Michelena, L. 1977. "El largo y difícil camino del euskera." In *El libro blanco del euskara.* Bilbao: Euskaltzaindia.

Mills, C. W. 1959. *The Sociological Imagination.* New York: Oxford University Press.

Morán, M. L. 1996–97. "Sociedad, cultura y política: Continuidad y novedad en el análisis cultural." *Zona Abierta* 77–78: 1–29.

Moreno Lara, X. 1977. "Los errores del franquismo en el País Vasco." *Nueva Historia* 1 (February): 82–91.

Moriones, I. 1976. *Euskadi y el Vaticano, 1935–1936.* Rome: n.p.

Moya, C. 1975. *El poder económico en España.* Madrid: Túcar.

Nisbet, R. A. 1970. *The Social Bond: An Introduction to the Study of Society.* New York: Knopf.

———. 1973. *The Quest for Community.* New York: Oxford University Press.

———. 1975. *El vínculo social.* Barcelona: Vicens Vives.

Núñez, L. C. 1977a. *Opresión y defensa en euskera.* San Sebastián: Txertoa.

———. 1977b. *La sociedad vasca actual.* San Sebastián: Txertoa.

Offe, K. 1990. *Contradicciones del Estado de Bienestar.* Madrid: Alianza.

Ormaetxea, J. M. 1997. *Orígenes y claves del cooperativismo de Mondragón.* N.p.: n.p.

Ortzi (Francisco Letamendia). 1975. *Historia de Euskadi.* Paris: Ruedo Ibérico.

Paramio, L. 1976. "Le bloc dominant dans l'Espagne de Franco." *Les Temps Modernes,* no. 357 bis.: 265–88.

Parsons, T. 1961. *The Structure of Social Action.* New York: Free Press of Glencoe.

———. 1974. *El sistema de las sociedades modernas.* Mexico City: Trillas.

Payne, S. G. 1974. *El nacionalismo vasco: De sus orígenes a la ETA.* Barcelona: Dopesa.

———, ed. 1976. *Politics and Society in Twentieth Century Spain.* New York: New Viewpoints.

Peña, J. M. 1984. *El Diario Vasco: 50 años en Guipúzcoa: Biografía de un periódico.* San Sebastián: Sociedad Vascongada de Publicaciones.

Pérez-Agote, A. 1976. *Medio ambiente e ideología en el capitalismo avanzado.* Madrid: Encuentros.

———. 1979a. "Racionalidad urbana y relaciones sociales: El Gran Bilbao (1945–1975)." *Saioak* 3: 3–57.

———. 1979b. "La signification sociologique de la planification urbaine. Le cas de Bilbao." In *Le pouvoir local,* edited by R. Ledrut, 81–95. Paris: Anthropos.

———. 1980. "L'arbitraire et le nécessaire de l'identité collective." In *Identités collectives et changements sociaux,* edited by P. Tap, 243–45. Toulouse: Privat.

————. 1984a. "La religión en Durkheim y el problema del centro simbólico de la sociedad en la sociología actual." In *Sociología contemporánea: Ocho temas a debate*, edited by L. Rodríguez Zúñiga and F. Bouza, 87–103. Madrid: Centro de Investigaciones Sociológicas.

————. 1984b. *La reproducción del nacionalismo: El caso vasco*. Madrid: Centro de Investigaciones Sociológicas-Siglo XXI.

————. 1987. *El nacionalismo vasco a la salida del franquismo*. Madrid: Centro de Investigaciones Sociológicas-Siglo XXI.

————. 1989a. "Cambio social e ideológico en Navarra (1936–1982): Algunas claves para su comprensión." *Revista Española de Investigaciones Sociológicas* 46: 7–21.

————, ed. 1989b. *Sociología del nacionalismo*. Bilbao: Servicio Editorial Universidad del País Vasco.

————. 1990. *Los lugares sociales de la religión: La secularización de la vida en el País Vasco*. Madrid: Centro de Investigaciones Sociológicas.

————. 1996a. "Are the New Social Movements Really Social?" Paper presented at the Second European Conference on Social Movements, Vitoria, Spain.

————. 1996b. "Nación y nacionalismo." In *Sociedad y política: Temas de sociología política*, edited by J. Benedicto and M. L. Morán, 109–38. Madrid: Alianza.

————. 1996c. "Paradoxes of a Nation." *Revista Española de Investigaciones Sociológicas* (English ed.), 1: 97–111.

————. 1999. "Globalización, crisis del Estado y anomia: La teoría social visita Europa." In *Globalización, riesgo y reflexividad: Tres temas de la teoría social contemporánea*, edited by R. Ramos and F. García Selgas, 57–72. Madrid: Centro de Investigaciones Sociológicas.

Pérez-Agote, A., J. Azcona, and A. Gurrutxaga. 1997. *Mantener la identidad: Los vascos del Río Carabelas*. Bilbao: Servicio Editorial Universidad del País Vasco.

Pérez-Agote, A., et al. 1999a. *Institucionalización política y reencantamiento de la sociedad: Las transformaciones en el mundo nacionalista*. Vitoria-Gasteiz: Gobierno Vasco.

Pérez-Agote, A., et al. 1999b. *Les nouveaux repères de l'identité collective en Europe*. Paris: L'Harmattan.

Pérez-Agote, A., et al. 2001. *El trabajo en la Comunidad autónoma vasca: Actividad, ocupación y paro*. Bilbao: BBK Gazte Lanbidean Fundazioa.

Potter, W. J. 1996. *An Analysis of Thinking and Research About Qualitative Methods*. Mahwah, N.J.: LEA, 1996.

Putnam, R. D. 2000. *Bowling Alone: The Collapse and Revival of American Community*. New York: Simon & Schuster.

Ramírez Goicoechea, E. 1984. "Cuadrillas en el País Vasco: Identidad local y revitalización étnica." *Revista Española de investigaciones Sociológicas* 25: 213–22.

————. 1991. *De jóvenes y sus identidades: Socio-antropología de la etnicidad en Euskadi*. Madrid: Centro de Investigaciones Sociológicas.

Ramos, R. "La formación histórica del Estado Nacional." In *Sociedad y política: Temas de sociología política*, edited by J. Benedicto and M. L. Morán, 35–67. Madrid: Alianza.

Ramos R., and F. García Selgas, eds. 1999. *Globalización, riesgo y reflexividad: Tres temas de la teoría social contemporánea*. Madrid: Centro de Investigaciones Sociológicas.

Ranke, L. 1979. *Pueblos y estados en la historia moderna*. Mexico City: Fondo de Cultura Económica.

Renaut, A. 1993. "Las lógicas de la nación." In *Teorías del nacionalismo*, edited by G. Delannoi and P-A. Taguieff, 37–62. Barcelona: Paidós.

Rodríguez Zúñiga, L., and F. Bouza, eds. 1984. *Sociología contemporánea: Ocho temas a debate*. Madrid: Centro de Investigaciones Sociológicas.

Rogowski, R. 1985. "Causes and Varieties of Nationalism: A Rationalist Account." In *New Nationalism of the Developed West*, edited by E. Tiryakian and R. Rogowski, 87–108. London: Allen Unwin.

Ruiz Olabuénaga, J. I., et al. 1998. *Sociología electoral vasca*. Bilbao: Universidad de Deusto.

Saiz Valdivielso, A. C. 1977. *Triunfo y tragedia del periodismo vasco (1900–1939)*. Madrid: Editora Nacional.

Sarasola, I. 1976. *Historia social de la literatura vasca*. Madrid: Akal.

Schutz, A. 1974. *Estudios sobre teoría social*. Buenos Aires: Amorrortu.

Scott, J. C. 1990. *Domination and Arts of Resistance: Hidden Transcripts*. New Haven, Conn.: Yale University Press.

Sennett, R. 1977. *The Fall of Public Man*. New York: Knopf.

Shils, E. 1975. *Center and Periphery: Essays in Macrosociology*. Chicago: University of Chicago Press.

Simmel, G. 1896–97. "Comment les formes sociales se maintiennent." *L'Année Sociologique* 1: 71–109.

———. 1977. *Filosofía del dinero*. Madrid: Instituto de Estudios Políticos.

Smith, A. 1971. *Theories of Nationalism*. New York: Harper & Row.

———. 1994. "Tres conceptos de nación." *Revista de Occidente* 161 (October): 7–22.

Smith, M. L. 1987. "Publishing Qualitative Research." *American Educational Research Journal* 24, no. 2: 173–83.

Snow, D. 1979. "A Dramaturgical Analysis of Movement Accommodation: Building Idiosyncrasy Credit as Movement Mobilization Strategy." *Symbolic Interaction* 2: 23–44.

Solozabal, J. 1975. *El primer nacionalismo vasco*. Madrid: Túcar.

Sommers, M. R. 1995a. "Narrating and Naturalizing Civil Society and Citizenship Theory: The Place of Political Culture and the Public Sphere." *Sociological Theory* 13, no. 3: 229–74.

———. 1995b. "What's Political or Cultural about Political Culture and the Public Sphere? Toward an Historical Sociology of Concepts Formation." *Sociological Theory* 13, no. 2: 113–44.

Spinoza, B. [1670] 1999. *Tractatus de intellectus emendatione, et de via, qua optime in veram rerum cognitionem dirigitur (Traité de l'amendement de l'intellect)*. Paris: Editions Allia.

Stone, L. 1981. "La Revolución inglesa." In *Revoluciones y rebeliones en la Europa moderna*, by J. H. Elliot and others, 67–121. Madrid: Alianza Editorial.

Sullivan, J. 1988. *ETA and Basque Nationalism: The Fight for Euskadi (1890–1986)*. London: Routledge.

Swidler, A. 1986. "Culture in Action: Symbols and Strategies." *American Sociological Review* 51: 273–86.

Tajfel, H. 1981. *Human Groups and Social Categories*. Cambridge: Cambridge University Press.

Tajfel, H., and J. C. Turner. 1986. "La teoría de la identidad social de la conducta intergrupal." In *Lecturas de psicología social*, edited by J. Morales and C. Huici, 225–59. Madrid: UNED.

Tap, P., ed. 1980. *Identités collectives et changements sociaux*. Toulouse: Privat.

Taylor-Gooby, P. 1991. *Social Change, Social Welfare, and Social Science*. Toronto: University of Toronto Press.

Tejerina, B. 1992. *Nacionalismo y lengua: Los procesos de cambio lingüístico en el País Vasco*. Madrid: Centro de Investigaciones Sociológicas.

Thomas, W. I. 1923. *The Unadjusted Girl*. Boston: Little Brown.

Tiryakian, E. A. 1985. "On the Significance of Differentiation." In *Macro Sociological Theory: Perspectives on Sociological Theory*, edited by S. N. Eisenstadt and H. J. Helle, 118–34. Beverly Hills: Sage.

———. 1989. "Nacionalismo, modernidad y sociología." In *Sociología del nacionalismo*, edited by A. Pérez-Agote, 143–61. Bilbao: Servicio Editorial Universidad del País Vasco.

———. "Dialectics of Modernity: Reenchantment and Dedifferentiation as Counterprocesses." In *Social Change and Modernity*, edited by H. Haferkamp and N. J. Smelser, 78–94. Berkeley and Los Angeles: University of California Press.

Tiryakian, E., and R. Rogowski, eds. 1985. *New Nationalism of the Developed West*. London: Allen Unwin.

Tiryakian, E., and N. Nevitte. 1985. "Nationalism and Modernity." In *New Nationalism of the Developed West*, edited by E. Tiryakian and R. Rogowski, 57–86. London: Allen Unwin.

Torrealdai, J. M. 1999. *La censura y el tema vasco*. N.p.: Kutxa.

———. 1977. *Euskal idazleak gaur*. Oñate-Arantzazu: Jakin.

Touraine, A. 1978. *La voix et le regard*. Paris: Seuil.

———. 1980. "Les deux faces de l'identité." In *Identités collectives et changements sociaux*, edited by P. Tap, 19–26. Toulouse: Privat.

Tuñón de Lara, M., ed. 1986. *La prensa de los siglos XIX y XX: Metodología, ideología e información: Aspectos económicos y tecnológicos*. Bilbao: Servicio Editorial Universidad del País Vasco.

Turner, B. S., ed. 1993. *Citizenship and Social Theory*. London: Sage.

Turner, J. C. n.d. *Redescubrir el grupo social*. Madrid: Morata.

Unzueta, P. 1979. "Diarios en Euskadi." Universidad del País Vasco. Photocopy.

Valle, M. S. 1997. *Técnicas cualitativas de investigación social: Reflexión metodológica y práctica profesional*. Madrid: Síntesis.

Van Deth, J. V. 1989. "Interest in Politics." In *Continuities in Political Action: A Longi-*

tudinal Study of Political Orientations in Western Democracies, by M. Kent Jennings, J. W. Deth, et al. Berlin: W. de Gruyter.

Vicens Vives, J. 1970. *Aproximación a la historia de España.* Madrid: Salvat.

Walter, G. 1971. *La revolución inglesa.* Barcelona: Grijalbo.

Weber, M. 1958. *The Protestant Ethic and the Spirit of Capitalism.* Translated by Talcott Parsons. New York: Scribner.

———. 1978. *Economy and Society: An Outline of Interpretive Sociology.* Translated by Ephraim Fischoff et al. Berkeley and Los Angeles: University of California Press.

———. 2002. "Politics as a Vocation." In *Violence: A Reader,* edited by Catherine Besteman, 13–18. New York: New York University Press.

Wieviorka, M. 1993. *La démocratie à l'épreuve: Nationalisme, populisme, ethnicité.* Paris: La Découverte.

Wuthnow, R., and M. Witten. 1988. "New Directions in the Study of Culture." *Annual Review of Sociology* 14: 49–67.

Ybarra, E. 1985. "El Correo Español–El Pueblo Vasco: Un periódico institución (1910–1985)." In *El Correo Español–El Pueblo Vasco,* 11–134. Bilbao: n.p.

Zulaika, J. 1988. *Basque Violence: Metaphor and Sacrament.* Reno: University of Nevada Press.

Index

Page references to tables are indicated with a "t" preceding the table number.

absolutism, 42–43

AEK. *See* Alfabetatze Euskalduntze Koordinakundea

Aguirre, José Antonio, 87

Ajuriaguerra, Juan, 85

Alfabetatze Euskalduntze Koordinakundea (Basque-language schools for adults): vs. HABE, 123, 134–37; promoting nationalist consciousness, 136

Alianza Popular (Popular Alliance), 112–13

amnesty committees, 89, 169, 175, 178–79, 181, 185–86; and youth, 188

L'Année Sociologique, (Simmel), 12–13

anomie, 7, 211n11

Antiterrorist Liberation Groups. *See* Grupos Antiterroristas de Liberación

AP. *See* Alianza Popular

Araba: Basque-language schools in, 83; Basque-nationalist vote in, xxx, 69t3.6; industrialization of, 60, 65, 208n11; newspapers in, during Franco Regime, 62t3.3; population trends in, 66t3.4

Arana, Sabino, 60, 84, 88

Aranzadi, Juan, 84

Arzallus, Xabier, 126

Association to Reestablish Basque Literacy Among Adults. *See* Helduen Alfabetatze Berreuskalduntzerako Erakundea

Basque Autonomous Community of Euskadi. *See* Euskadi

Basque Autonomous Police, 121, 146–47, 221n12

Basque Country

—Basque-nationalist vote in, 69t3.6, 158t6.2

—and education, 63–64, 104–6

—evolution of nationalism in, xx–xxii, xxx–xxxi, 38, 55, 60–61; political conflict in, 56–59, 70–73, 208n8, 211n12

—during Franco Regime: and Catholic Church, 102–6; decree against, 97; social solidarity, 79, 88; violence and oppression in, 115–16

—government of, xxix, 164–65, 220–21n1

—industrialization in, xxx, 59–60, 61, 65, 68, 213n2; Araba's, 208n11; Navarre's, 100–101

—nationalism, xi, xxix–xxxii, 72–73, 89, 162–65, 190–91, 194–95, 196–97, 224n4; associative framework of, 175–91; decline in interest in politics of, 174–75, 223n16; future of, xxxiv–xxxv; generations of, 193–95; and intersubjective framework of, 165–75; lack of solidarity in, 204–5; political institutionalization of, 195–96

—newspapers in, 62t3.3, 63, 213–14n6

—religiosity vs. secularization of, 107–13

—and Spanish state, xviii–xx, xxii, 32, 37–38, 39, 52, 56, 72–73, 196 (*see also* Euskadi; Spain)

Basque culture: dance groups, 92, 176, 180, 182–83, 184, 187; de-politicizing of, 182–85, 187, 194; hiking clubs, 93–

Ertzaintza. *See* Basque Autonomous
Police
essentialism, 9–10, 15
ETA. *See* Euskadi ta Askatasuna
ethnicity, 29–31, 37–39; and nationalism,
47, 51–52
European Union, 46, 207n6
Euskadi, xx, 32; and Basque identity, 190–
91; Basque Government, disillusionment with, 139–46; Basque language,
122–23; population trends in, 66–
67tt3.4–3.5; religiosity of, 109–13,
110–11tt4.12–14; unemployment in,
170, 222n13, 223–24n2. *See also*
Basque Country
Euskadiko Ezkerra (Euskadi Left), 130,
144–46, 152, 222n.8; and Basque language, 131–32, 133, 137; and *cuadrillas*,
169; and ETA violence, 147, 164
Euskadi ta Askatasuna (Euskadi and
Freedom), 79, 83–84, 85, 87–90, 98
—and Basque language, 83–85, 90–91, 99
—and Burgos trials, 94, 219n38
—erosion of image of, 153–54
—and Franco Regime: during, 71, 72, 79,
94, 98, 194, 197; post, 72–73, 163–65,
193, 197–98, 204–5
—groups: ETA-V, 65, 78; ETA-VI, 78,
216n12; youth, 98, 152, 200, 217n19
—and GAL, 139–40, 153
—and Gesto por la Paz (A Gesture for
Peace), 198–99
—and Lemoniz (nuclear power station),
221n13
—Marxism development within, 100
—and membership recruitment, 91–92,
94, 219n37
—political organizations under, 163
—and religion, 77, 85–88, 110
—and violence, 69–70, 94, 99–100, 101–2,
114–17, 147–55, 163, 197, 221n13;
acceptance of, 72, 73, 101–2, 117, 121,
165; opposition to, 204–5; in response
to repression, 94, 114, 162

—Zabala kidnapping by, 65
euskaldunberris (new Basque speakers),
84
Euskal Herrian Euskaraz (linguistic
group), 132
Euskal Iraultzarako Alderdia (Basque
Revolutionary Party), 163, 222n8. *See
also* Euskadiko Ezkerra
euskaltegis (Basque-language learning
centers), 135–36. *See also* educational
system
Euskara. *See* Basque language
Eusko Alkartasuna (Basque Solidarity),
112, 197
Eusko Gaztedi (Basque Nationalist Party
Youth), 85, 217n19

familial relations: and Basque nationalism, 75, 80–81, 89, 97–98; generational
radicalization of, 88–91, 98
feudalism, 42
Fichte, Johann Gottlieb, 37
fieldwork guidelines: factors for interviews, xxxii–xxxiv
foral autonomy, early nineteenth century, 58, 59
France, xx, 37, 38, 39; and GAL, 139–40,
153
Franco Regime
—Basque-identity definitions, during, 38,
212n5
—Basque nationalism: during, xxi, xxv–
xxvi, xxvii, xxxi, 50, 56, 74–118,
80t4.1, 194, 218n27; and Catholic
Church, 72, 76, 96–97, 102, 103–4; and
lack of leadership, during, 77–78,
216n10; radicalization of, 68–70; stages
of, 95, 218n27 (*see also* nationalism)
—class structures/population trends
during, 61–68, 67t3.5, 69t3.7
—and ETA, during, 71, 72, 79, 94, 98, 194,
197
—and intersubjective framework, xxxi,
173–74

—evolution of: Basque, xx–xxii, xxx–
xxxi, 55–61, 70; in Eastern European
countries, 46
—and history, 45, 51–52, 211n12, 212–
13n14
—inclusive vs. exclusive, 31
—in French Revolution, 34
—as nineteenth-century invention, 33–
34, 35, 36
—peripheral, 29–31, 42, 45, 47, 49, 51–
52, 56
—as politicization of collective identity,
29–52
—radical, 140–41, 221n11; vs. moderate
expressions of nationalism, 202–3
—and religion, 34–35, 75–76, 215–16n4;
Catholic Church's role, in Basque, 106
—Third World, 45–46, 47
—"we" conflicts, xix–xx, 207–8n7
Nationalism: Five Roads to Modernity
(Greenfield), xvii
National Movement. *See under* Franco
Regime
nation-states. *See under* nation
Navarre: Basque Country, as part of, xx;
Basque nationalism, development in,
69t3.6; *ikastolas* in, 83; industrialization of, 60, 100–101, 208n11; newspapers in, during Franco Regime, 62t3.3;
population trends in, 66t3.4
newspapers: post-Franco Regime, 214–
15n7. *See also under* Franco Regime,
mass media
Nietsche, Friedrich, 212–13n14
Nisbet, Robert A., 12, 14, 35, 210n8
Núñez, Luís C., 218n31, 223n1

objective history, xx
ochotes, 91, 217n22
Old Regime, xx, 57, 59, 96

Pamplona/Iruñea: population trends in,
67t3.5, 101
Parsons, Talcott, 95

Partido Nacionalista Vasco (Basque Nationalist Party)
—and Basque Youth, 85, 86–87, 177,
217n19
—and *cuadrillas*, 169
—EA, as splinter of, 112–13, 197
—and ETA violence, 147, 152
—formation of, 57, 59
—Franco Regime: and Basque language
in, 131–32, 133, 137; during, 64–65, 68,
78, 83, 89–90, 98, 116–17; post-, 163
—older-generation support for, xxvii,
xxviii
—and religion, 112–13
—and social classes, 64–65
—and Spanish state, 142, 144–45
—and Statute of Autonomy, 139, 145
—tensions within, 164–65
Partido Socialista Obrero Español (Spanish Socialist Workers' Party), 113, 145
patrimonial state, 43
Peace of Westphalia (1648), 35
performativity, xxiv, 15–16, 23–24, 46;
statements, xiv, xv, 4
peripheral nationalism, 29–31, 42, 45, 47,
51–52, 56, 211n1; vs. central nationalism, 30–31; and social movements,
during 1970s–1980s, 49
plural nation, 39. *See also under* nation,
and multiple ethnicities
PNV. *See* Partido Nacionalista Vasco
political parties, participation in, 160–62,
222n3
Popular Alliance. *See* Alianza Popular
Popular Unity. *See* Herri Batasuna
population trends: in Basque Country,
xxx–xxxi, 65, 66t3.4, 67t3.5, 68–70; in
Bilbao/Bilbo, 67t3.5; during Franco
Regime, 68, 69t3.7; during nineteenth
century, 58; in Pamplona/Iruñea, 67t3.5;
in San Sebastián/Donostia, 67t3.5;
during twentieth century, 70t3.8,
215n13; in Vitoria/Gasteiz, 67t3.5
poteo, xxx, xxxi, xxxii, 172; alcohol con-

sumption at, 173; bar-owners, 170; decline
of, 168, 169, 171, 172–73, 174; generational differences, in performing, 168,
173; for political socialization, 76, 93–94,
101, 165–66, 216n13. *See also* cuadrillas
Potter, W. James, xxv
prisoners: Basque nationalist, 99, 115–16,
148, 203–4, 224n6; and Burgos trials,
94, 219n38; and *cuadrillas*, 169, 178–
79; demand for repatriation of, 203–4,
224n7; families in support of, 186;
numbers of, 80t4.1, 223n1; during
post-Franco Regime, 139, 196; and pro-
amnesty committees, 89, 169, 178–79,
181, 185–86, 188
privatism: and privatization of life, 159–
62, 221–22n1, 223n17; and youth,
186–88
pro-amnesty committees. *See* amnesty
committees; prisoners
PSOE. *See* Partido Socialista Obrero
Español
Putnam, Robert D., 165

qualitative methodology of nationalism
research, xxv–xxxv

racism, of Basque nationalism, 60
radio. *See under* Franco Regime, mass
media
rationalist theory, xiii, 207n1. *See also*
Rogowski, Ronald
Reformation, 34
Religion
—and Basque nationalism, 61, 75–76, 77,
83, 85–88, 102–6, 177, 217n18; and
clergy, 102–6, 219n40, 220n46
—Catholic Church, 61, 76, 96; and
Catalonia, 219n41; and communist
Poland, 215–16n4; and generational
influences in, 112, 220n49; role of, in
education, 104–6, 106t4.6; and state
issues, during nineteenth century, 96

—changes in groups associated with,
175–76, 179–80, 182, 186–87
—Confirmation catechumen, 187, 189
—and ETA, 77, 85–88, 110
—and Franco Regime, 76, 96–97
—and literature, 103, 104–5
—and political allegiance, 112–13
—post-Confirmation groups, 189,
220n49
—privatism and privatization of life in,
188–89
—secularization process in 1970s, 110–13
Renaissance, 34
Renaut, Alain, 37
Rogowski, Ronald: rationalist theory of,
xiii

Sarasola, Ibon, 219n40
Schutz, A., 10
scientific discourse, and social definitions, 4
scientific method, 32
Scott, James C., 74
scout movement, 177
Secretaría de la Política Lingüística (Department of Linguistic Policy), 122
Shils, Edward A., 95
Silence: as response to repression, 80–81,
89, 99; ETA's violence in response, 114,
162
Simmel, Georg, 10, 12–13
Smith, Anthony, xviii, 37–39
social actor: and collective identities, 17–
28
social aggregate, 210n8
social capital, 165
social conflict: and collective identity, 26–
28, 46–47; and peripheral nationalism,
29–31, 211n2
Social Construction of Reality, The
(Berger and Luckmann), 6
social definitions: of collective reality, 32–
33
social identities: and absolute objectifica-